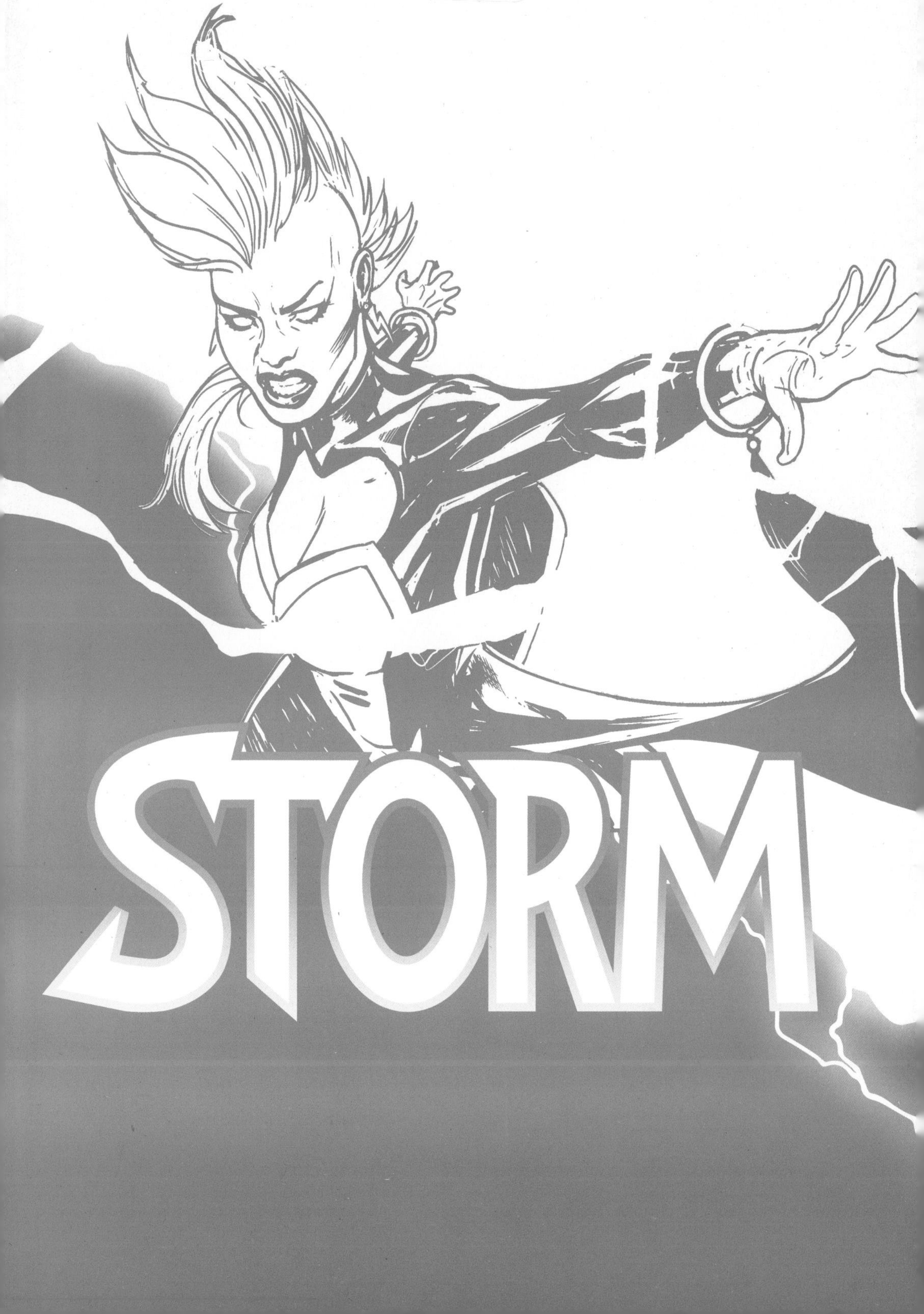
STORM

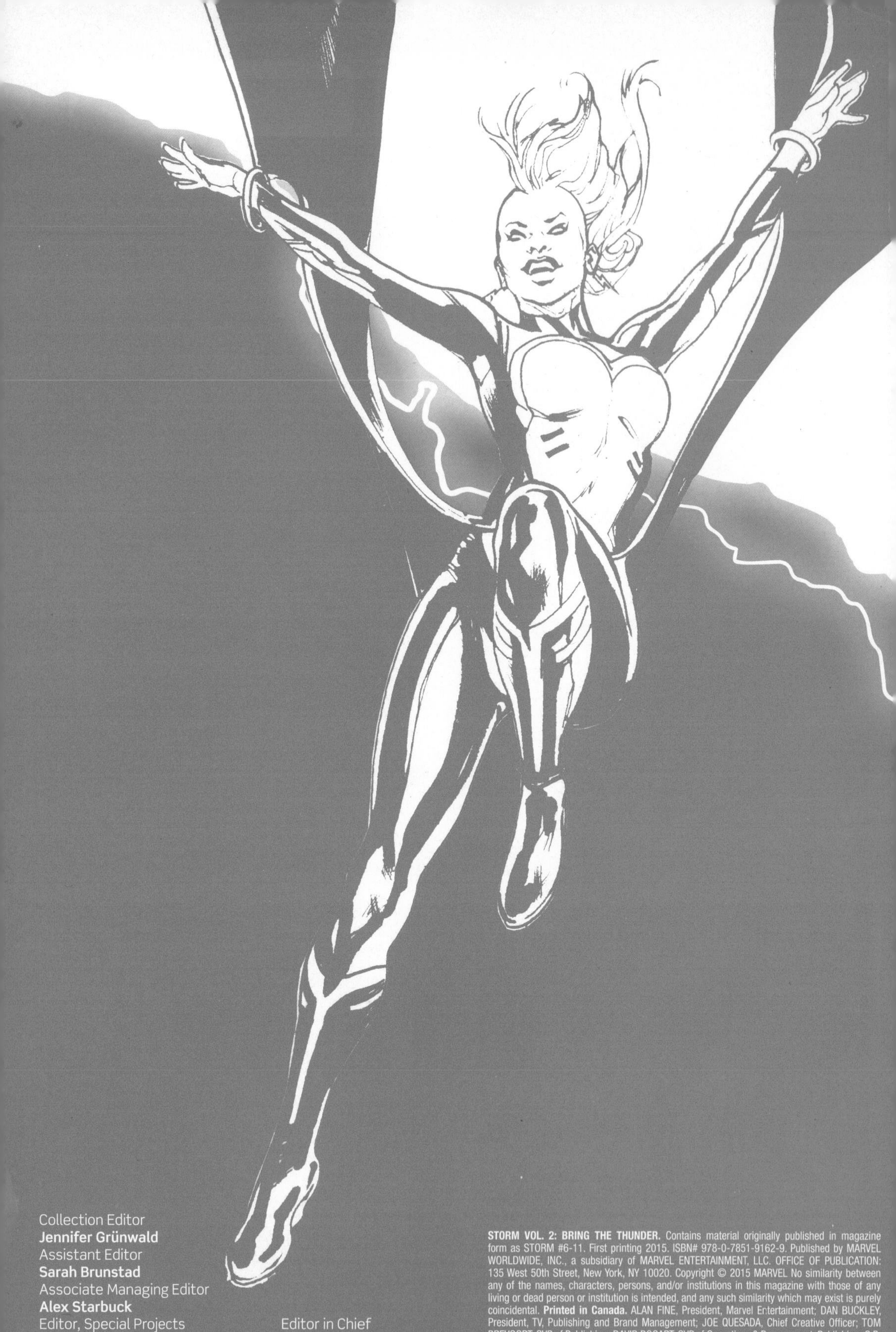

Collection Editor
Jennifer Grünwald
Assistant Editor
Sarah Brunstad
Associate Managing Editor
Alex Starbuck
Editor, Special Projects
Mark D. Beazley
Senior Editor, Special Projects
Jeff Youngquist
SVP Print, Sales & Marketing
David Gabriel
Book Design
Jay Bowen

Editor in Chief
Axel Alonso
Chief Creative Officer
Joe Quesada
Publisher
Dan Buckley
Executive Producer
Alan Fine

STORM VOL. 2: BRING THE THUNDER. Contains material originally published in magazine form as STORM #6-11. First printing 2015. ISBN# 978-0-7851-9162-9. Published by MARVEL WORLDWIDE, INC., a subsidiary of MARVEL ENTERTAINMENT, LLC. OFFICE OF PUBLICATION: 135 West 50th Street, New York, NY 10020. **Printed in Canada.** ALAN FINE, President, Marvel Entertainment; DAN BUCKLEY, President, TV, Publishing and Brand Management; JOE QUESADA, Chief Creative Officer; TOM BREVOORT, SVP of Publishing; DAVID BOGART, SVP of Operations & Procurement, Publishing; C.B. CEBULSKI, VP of International Development & Brand Management; DAVID GABRIEL, SVP Print, Sales & Marketing; JIM O'KEEFE, VP of Operations & Logistics; DAN CARR, Executive Director of Publishing Technology; SUSAN CRESPI, Editorial Operations Manager; ALEX MORALES, Publishing Operations Manager; STAN LEE, Chairman Emeritus. For information regarding advertising in Marvel Comics or on Marvel.com, please contact Jonathan Rheingold, VP of Custom Solutions & Ad Sales, at jrheingold@marvel.com. For Marvel subscription inquiries, please call 800-217-9158. **Manufactured between 5/15/2015 and 6/22/2015 by SOLISCO PRINTERS, SCOTT, QC, CANADA.**

10 9 8 7 6 5 4 3 2 1

THIEF. GODDESS. HEADMISTRESS. QUEEN. THE X-MAN CALLED STORM
HAS ALWAYS DEFIED A SINGLE TITLE. AND HER DESIRE TO BETTER
THE WORLD HAS NEVER BEEN LIMITED TO HER OWN KIND.

STORM

BRING THE THUNDER

WRITER **GREG PAK**

ISSUES #6-9
PENCILER: **AL BARRIONUEVO** WITH **NEIL EDWARDS** (#9)
INKER: **TOM PALMER** WITH **ED TADEO** (#8)

ISSUE #10
PENCILER: **VICTOR IBAÑEZ** WITH **AL BARRIONUEVO** & **NEIL EDWARDS**
INKERS: **VICTOR IBAÑEZ** WITH **ED TADEO**

ISSUE #11
ARTISTS: **VICTOR IBAÑEZ** WITH **NEIL EDWARDS**

COLORIST
RUTH REDMOND
LETTERERS
VC'S JOE SABINO (#6) **CORY PETIT** (#7-11)
COVER ART
STEPHANIE HANS
ASSISTANT EDITOR **ALANNA SMITH**
EDITOR **DANIEL KETCHUM**
X-MEN GROUP EDITOR **MIKE MARTS**

PREVIOUSLY...

Mourning the death of her teammate and lover, Wolverine, Storm went to the aid of their mutual acquaintance Yukio, hoping to gain a sense of closure by concluding some of Logan's unfinished business. However, Storm was unprepared to find Yukio embroiled in the activities of warring clans in Las Vegas — clans led by longtime X-Men foe Moses Magnum, Davis Harmon and Eaglestar International Arms Manufacturing, and Kuva of the Breakworld — the tentative peace kept only through the institution of combat in an underground fight club to settle disputes. Challenged for her seat of power by Kuva, Yukio appointed the reluctant Storm as her champion. And while Storm did fight and take a beating on Yukio's behalf, Storm was crestfallen to find that Yukio had only used her as a diversion... and killed Kuva herself behind the scenes!

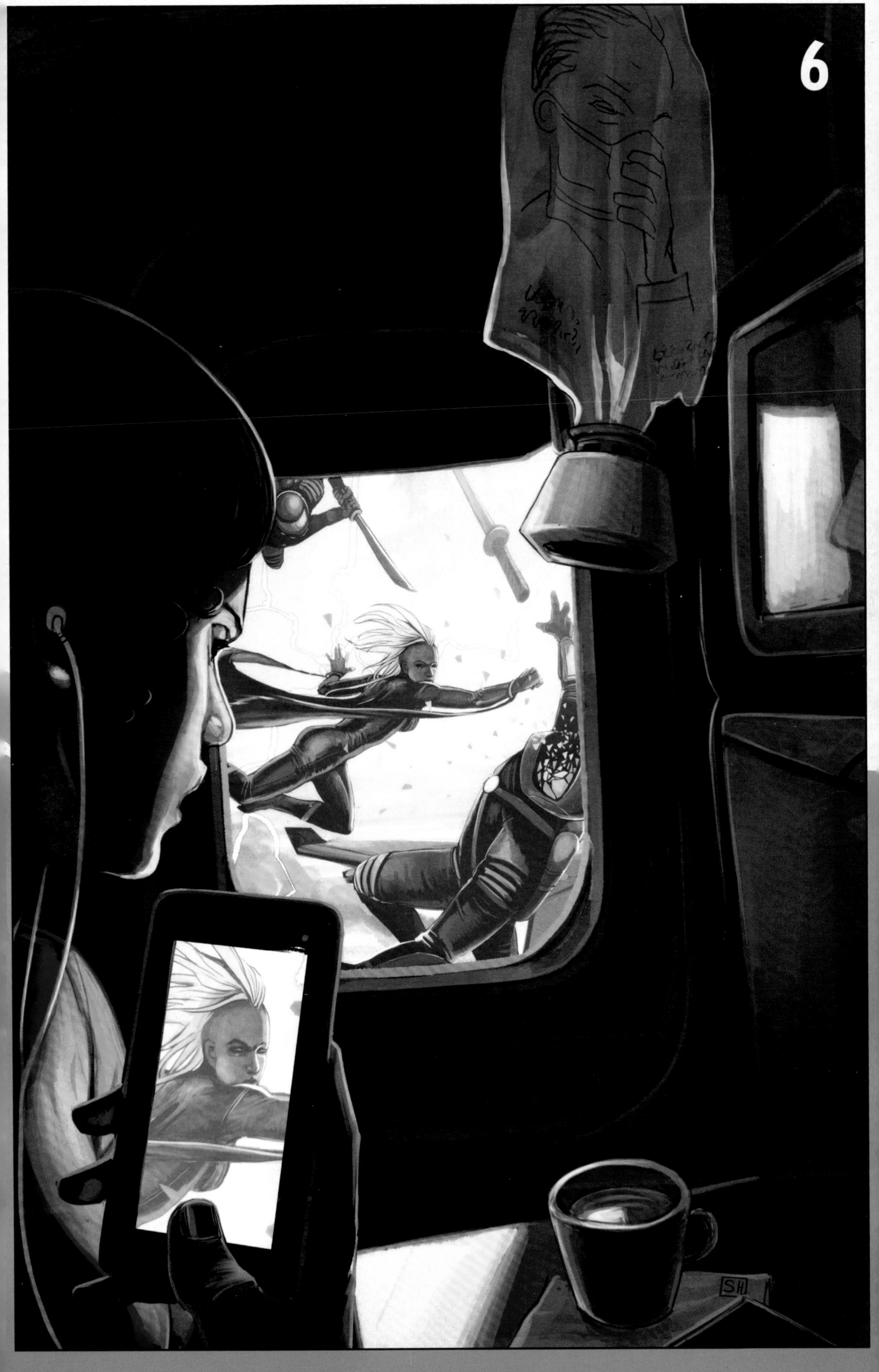

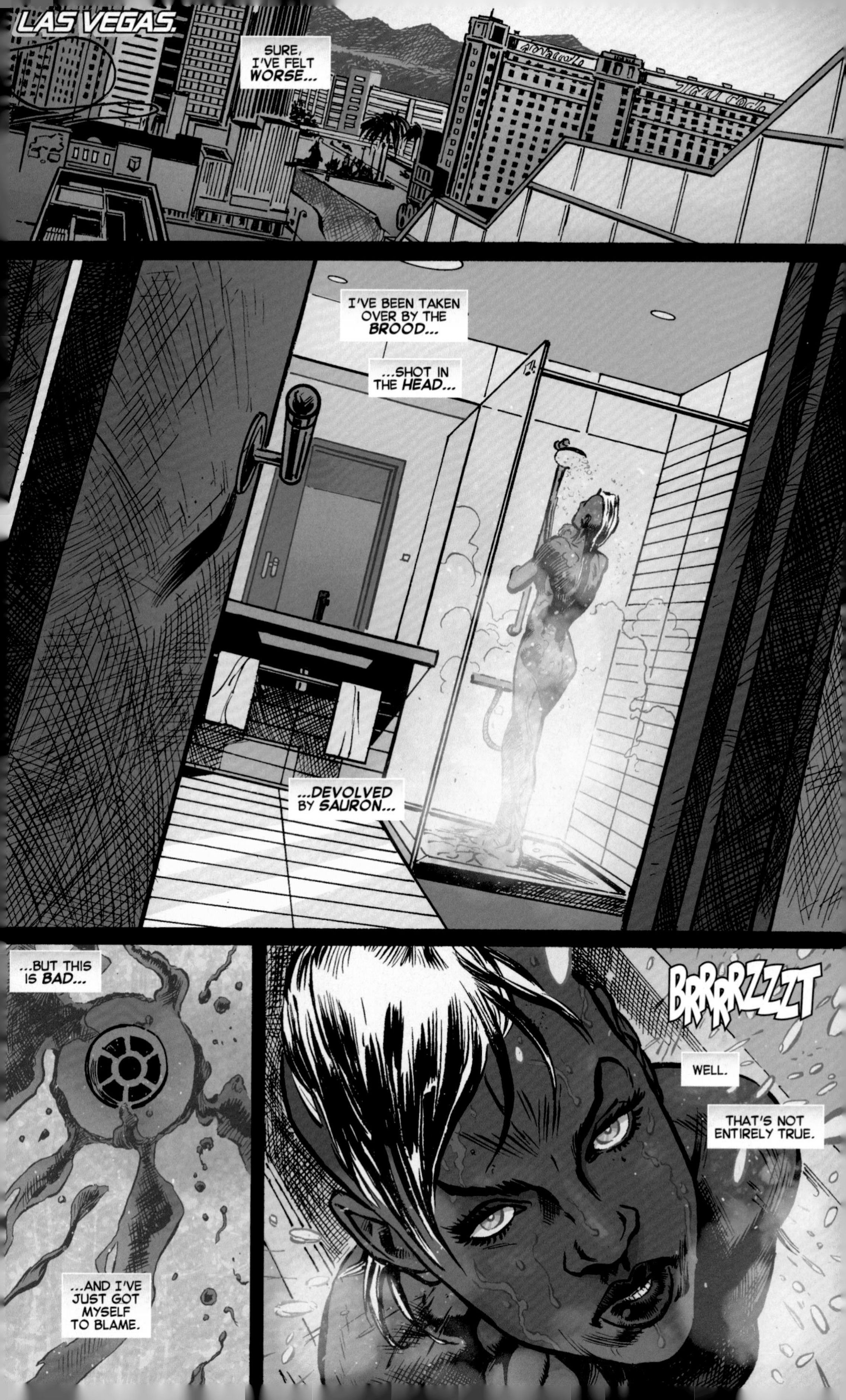
LAS VEGAS.
SURE, I'VE FELT WORSE...
I'VE BEEN TAKEN OVER BY THE BROOD...
...SHOT IN THE HEAD...
...DEVOLVED BY SAURON...
...BUT THIS IS BAD...
...AND I'VE JUST GOT MYSELF TO BLAME.
BRRRRZZZT
WELL.
THAT'S NOT ENTIRELY TRUE.

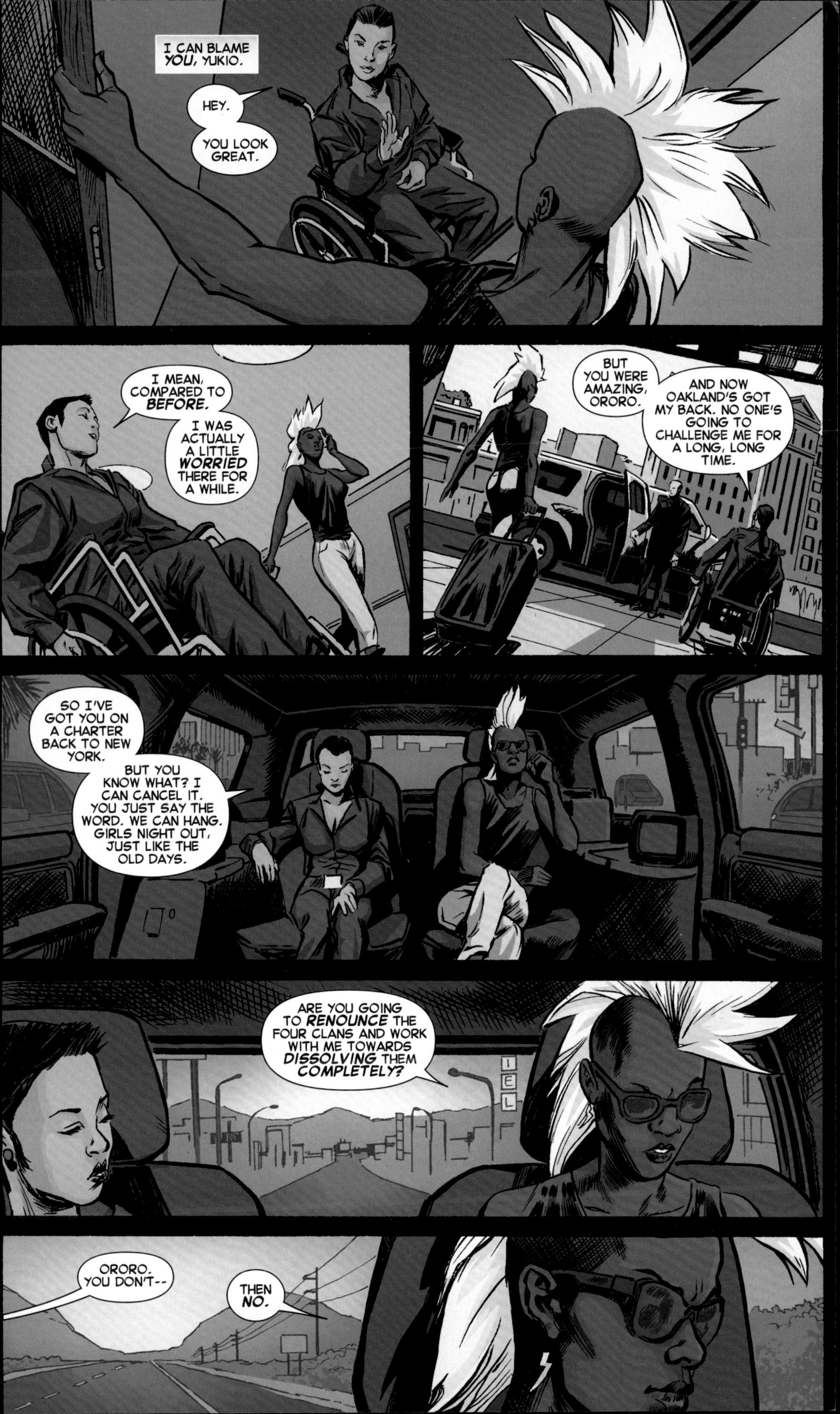
I CAN BLAME YOU, YUKIO.
HEY.
YOU LOOK GREAT.
I MEAN, COMPARED TO BEFORE.
I WAS ACTUALLY A LITTLE WORRIED THERE FOR A WHILE.
BUT YOU WERE AMAZING, ORORO.
AND NOW OAKLAND'S GOT MY BACK. NO ONE'S GOING TO CHALLENGE ME FOR A LONG, LONG TIME.
SO I'VE GOT YOU ON A CHARTER BACK TO NEW YORK.
BUT YOU KNOW WHAT? I CAN CANCEL IT. YOU JUST SAY THE WORD. WE CAN HANG. GIRLS NIGHT OUT, JUST LIKE THE OLD DAYS.
ARE YOU GOING TO RENOUNCE THE FOUR CLANS AND WORK WITH ME TOWARDS DISSOLVING THEM COMPLETELY?
ORORO. YOU DON'T--
THEN NO.

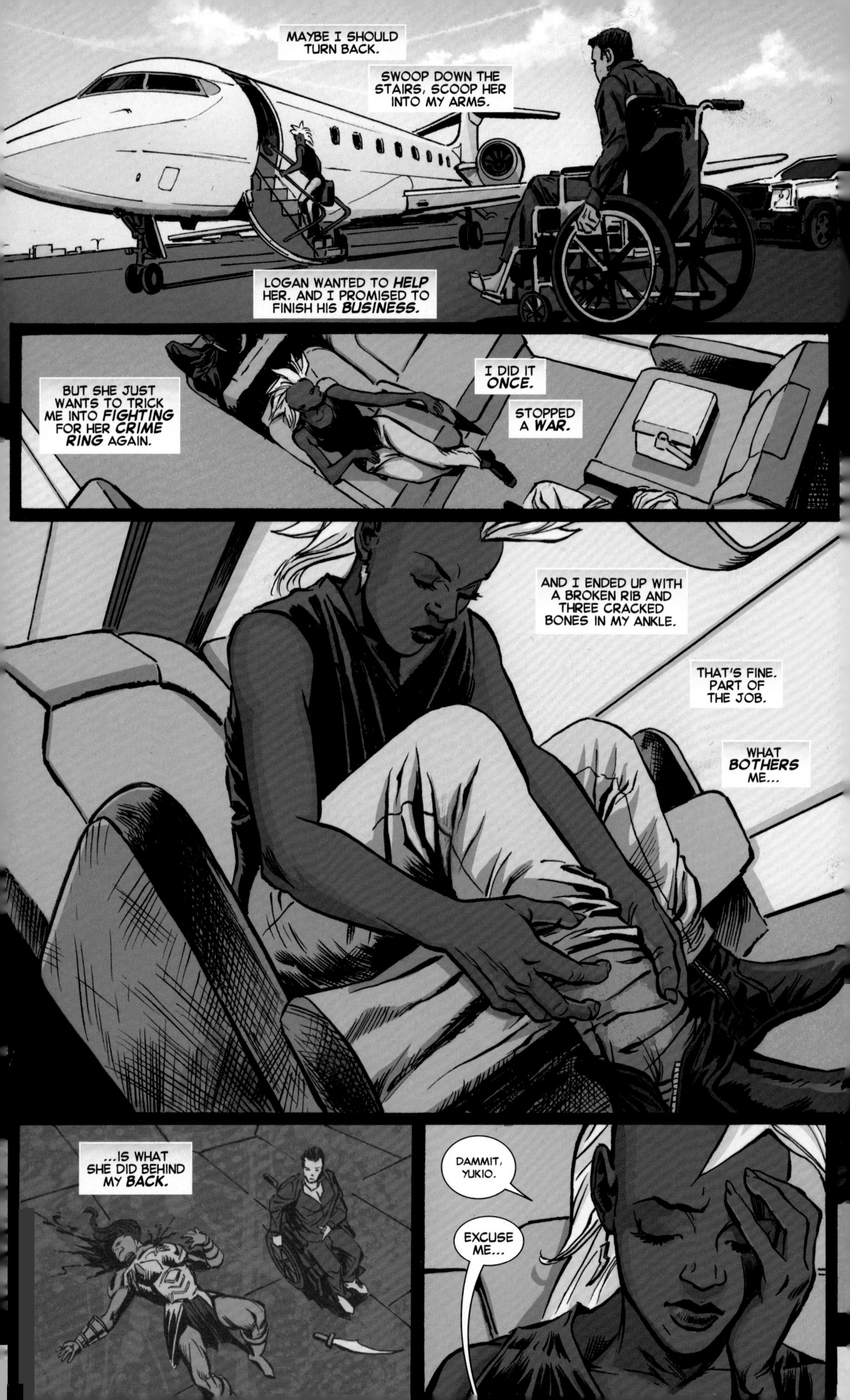
MAYBE I SHOULD TURN BACK.
SWOOP DOWN THE STAIRS, SCOOP HER INTO MY ARMS.
LOGAN WANTED TO HELP HER. AND I PROMISED TO FINISH HIS BUSINESS.
BUT SHE JUST WANTS TO TRICK ME INTO FIGHTING FOR HER CRIME RING AGAIN.
I DID IT ONCE.
STOPPED A WAR.
AND I ENDED UP WITH A BROKEN RIB AND THREE CRACKED BONES IN MY ANKLE.
THAT'S FINE. PART OF THE JOB.
WHAT BOTHERS ME...
...IS WHAT SHE DID BEHIND MY BACK.
DAMMIT, YUKIO.
EXCUSE ME...

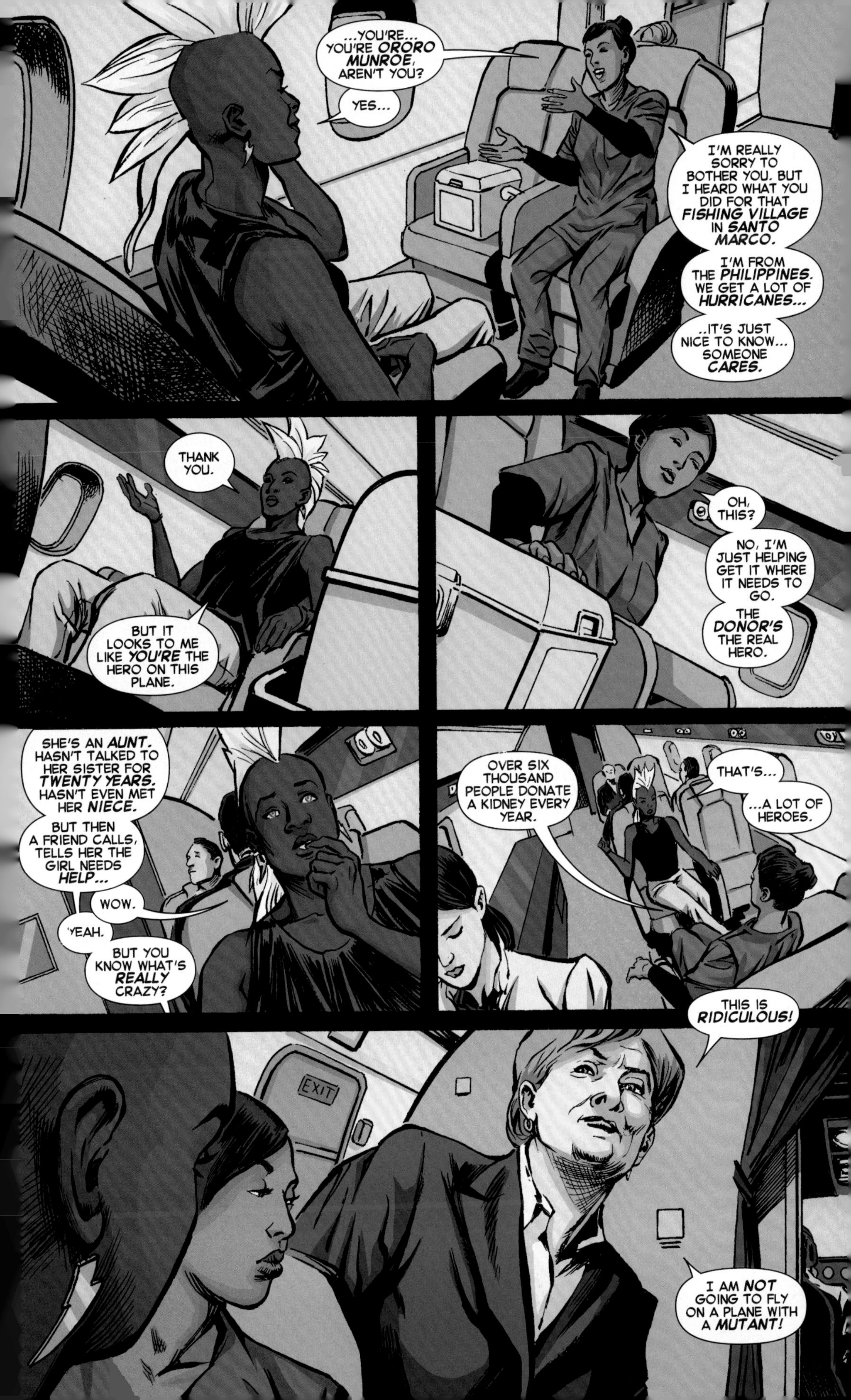
...YOU'RE... YOU'RE ORORO MUNROE, AREN'T YOU?
YES...
I'M REALLY SORRY TO BOTHER YOU. BUT I HEARD WHAT YOU DID FOR THAT FISHING VILLAGE IN SANTO MARCO.
I'M FROM THE PHILIPPINES. WE GET A LOT OF HURRICANES...
..IT'S JUST NICE TO KNOW... SOMEONE CARES.
THANK YOU.
BUT IT LOOKS TO ME LIKE YOU'RE THE HERO ON THIS PLANE.
OH, THIS?
NO, I'M JUST HELPING GET IT WHERE IT NEEDS TO GO.
THE DONOR'S THE REAL HERO.
SHE'S AN AUNT. HASN'T TALKED TO HER SISTER FOR TWENTY YEARS. HASN'T EVEN MET HER NIECE.
BUT THEN A FRIEND CALLS, TELLS HER THE GIRL NEEDS HELP...
WOW.
YEAH.
BUT YOU KNOW WHAT'S REALLY CRAZY?
OVER SIX THOUSAND PEOPLE DONATE A KIDNEY EVERY YEAR.
THAT'S...
...A LOT OF HEROES.
THIS IS RIDICULOUS!
EXIT
I AM NOT GOING TO FLY ON A PLANE WITH A MUTANT!

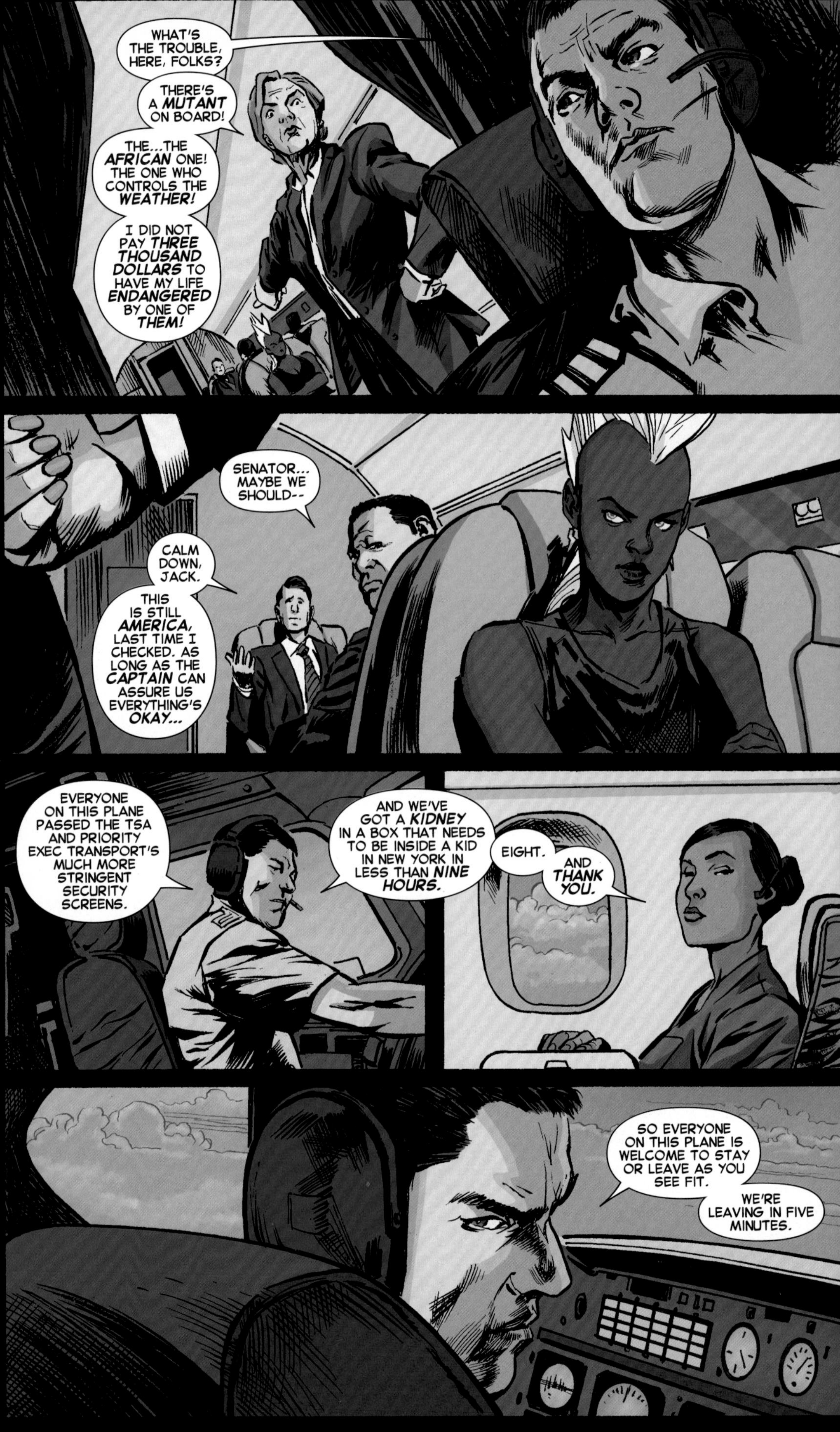
WHAT'S THE TROUBLE, HERE, FOLKS?
THERE'S A *MUTANT* ON BOARD!
THE...THE *AFRICAN* ONE! THE ONE WHO CONTROLS THE *WEATHER!*
I DID NOT PAY *THREE THOUSAND DOLLARS* TO HAVE MY LIFE *ENDANGERED* BY ONE OF *THEM!*
SENATOR... MAYBE WE SHOULD--
CALM DOWN, JACK.
THIS IS STILL *AMERICA,* LAST TIME I CHECKED. AS LONG AS THE *CAPTAIN* CAN ASSURE US EVERYTHING'S *OKAY...*
EVERYONE ON THIS PLANE PASSED THE TSA AND PRIORITY EXEC TRANSPORT'S MUCH MORE STRINGENT SECURITY SCREENS.
AND WE'VE GOT A *KIDNEY* IN A BOX THAT NEEDS TO BE INSIDE A KID IN NEW YORK IN LESS THAN *NINE HOURS.*
EIGHT.
AND *THANK YOU.*
SO EVERYONE ON THIS PLANE IS WELCOME TO STAY OR LEAVE AS YOU SEE FIT.
WE'RE LEAVING IN FIVE MINUTES.

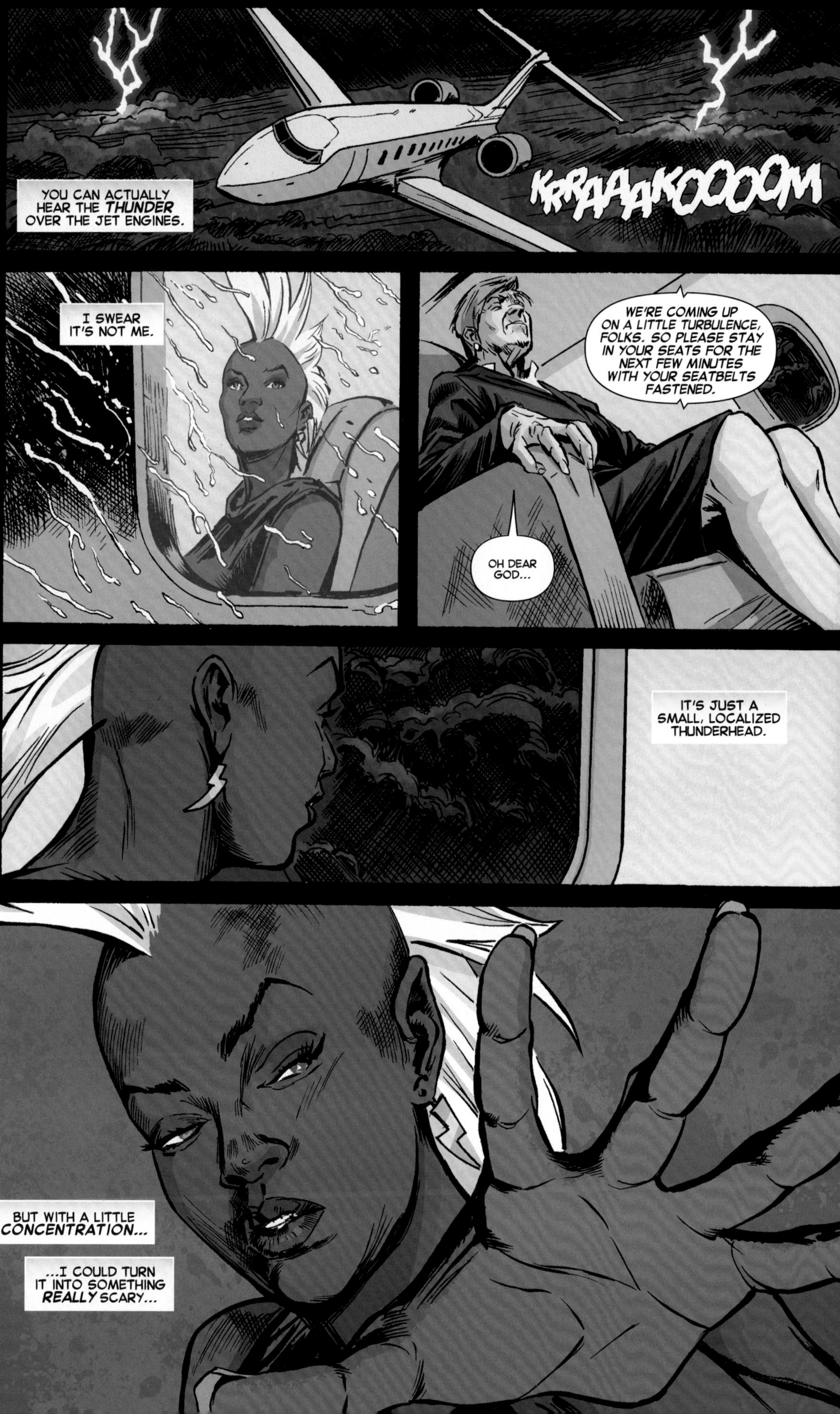
YOU CAN ACTUALLY HEAR THE THUNDER OVER THE JET ENGINES.
KRRAAAKOOOOM
I SWEAR IT'S NOT ME.
WE'RE COMING UP ON A LITTLE TURBULENCE, FOLKS. SO PLEASE STAY IN YOUR SEATS FOR THE NEXT FEW MINUTES WITH YOUR SEATBELTS FASTENED.
OH DEAR GOD...
IT'S JUST A SMALL, LOCALIZED THUNDERHEAD.
BUT WITH A LITTLE CONCENTRATION...
...I COULD TURN IT INTO SOMETHING REALLY SCARY...

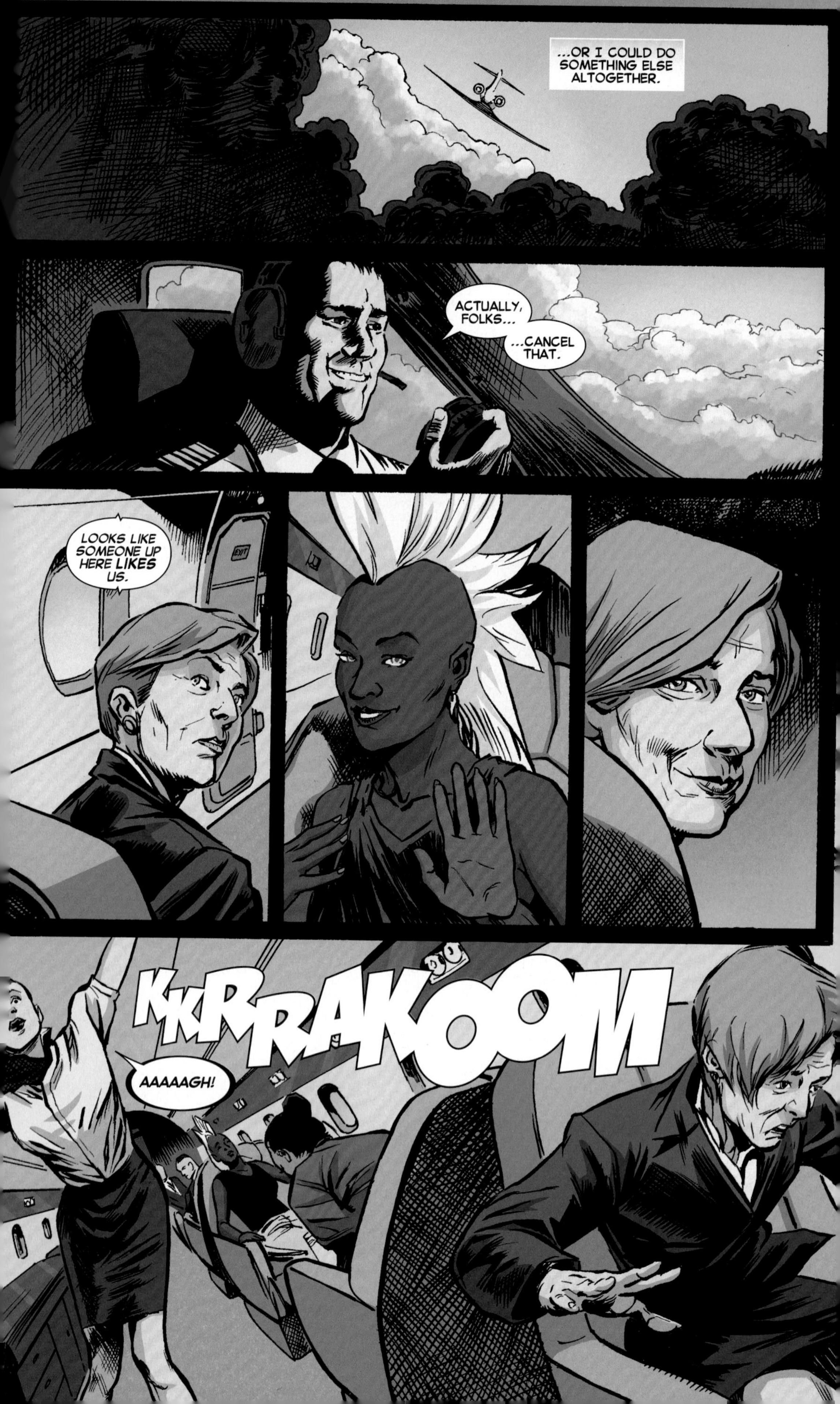
...OR I COULD DO SOMETHING ELSE ALTOGETHER.
ACTUALLY, FOLKS...
...CANCEL THAT.
LOOKS LIKE SOMEONE UP HERE LIKES US.
KKRRAKOOM
AAAAAGH!

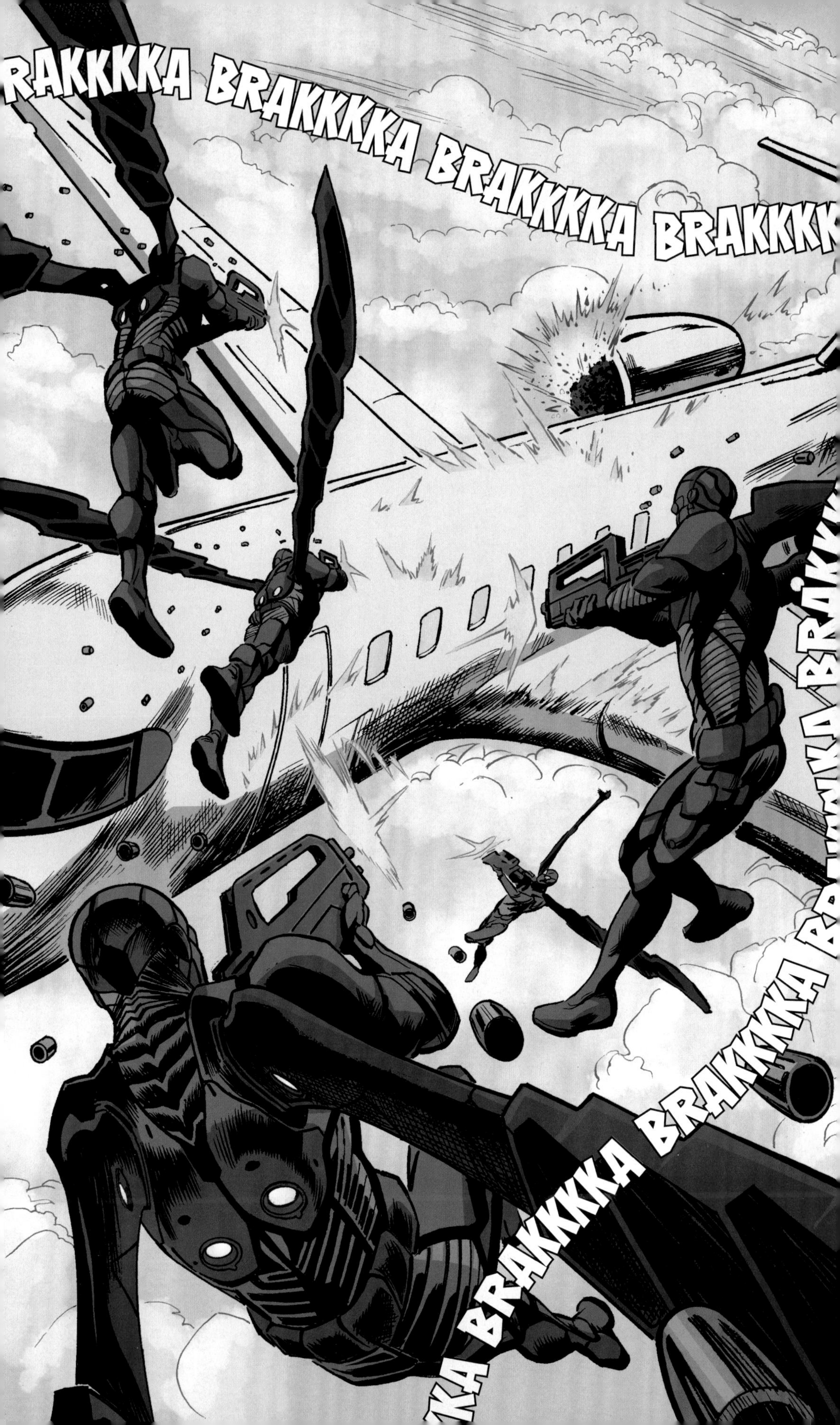
RAKKKA BRAKKKKA BRAKKKKA BRAKKKK
KA BRAKKKKA BRAKKKKA BRAKKKKA BRA

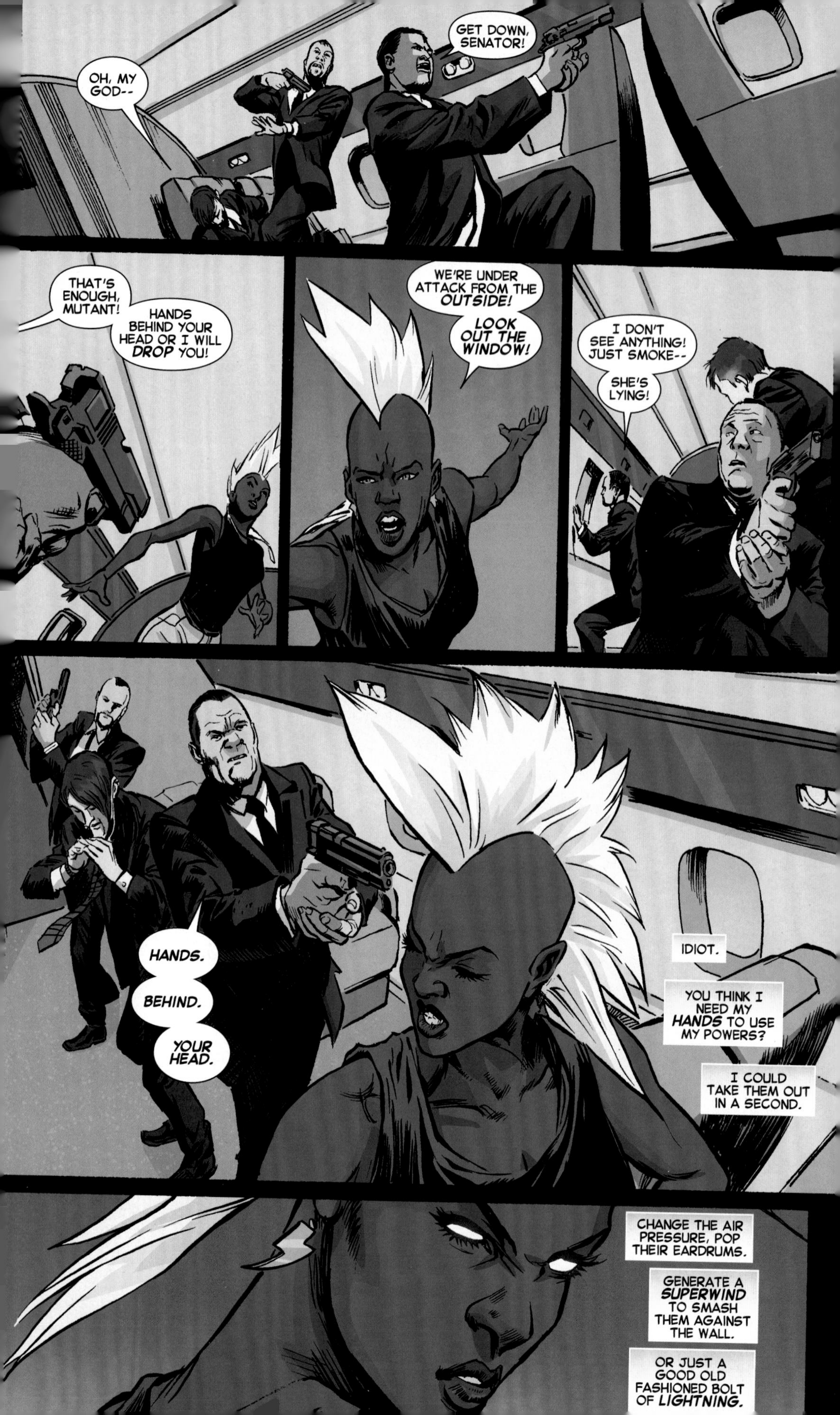
GET DOWN, SENATOR!
OH, MY GOD--
THAT'S ENOUGH, MUTANT!
HANDS BEHIND YOUR HEAD OR I WILL DROP YOU!
WE'RE UNDER ATTACK FROM THE OUTSIDE!
LOOK OUT THE WINDOW!
I DON'T SEE ANYTHING! JUST SMOKE--
SHE'S LYING!
HANDS.
BEHIND.
YOUR HEAD.
IDIOT.
YOU THINK I NEED MY HANDS TO USE MY POWERS?
I COULD TAKE THEM OUT IN A SECOND.
CHANGE THE AIR PRESSURE, POP THEIR EARDRUMS.
GENERATE A SUPERWIND TO SMASH THEM AGAINST THE WALL.
OR JUST A GOOD OLD FASHIONED BOLT OF LIGHTNING.

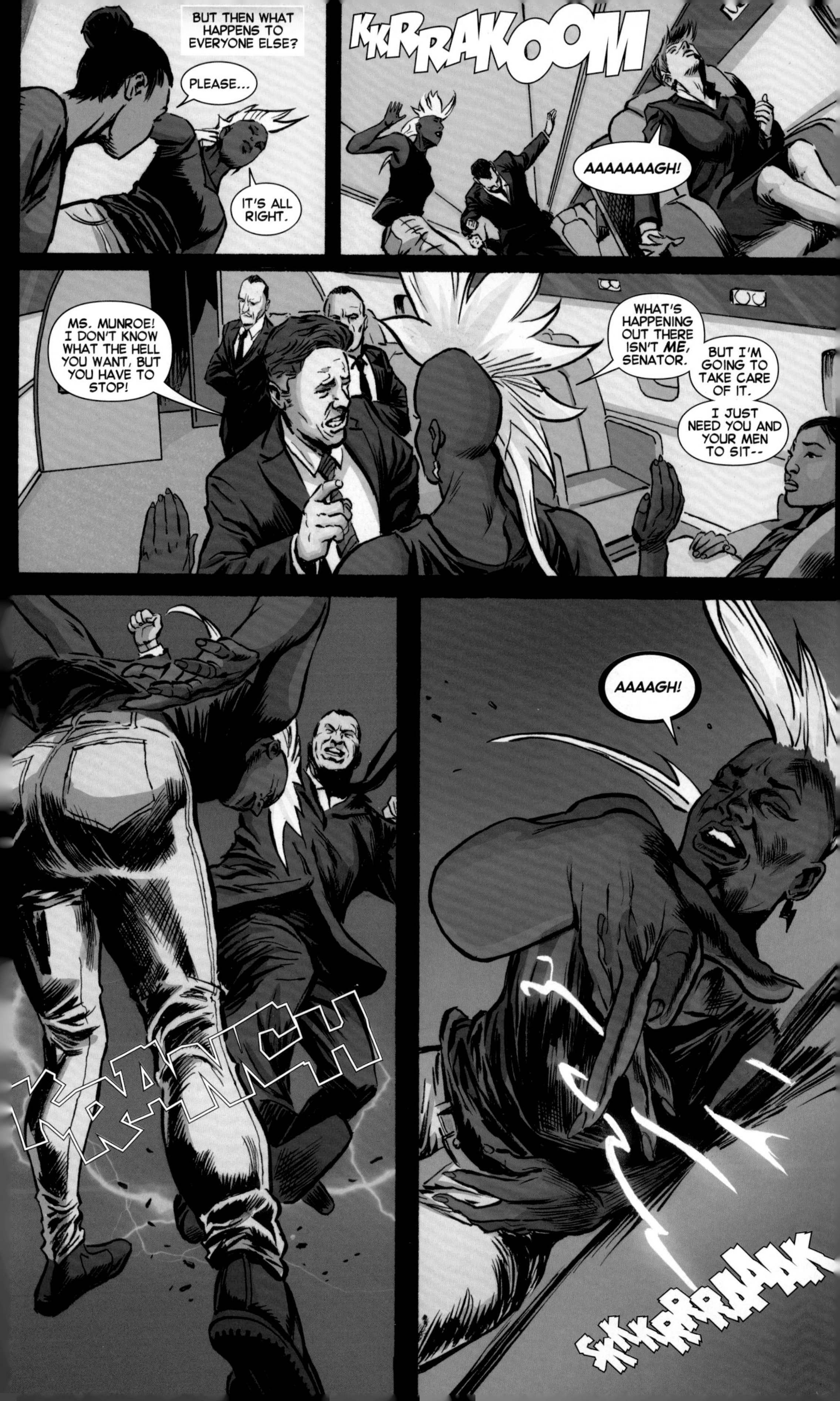

BUT THEN WHAT HAPPENS TO EVERYONE ELSE?
PLEASE...
IT'S ALL RIGHT.
KKRRAKOOM
AAAAAAAGH!
MS. MUNROE! I DON'T KNOW WHAT THE HELL YOU WANT, BUT YOU HAVE TO STOP!
WHAT'S HAPPENING OUT THERE ISN'T ME, SENATOR.
BUT I'M GOING TO TAKE CARE OF IT.
I JUST NEED YOU AND YOUR MEN TO SIT--
KRANCH
AAAAGH!
SKKRRRAAAK

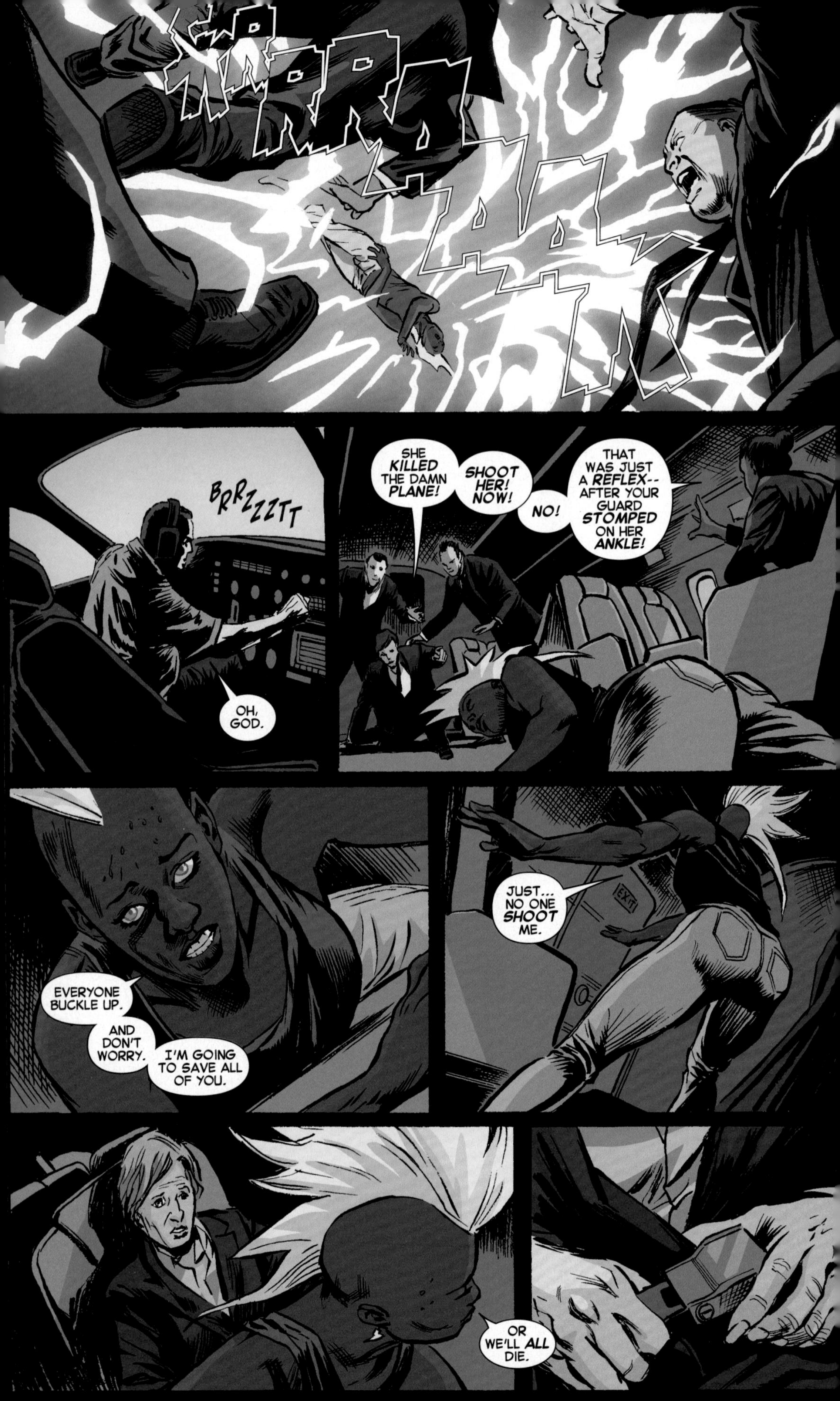
BRRZZZTT
OH, GOD.
SHE KILLED THE DAMN PLANE!
SHOOT HER! NOW!
NO!
THAT WAS JUST A REFLEX--AFTER YOUR GUARD STOMPED ON HER ANKLE!
EVERYONE BUCKLE UP.
AND DON'T WORRY.
I'M GOING TO SAVE ALL OF YOU.
JUST... NO ONE SHOOT ME.
EXIT
OR WE'LL ALL DIE.

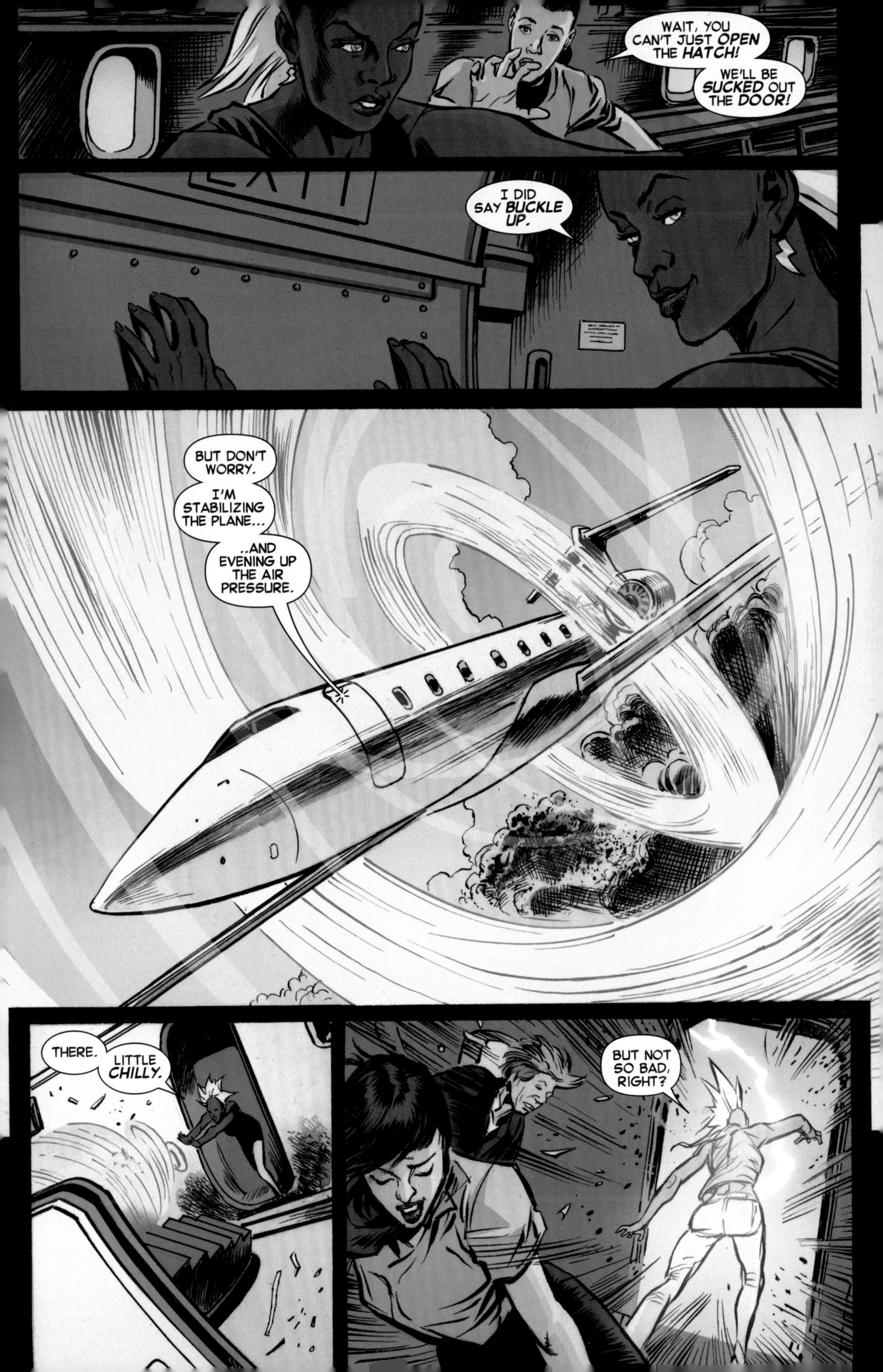
WAIT, YOU CAN'T JUST OPEN THE HATCH!
WE'LL BE SUCKED OUT THE DOOR!
I DID SAY BUCKLE UP.
BUT DON'T WORRY.
I'M STABILIZING THE PLANE...
..AND EVENING UP THE AIR PRESSURE.
THERE.
LITTLE CHILLY.
BUT NOT SO BAD, RIGHT?

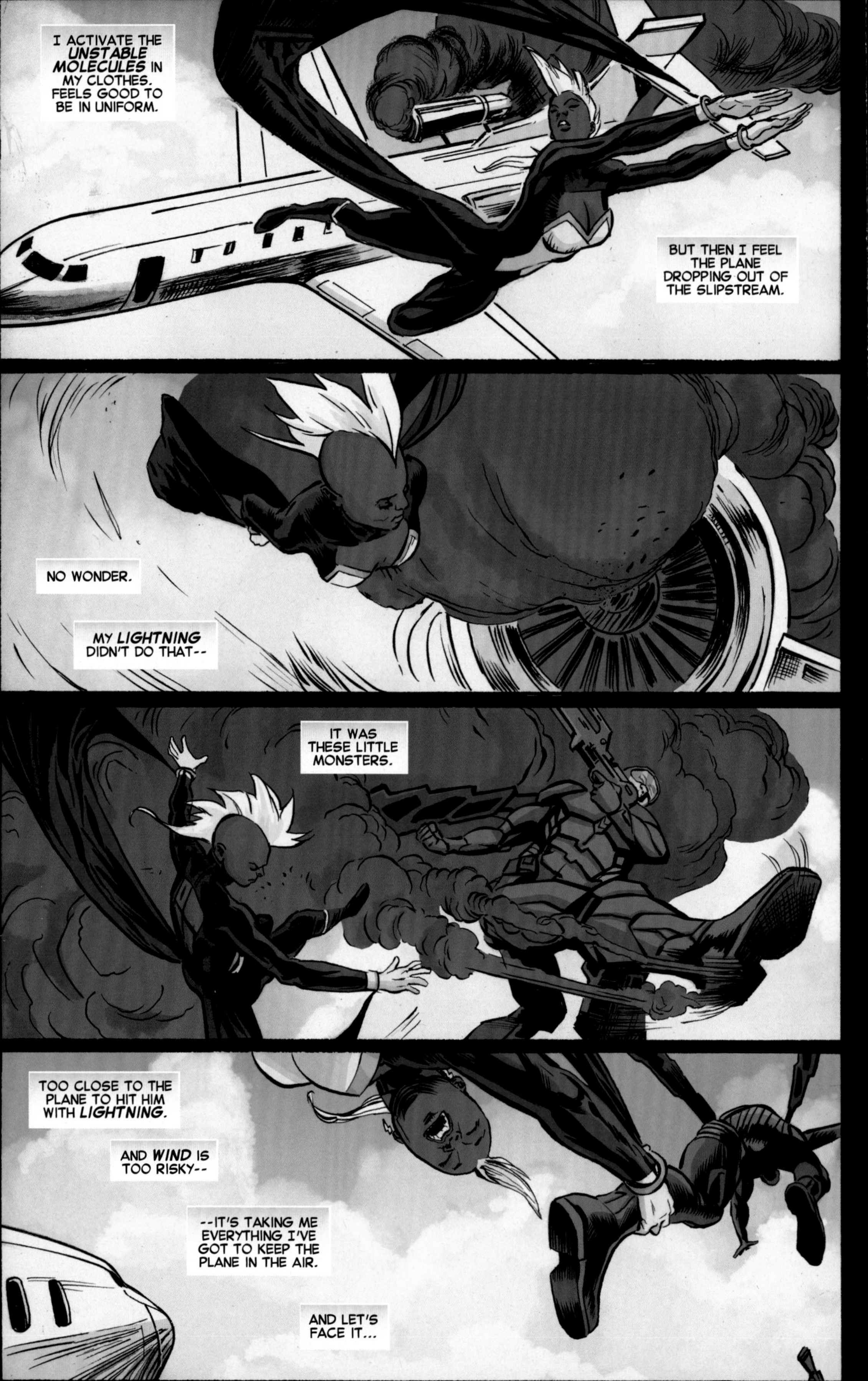
I ACTIVATE THE UNSTABLE MOLECULES IN MY CLOTHES. FEELS GOOD TO BE IN UNIFORM.
BUT THEN I FEEL THE PLANE DROPPING OUT OF THE SLIPSTREAM.
NO WONDER.
MY LIGHTNING DIDN'T DO THAT--
IT WAS THESE LITTLE MONSTERS.
TOO CLOSE TO THE PLANE TO HIT HIM WITH LIGHTNING.
AND WIND IS TOO RISKY--
--IT'S TAKING ME EVERYTHING I'VE GOT TO KEEP THE PLANE IN THE AIR.
AND LET'S FACE IT...

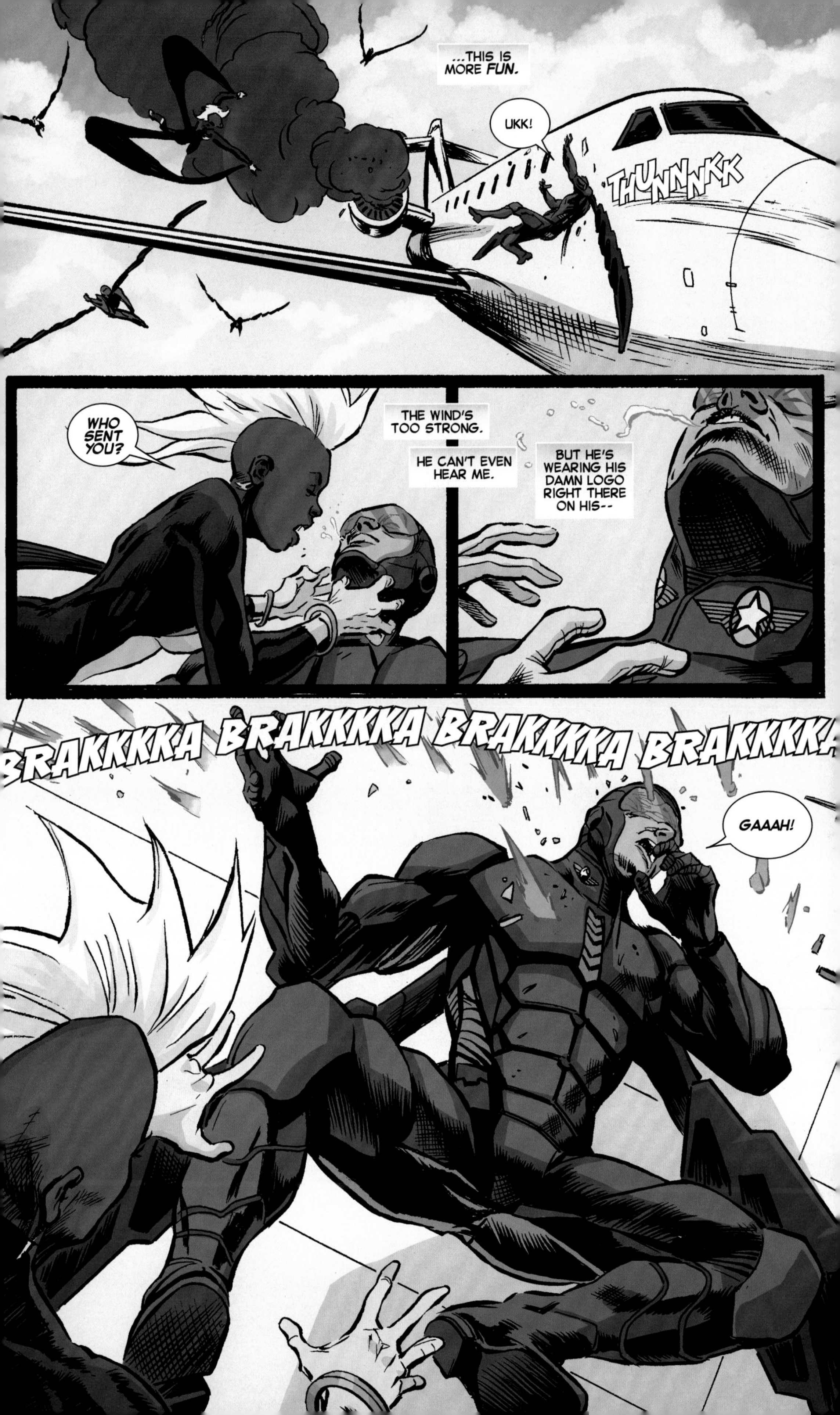
...THIS IS MORE FUN.
UKK!
THUNNNKK
WHO SENT YOU?
THE WIND'S TOO STRONG.
HE CAN'T EVEN HEAR ME.
BUT HE'S WEARING HIS DAMN LOGO RIGHT THERE ON HIS--
BRAKKKKA BRAKKKKA BRAKKKKA BRAKKKK
GAAAH!

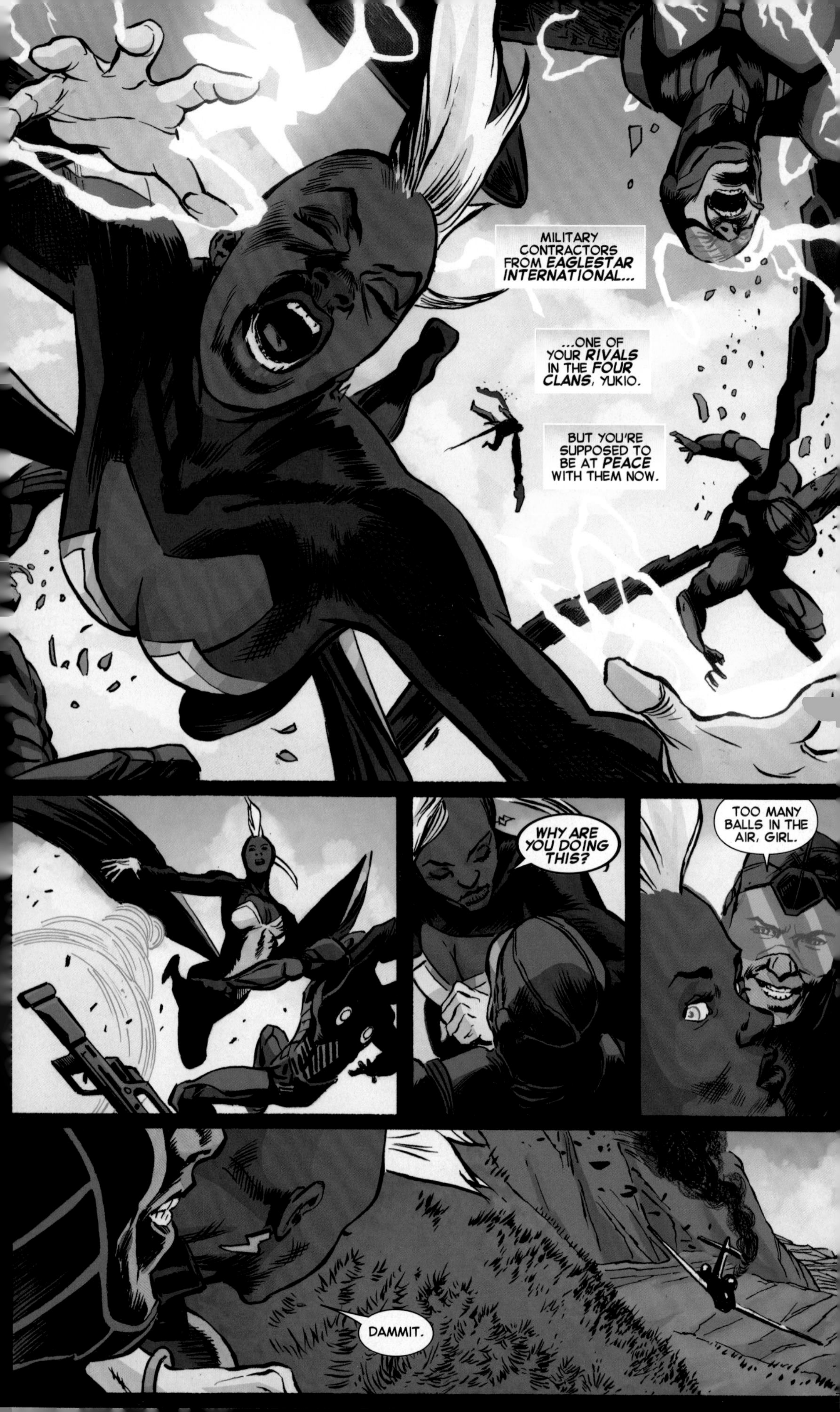
MILITARY CONTRACTORS FROM EAGLESTAR INTERNATIONAL...
...ONE OF YOUR RIVALS IN THE FOUR CLANS, YUKIO.
BUT YOU'RE SUPPOSED TO BE AT PEACE WITH THEM NOW.
WHY ARE YOU DOING THIS?
TOO MANY BALLS IN THE AIR, GIRL.
DAMMIT.

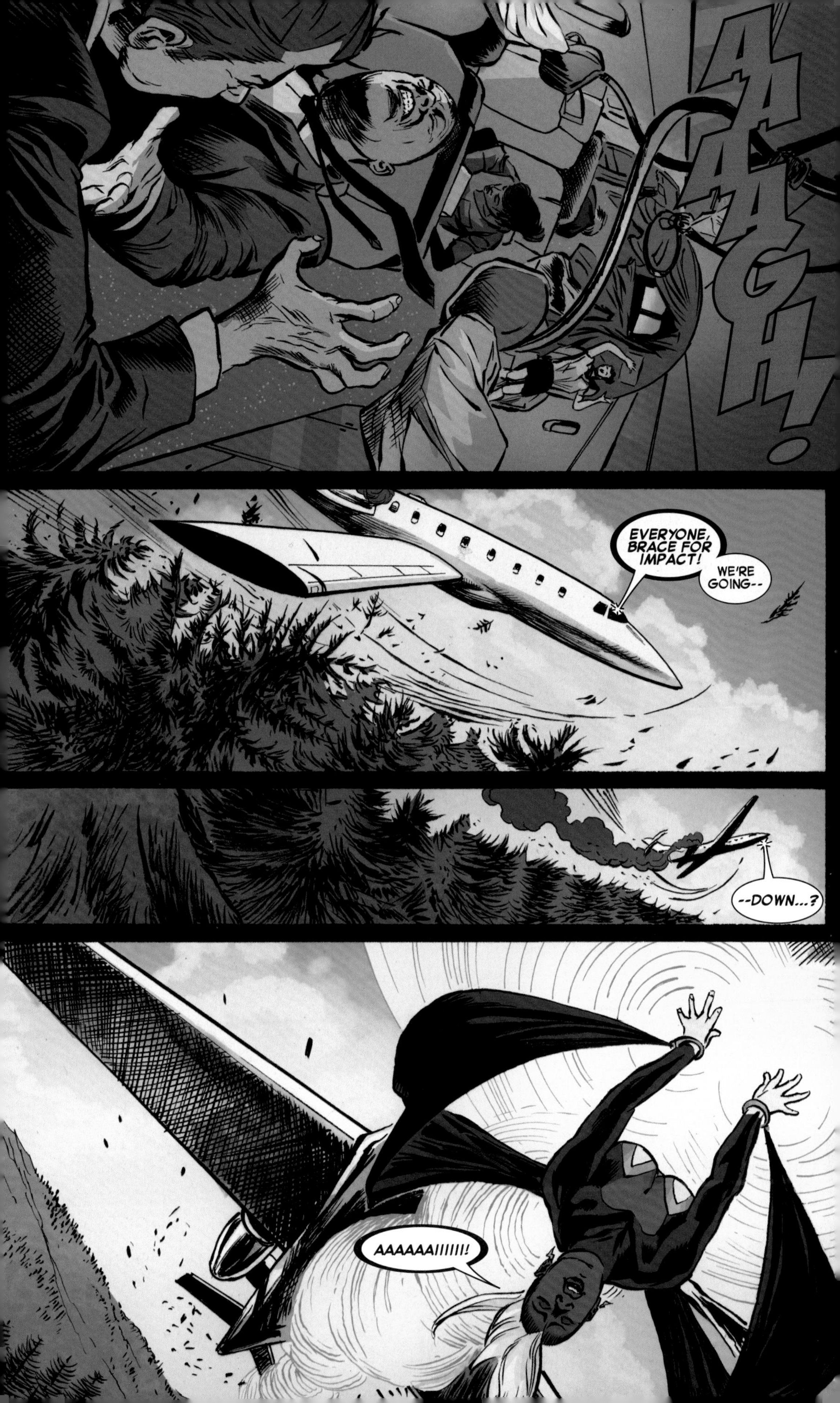
AAAGH!
EVERYONE, BRACE FOR IMPACT!
WE'RE GOING--
--DOWN...?
AAAAAAIIIIII!

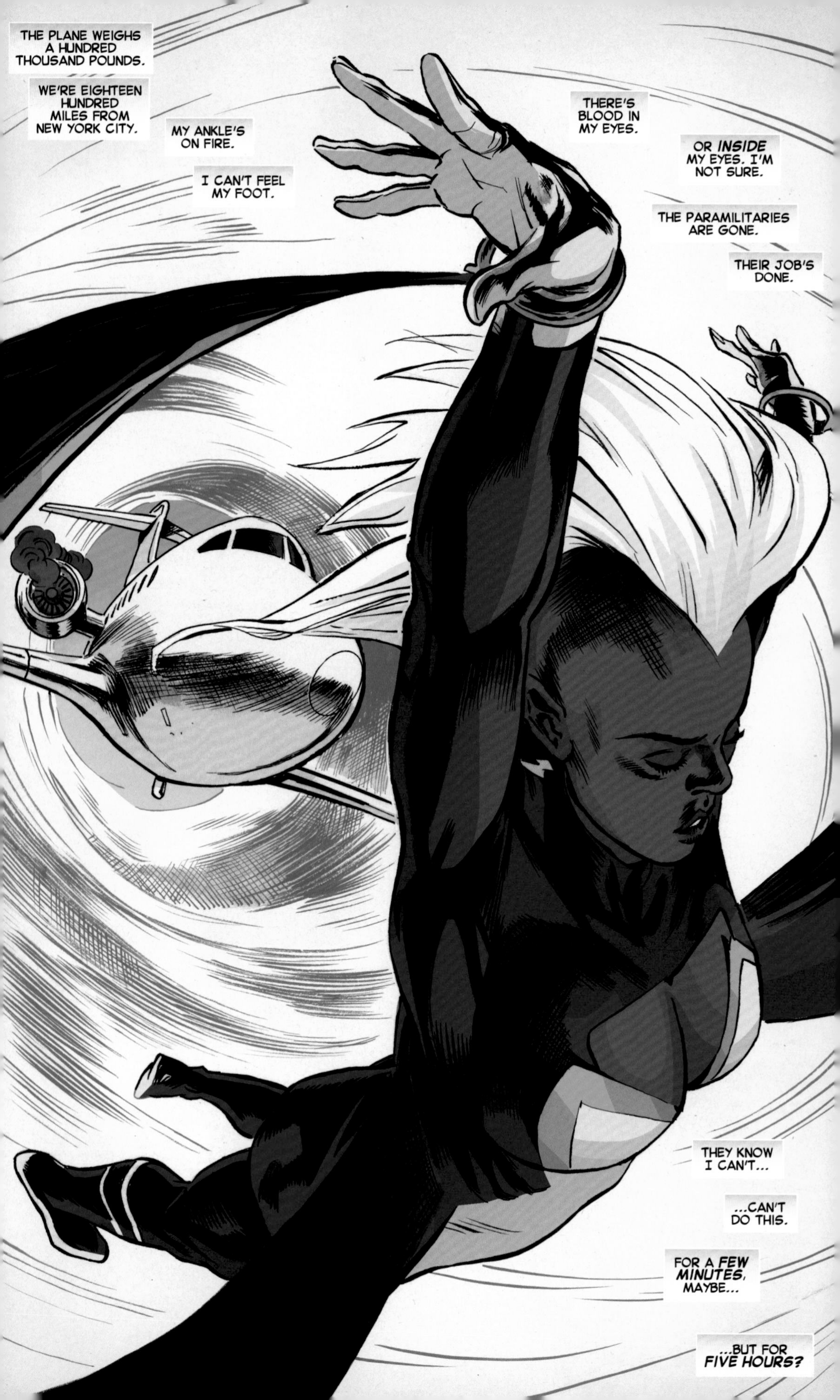
THE PLANE WEIGHS A HUNDRED THOUSAND POUNDS.
WE'RE EIGHTEEN HUNDRED MILES FROM NEW YORK CITY.
MY ANKLE'S ON FIRE.
I CAN'T FEEL MY FOOT.
THERE'S BLOOD IN MY EYES.
OR *INSIDE* MY EYES. I'M NOT SURE.
THE PARAMILITARIES ARE GONE.
THEIR JOB'S DONE.
THEY KNOW I CAN'T...
...CAN'T DO THIS.
FOR A *FEW MINUTES*, MAYBE...
...BUT FOR *FIVE HOURS?*

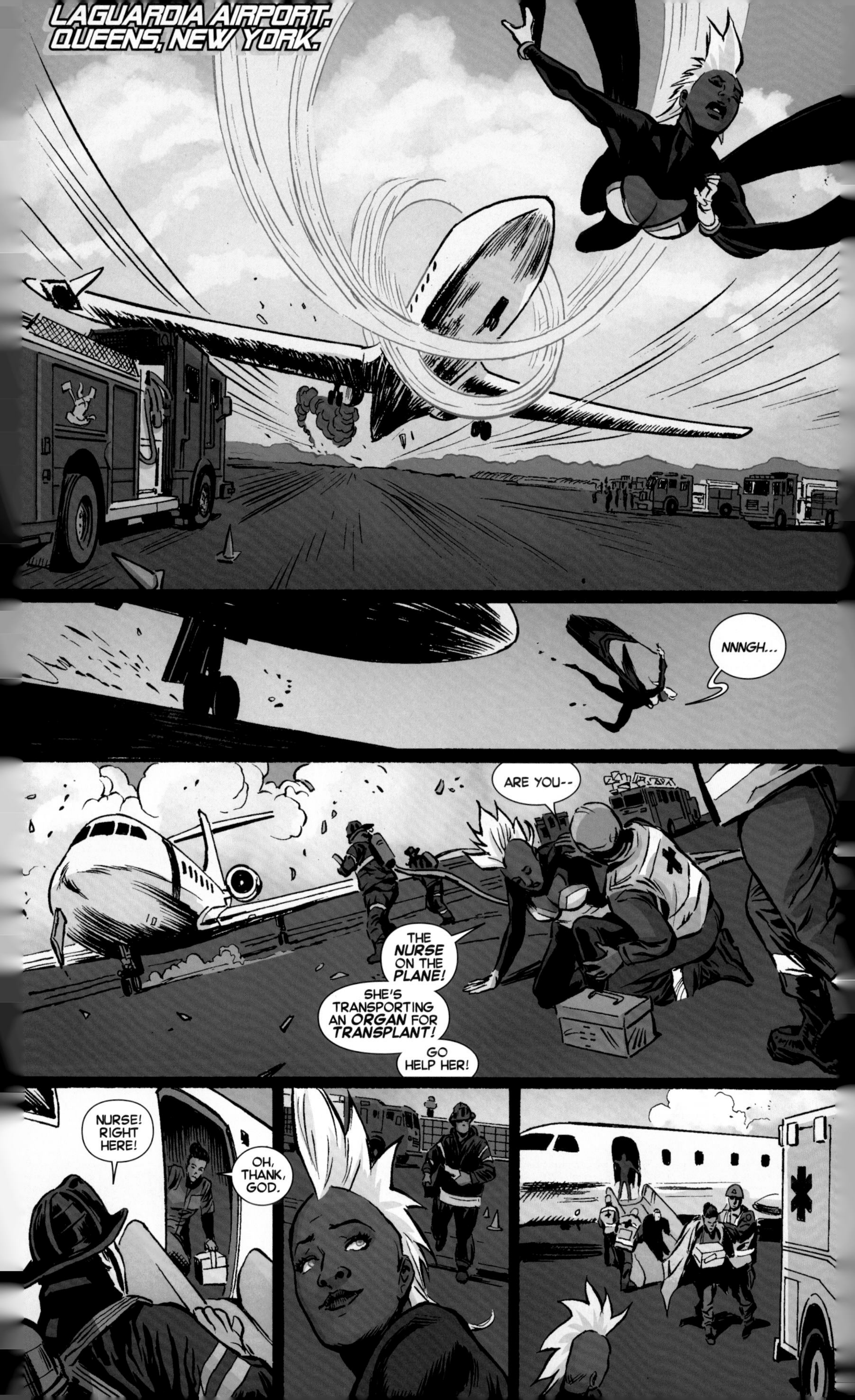
LAGUARDIA AIRPORT. QUEENS, NEW YORK.
NNNGH...
ARE YOU--
THE NURSE ON THE PLANE!
SHE'S TRANSPORTING AN ORGAN FOR TRANSPLANT!
GO HELP HER!
NURSE! RIGHT HERE!
OH, THANK, GOD.

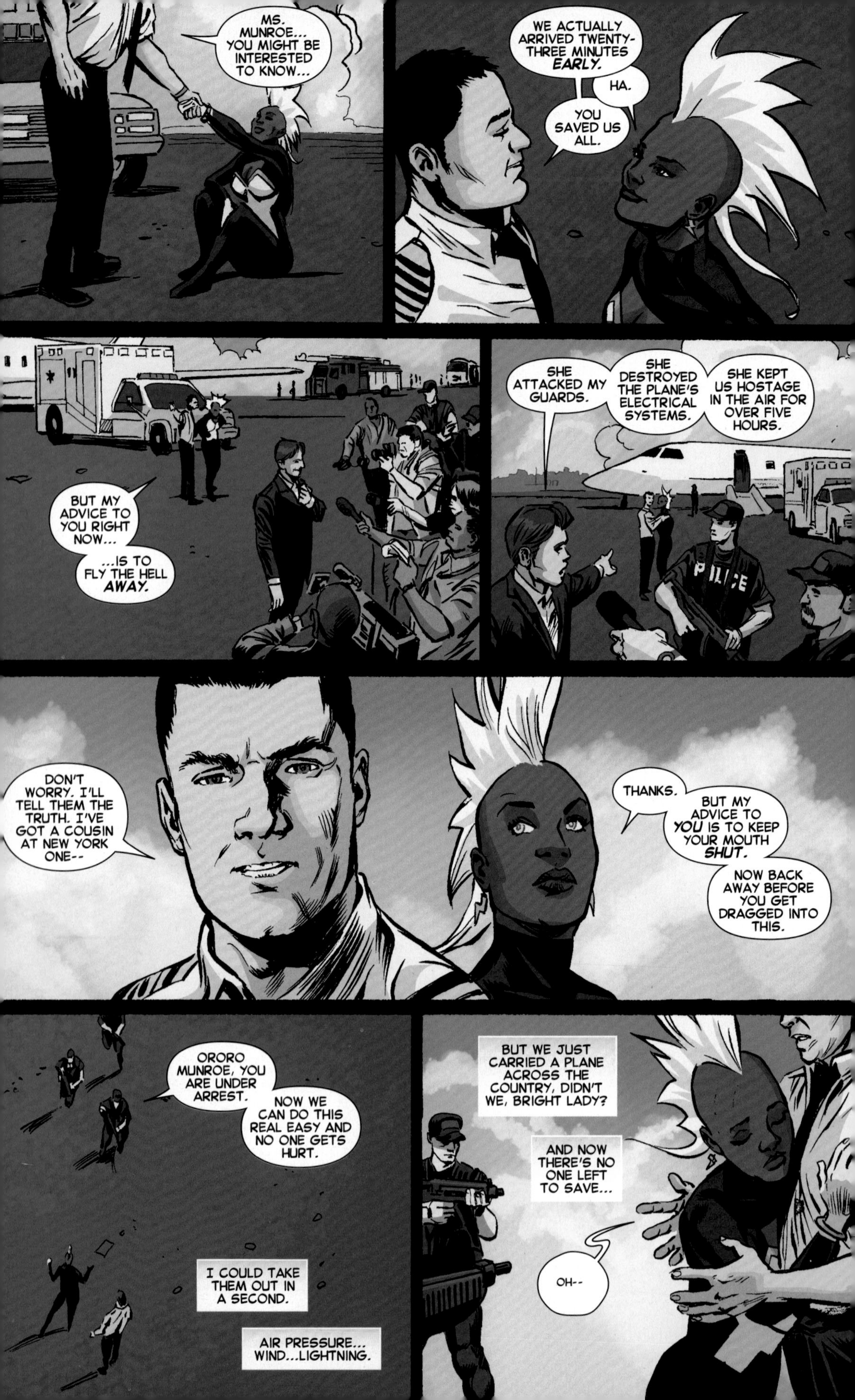
MS. MUNROE... YOU MIGHT BE INTERESTED TO KNOW...
WE ACTUALLY ARRIVED TWENTY-THREE MINUTES EARLY.
HA.
YOU SAVED US ALL.
BUT MY ADVICE TO YOU RIGHT NOW...
...IS TO FLY THE HELL AWAY.
SHE ATTACKED MY GUARDS.
SHE DESTROYED THE PLANE'S ELECTRICAL SYSTEMS.
SHE KEPT US HOSTAGE IN THE AIR FOR OVER FIVE HOURS.
POLICE
DON'T WORRY. I'LL TELL THEM THE TRUTH. I'VE GOT A COUSIN AT NEW YORK ONE--
THANKS.
BUT MY ADVICE TO YOU IS TO KEEP YOUR MOUTH SHUT.
NOW BACK AWAY BEFORE YOU GET DRAGGED INTO THIS.
ORORO MUNROE, YOU ARE UNDER ARREST.
NOW WE CAN DO THIS REAL EASY AND NO ONE GETS HURT.
I COULD TAKE THEM OUT IN A SECOND.
AIR PRESSURE... WIND...LIGHTNING.
BUT WE JUST CARRIED A PLANE ACROSS THE COUNTRY, DIDN'T WE, BRIGHT LADY?
AND NOW THERE'S NO ONE LEFT TO SAVE...
OH--

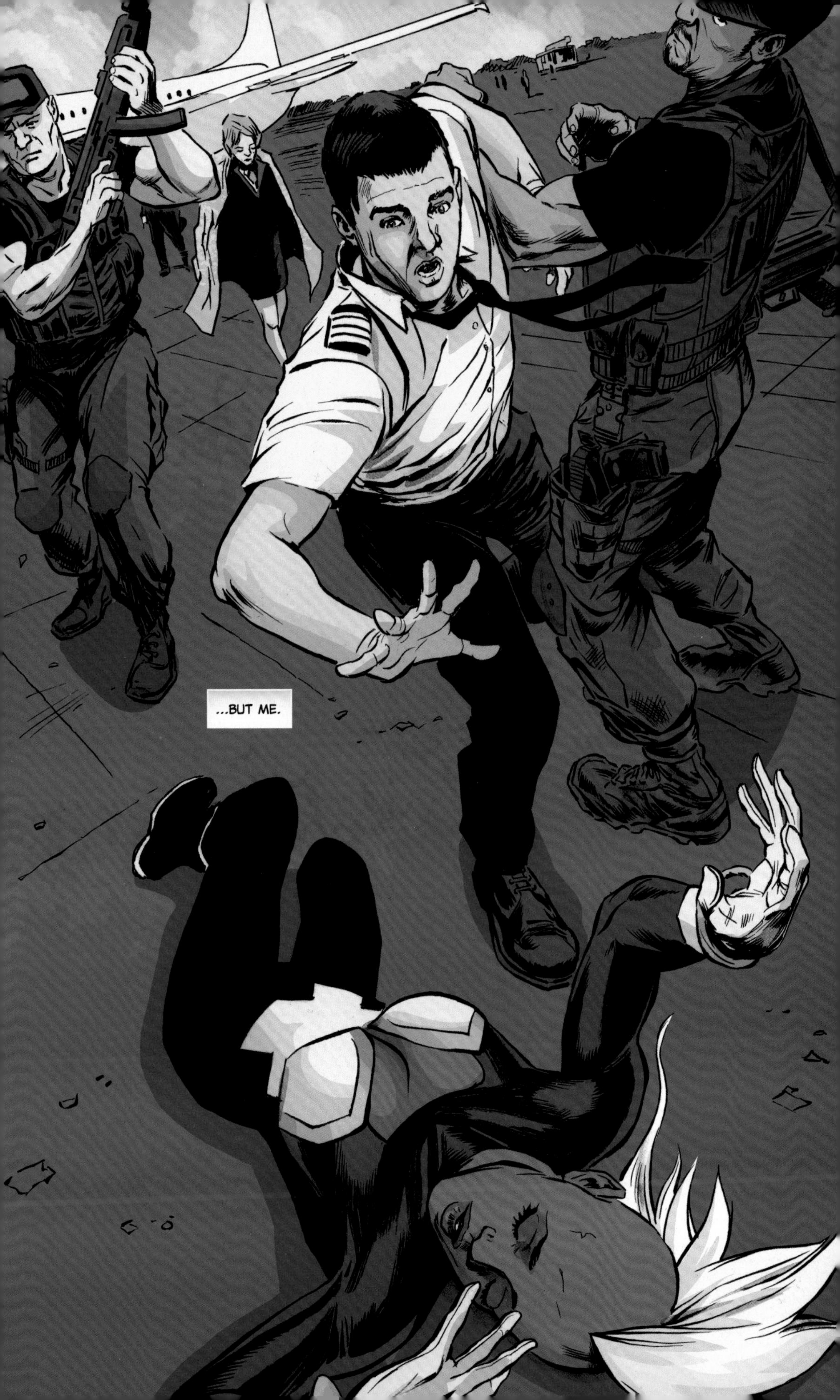
...BUT ME.

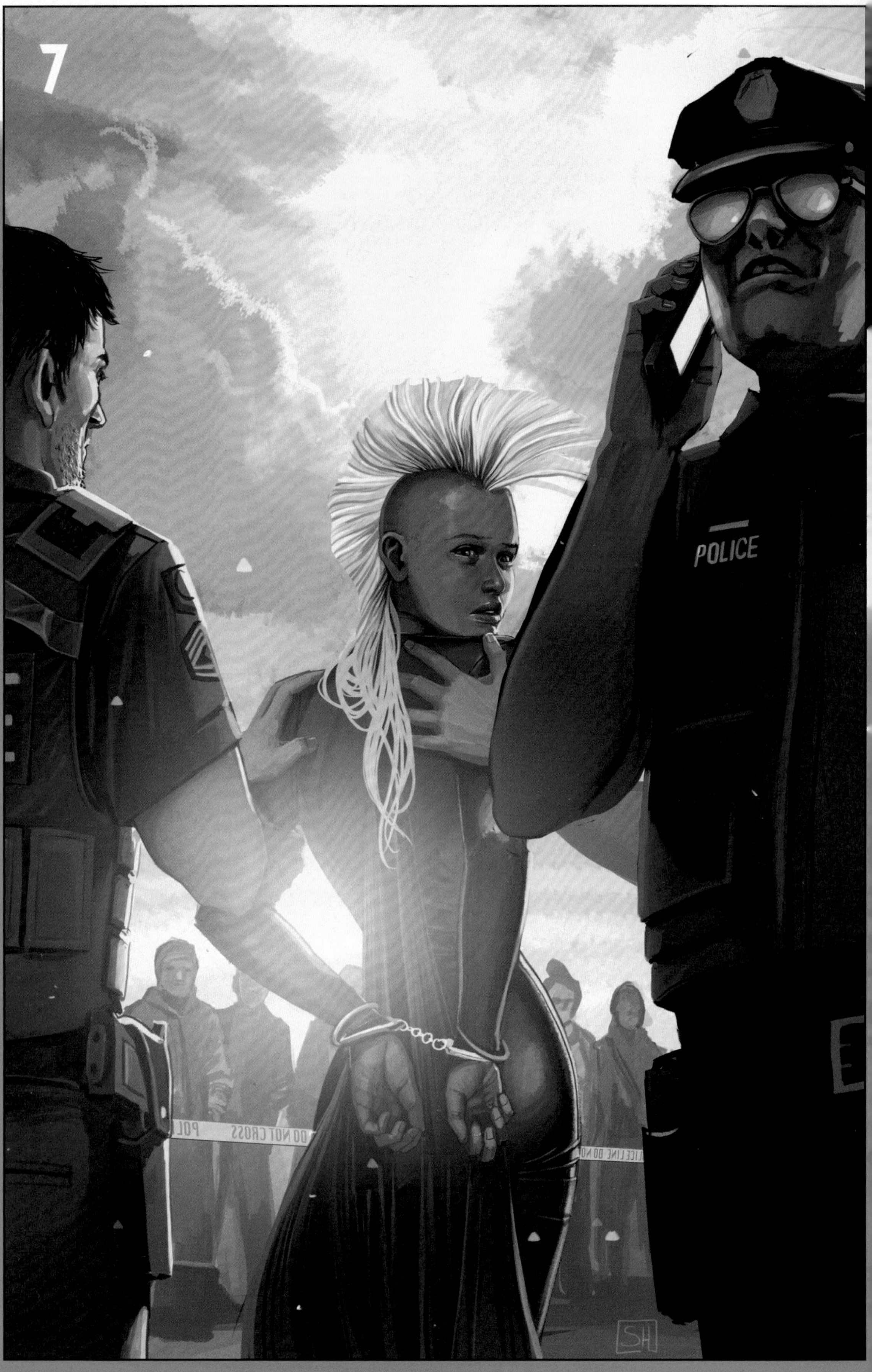

7
POLICE

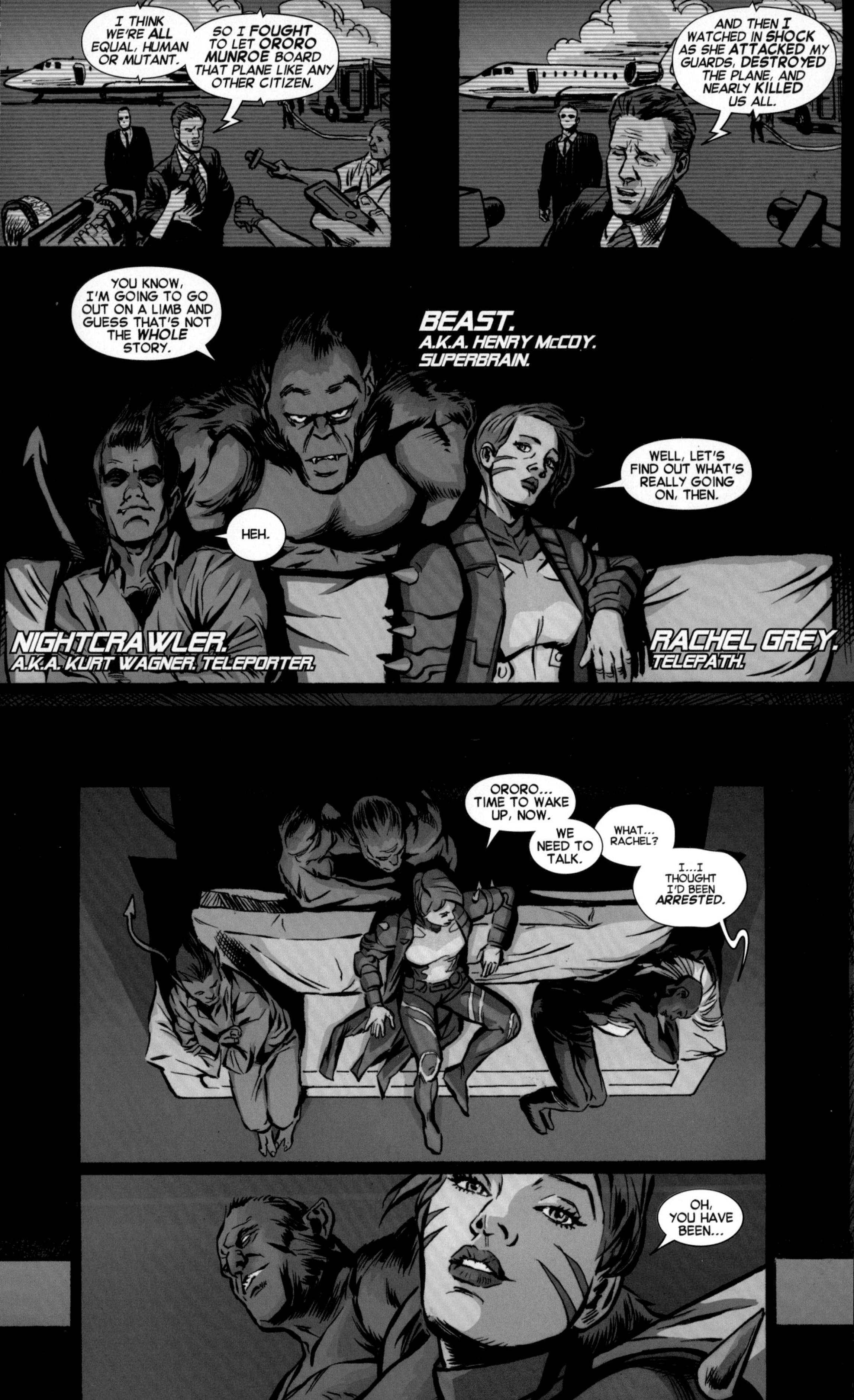
I THINK WE'RE ALL EQUAL, HUMAN OR MUTANT.
SO I FOUGHT TO LET ORORO MUNROE BOARD THAT PLANE LIKE ANY OTHER CITIZEN.
AND THEN I WATCHED IN SHOCK AS SHE ATTACKED MY GUARDS, DESTROYED THE PLANE, AND NEARLY KILLED US ALL.
YOU KNOW, I'M GOING TO GO OUT ON A LIMB AND GUESS THAT'S NOT THE WHOLE STORY.
BEAST. A.K.A. HENRY McCOY. SUPERBRAIN.
HEH.
WELL, LET'S FIND OUT WHAT'S REALLY GOING ON, THEN.
NIGHTCRAWLER. A.K.A. KURT WAGNER. TELEPORTER.
RACHEL GREY. TELEPATH.
ORORO... TIME TO WAKE UP, NOW.
WE NEED TO TALK.
WHAT... RACHEL?
I...I THOUGHT I'D BEEN ARRESTED.
OH, YOU HAVE BEEN...

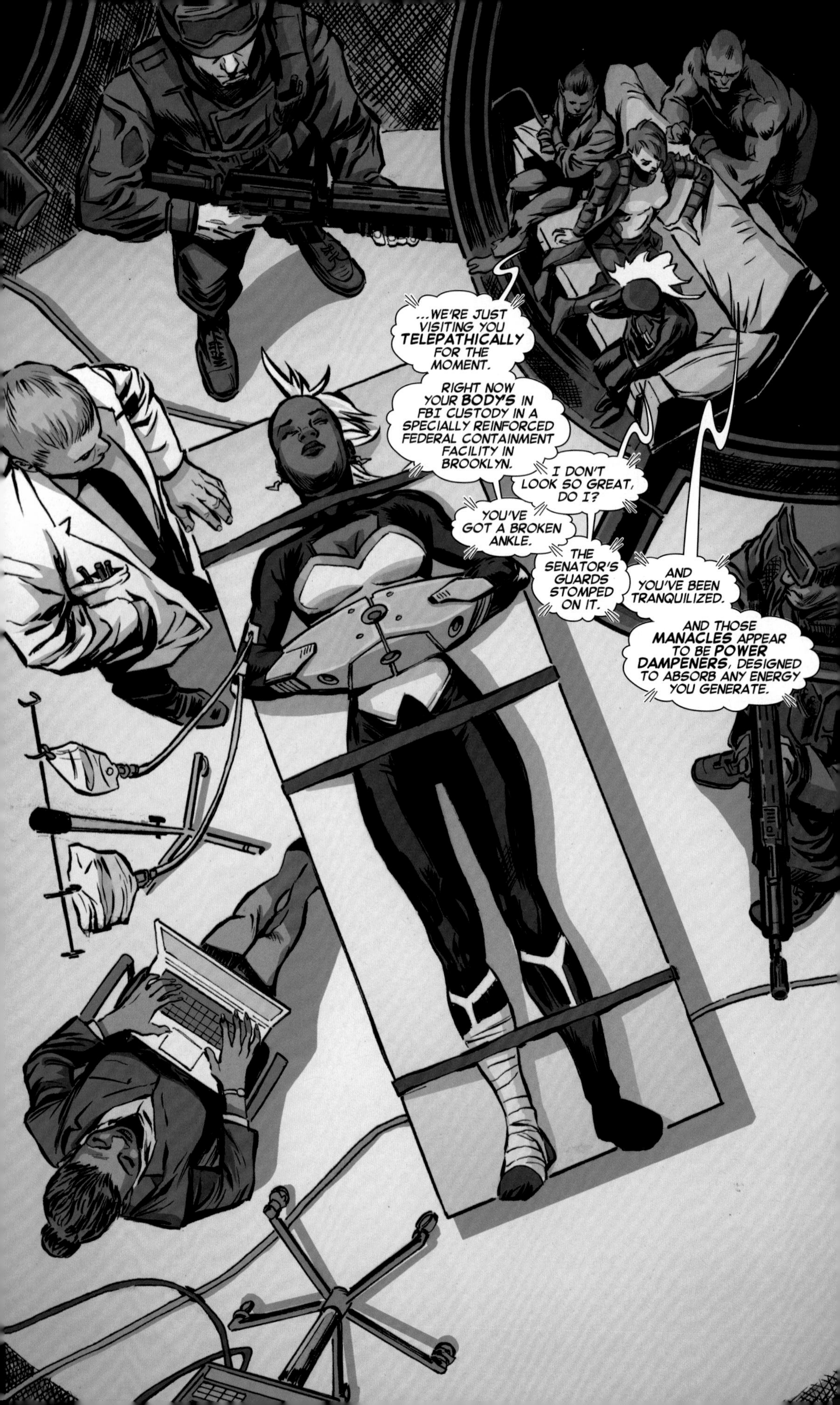

...WE'RE JUST VISITING YOU TELEPATHICALLY FOR THE MOMENT.
RIGHT NOW YOUR BODY'S IN FBI CUSTODY IN A SPECIALLY REINFORCED FEDERAL CONTAINMENT FACILITY IN BROOKLYN.
I DON'T LOOK SO GREAT, DO I?
YOU'VE GOT A BROKEN ANKLE.
THE SENATOR'S GUARDS STOMPED ON IT.
AND YOU'VE BEEN TRANQUILIZED.
AND THOSE MANACLES APPEAR TO BE POWER DAMPENERS, DESIGNED TO ABSORB ANY ENERGY YOU GENERATE.

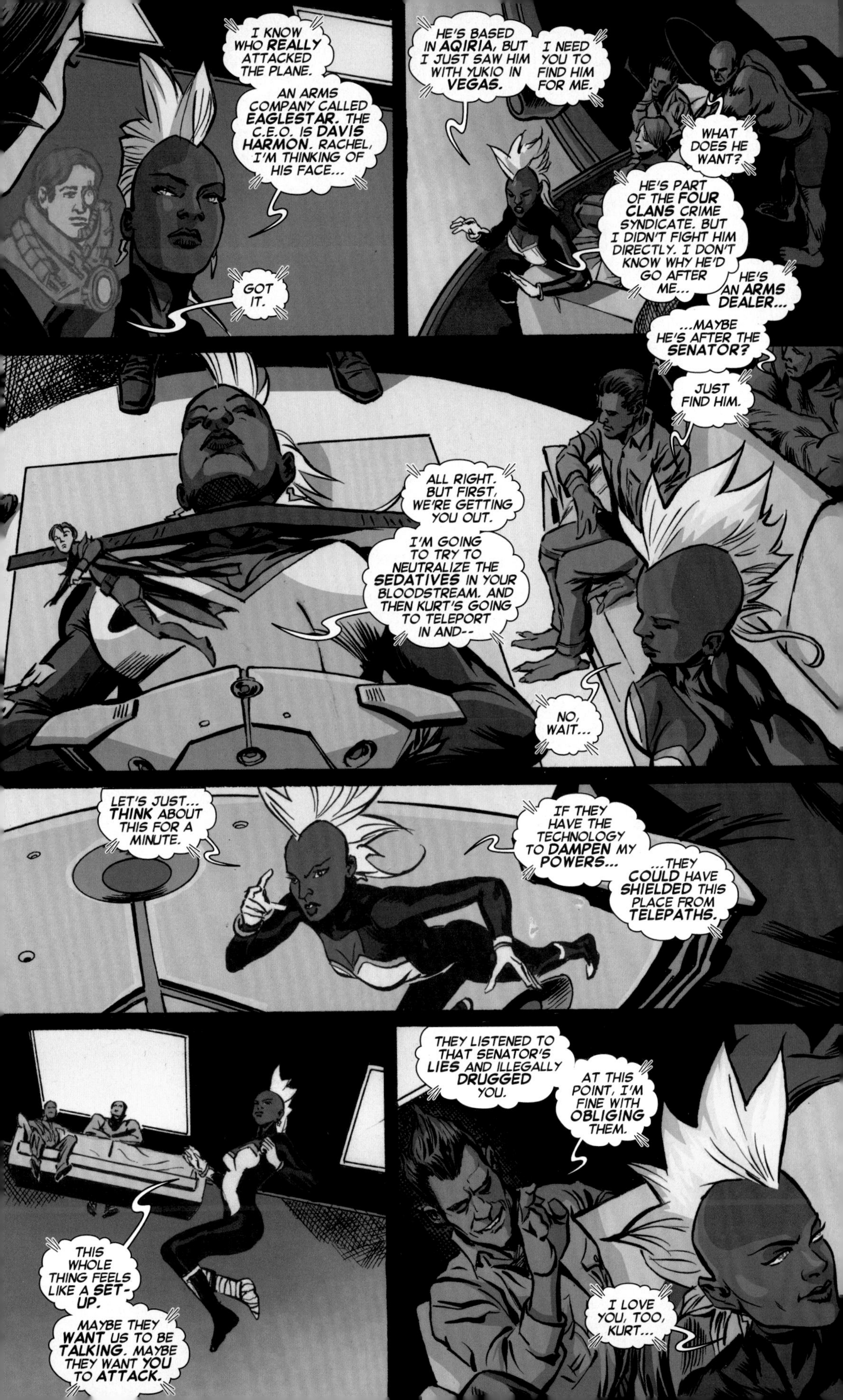

I KNOW WHO REALLY ATTACKED THE PLANE.
AN ARMS COMPANY CALLED EAGLESTAR. THE C.E.O. IS DAVIS HARMON. RACHEL, I'M THINKING OF HIS FACE...
GOT IT.
HE'S BASED IN AQIRIA, BUT I JUST SAW HIM WITH YUKIO IN VEGAS.
I NEED YOU TO FIND HIM FOR ME.
WHAT DOES HE WANT?
HE'S PART OF THE FOUR CLANS CRIME SYNDICATE. BUT I DIDN'T FIGHT HIM DIRECTLY. I DON'T KNOW WHY HE'D GO AFTER ME...
HE'S AN ARMS DEALER...
...MAYBE HE'S AFTER THE SENATOR?
JUST FIND HIM.
ALL RIGHT. BUT FIRST, WE'RE GETTING YOU OUT.
I'M GOING TO TRY TO NEUTRALIZE THE SEDATIVES IN YOUR BLOODSTREAM. AND THEN KURT'S GOING TO TELEPORT IN AND--
NO, WAIT...
LET'S JUST... THINK ABOUT THIS FOR A MINUTE.
IF THEY HAVE THE TECHNOLOGY TO DAMPEN MY POWERS...
...THEY COULD HAVE SHIELDED THIS PLACE FROM TELEPATHS.
THIS WHOLE THING FEELS LIKE A SET-UP.
MAYBE THEY WANT US TO BE TALKING. MAYBE THEY WANT YOU TO ATTACK.
THEY LISTENED TO THAT SENATOR'S LIES AND ILLEGALLY DRUGGED YOU.
AT THIS POINT, I'M FINE WITH OBLIGING THEM.
I LOVE YOU, TOO, KURT...

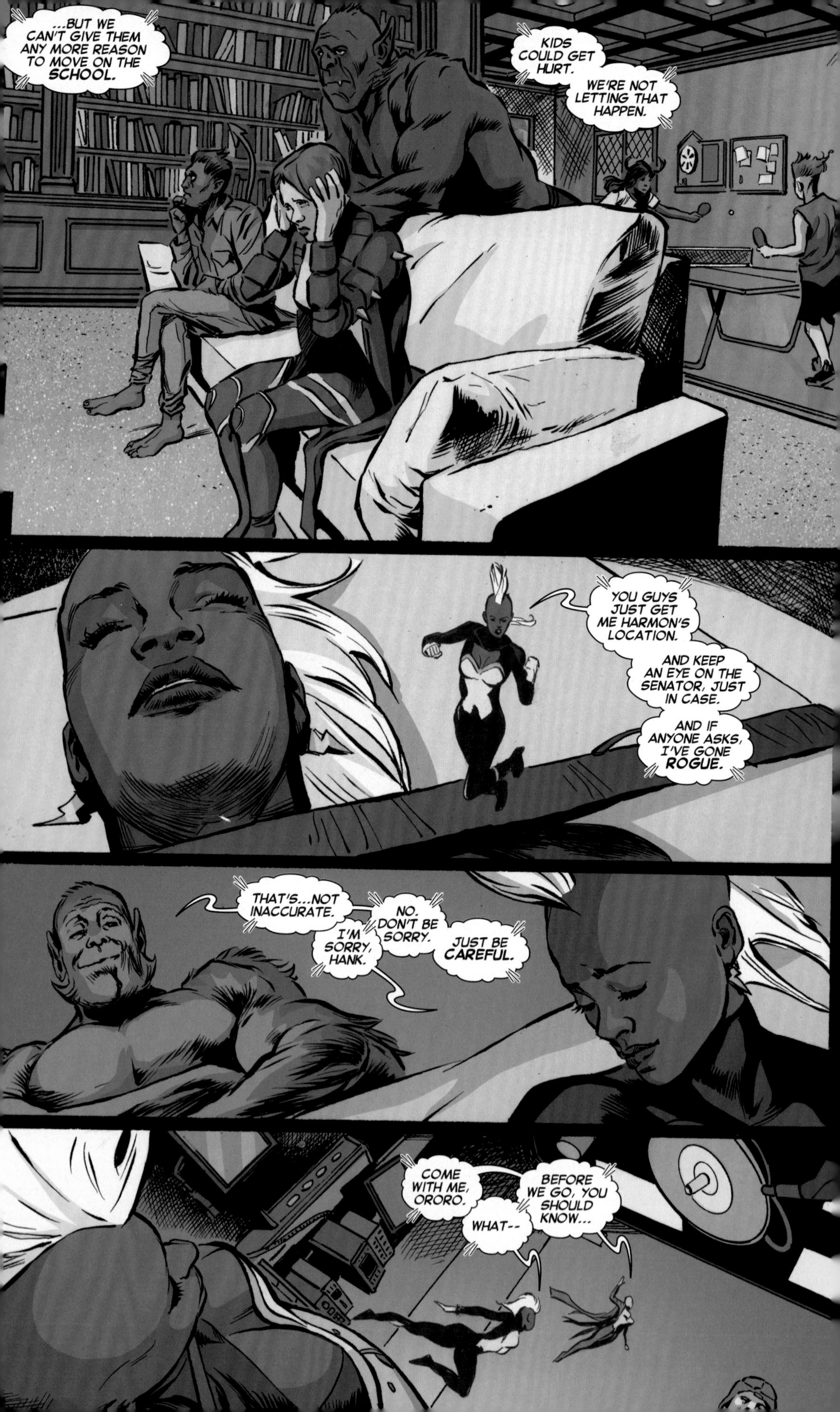
...BUT WE CAN'T GIVE THEM ANY MORE REASON TO MOVE ON THE SCHOOL.
KIDS COULD GET HURT.
WE'RE NOT LETTING THAT HAPPEN.
YOU GUYS JUST GET ME HARMON'S LOCATION.
AND KEEP AN EYE ON THE SENATOR, JUST IN CASE.
AND IF ANYONE ASKS, I'VE GONE ROGUE.
THAT'S...NOT INACCURATE.
I'M SORRY, HANK.
NO. DON'T BE SORRY.
JUST BE CAREFUL.
COME WITH ME, ORORO.
WHAT--
BEFORE WE GO, YOU SHOULD KNOW...

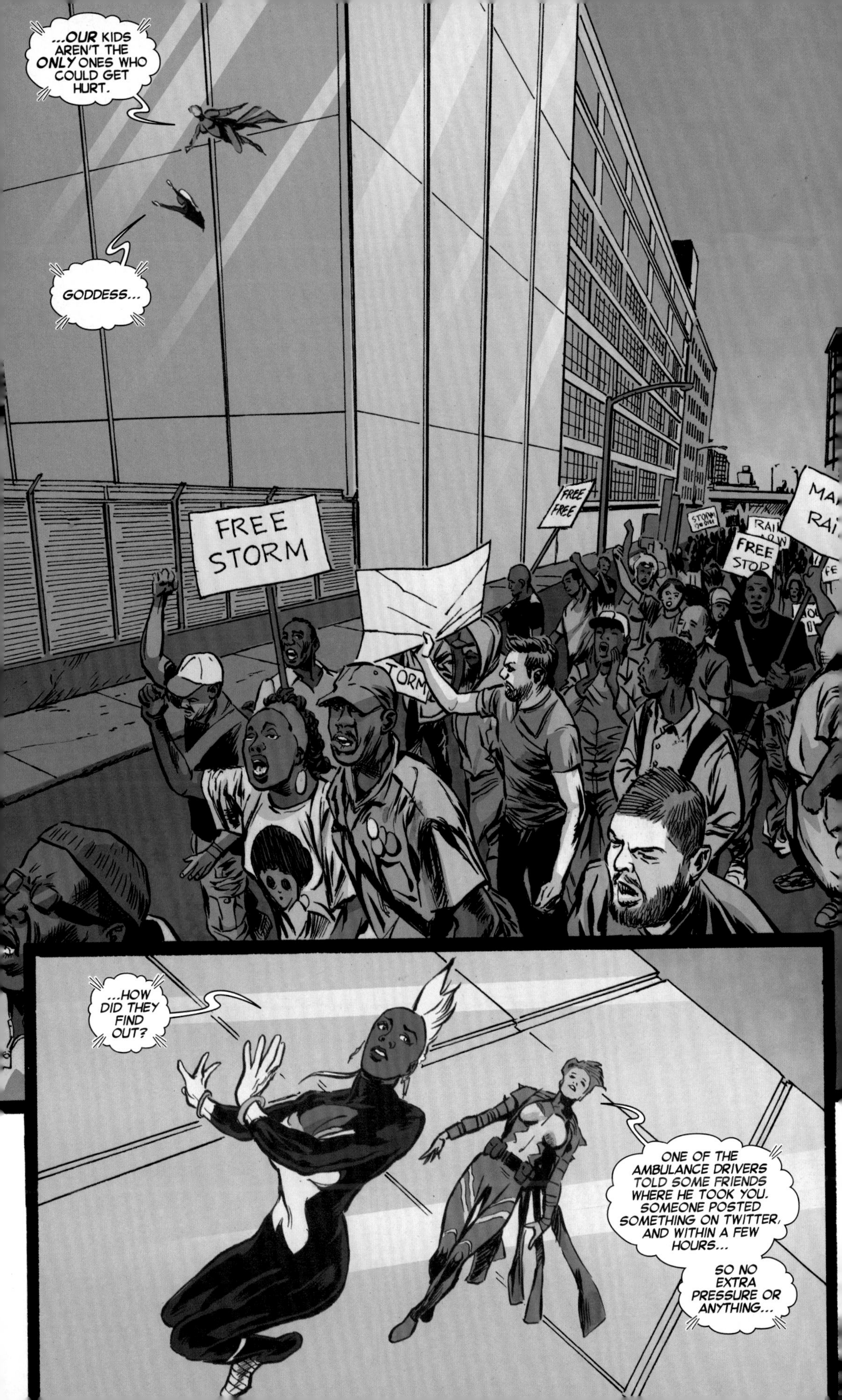
...OUR KIDS AREN'T THE ONLY ONES WHO COULD GET HURT.
GODDESS...
FREE STORM
FREE FREE
FREE STOR
...HOW DID THEY FIND OUT?
ONE OF THE AMBULANCE DRIVERS TOLD SOME FRIENDS WHERE HE TOOK YOU. SOMEONE POSTED SOMETHING ON TWITTER, AND WITHIN A FEW HOURS...
SO NO EXTRA PRESSURE OR ANYTHING...

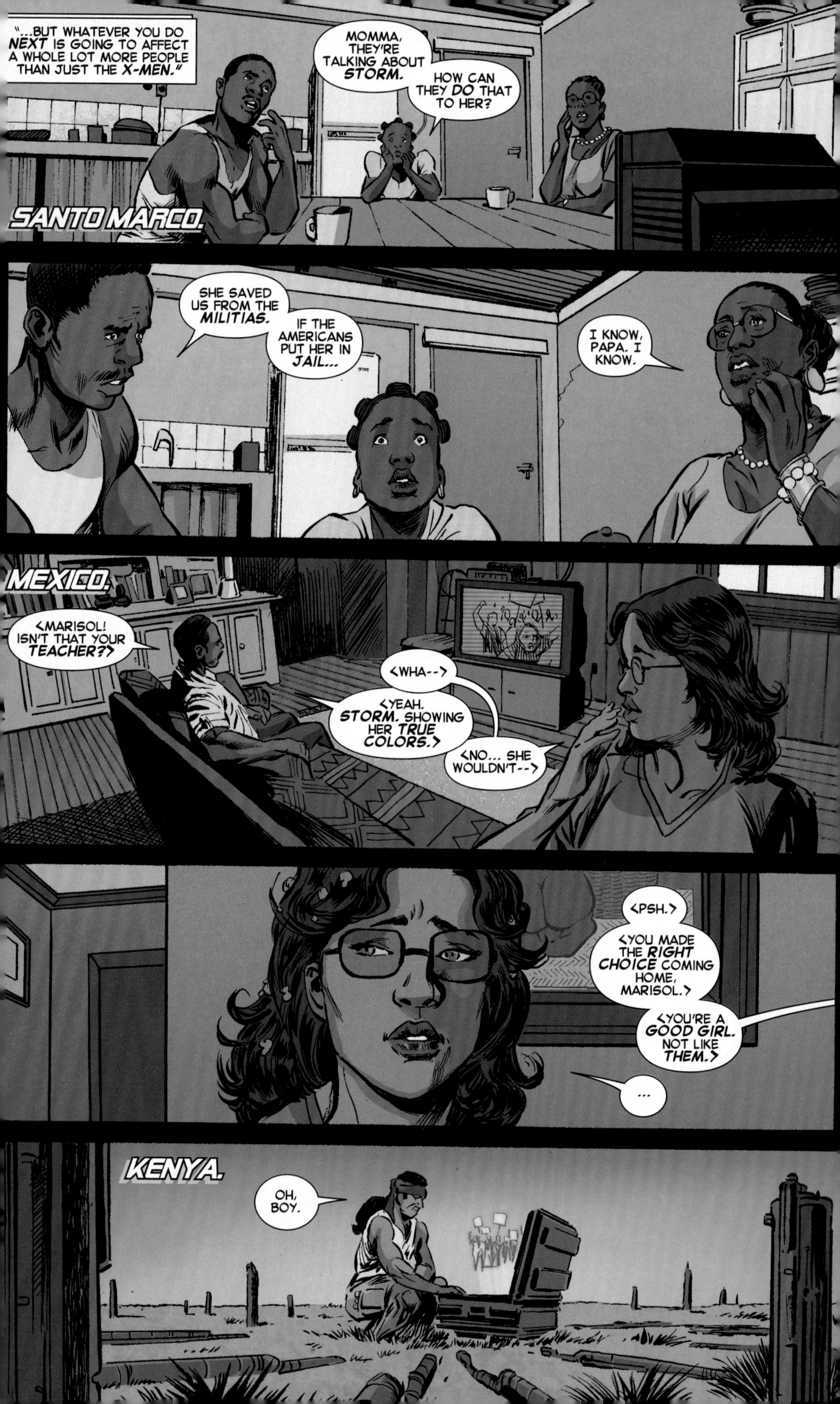
"...BUT WHATEVER YOU DO NEXT IS GOING TO AFFECT A WHOLE LOT MORE PEOPLE THAN JUST THE X-MEN."
MOMMA, THEY'RE TALKING ABOUT STORM.
HOW CAN THEY DO THAT TO HER?
SANTO MARCO.
SHE SAVED US FROM THE MILITIAS.
IF THE AMERICANS PUT HER IN JAIL...
I KNOW, PAPA. I KNOW.
MEXICO.
<MARISOL! ISN'T THAT YOUR TEACHER?>
<WHA-->
<YEAH. STORM. SHOWING HER TRUE COLORS.>
<NO... SHE WOULDN'T-->
<PSH.>
<YOU MADE THE RIGHT CHOICE COMING HOME, MARISOL.>
<YOU'RE A GOOD GIRL. NOT LIKE THEM.>
...
KENYA.
OH, BOY.

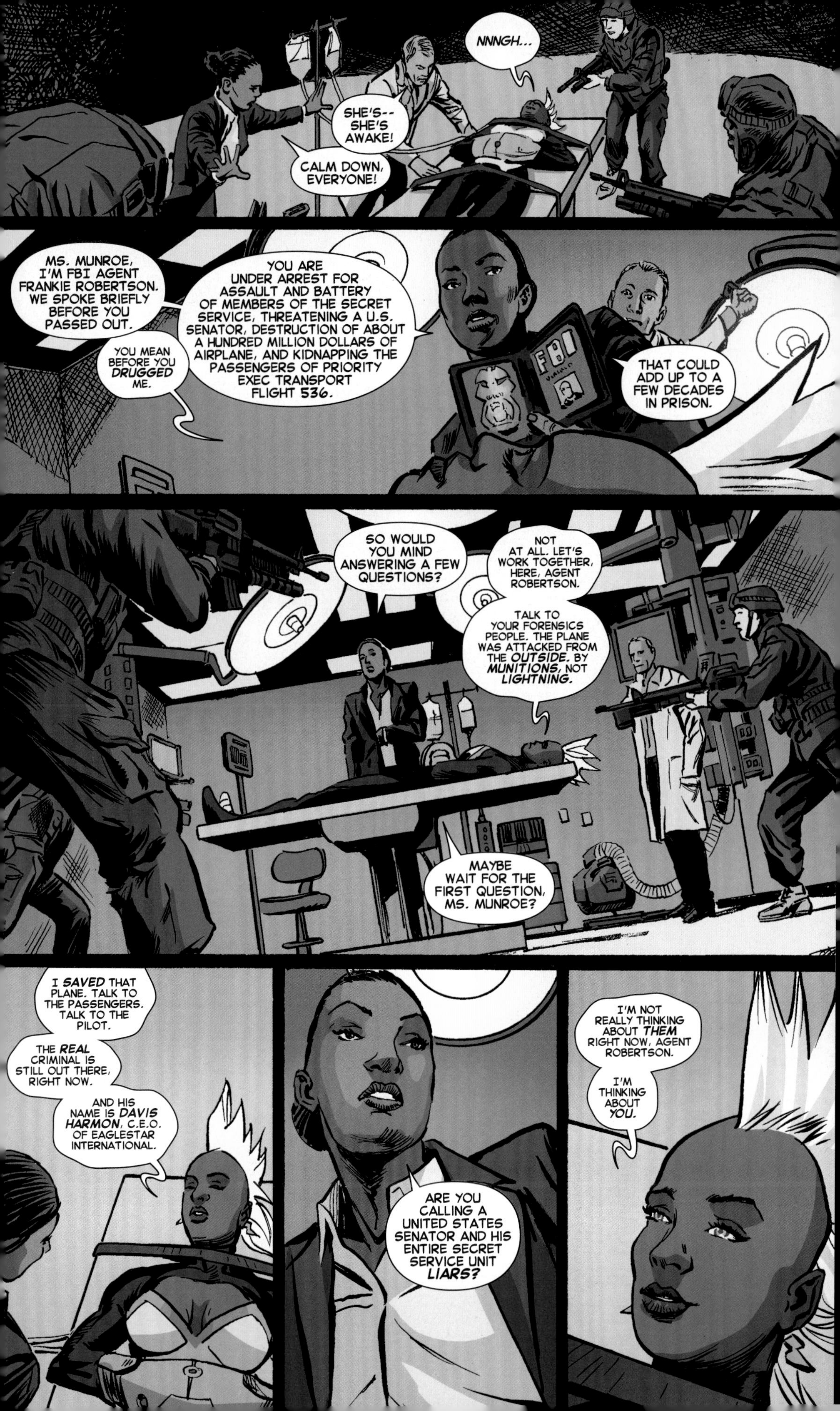

NNNGH...
SHE'S-- SHE'S AWAKE!
CALM DOWN, EVERYONE!
MS. MUNROE, I'M FBI AGENT FRANKIE ROBERTSON. WE SPOKE BRIEFLY BEFORE YOU PASSED OUT.
YOU MEAN BEFORE YOU DRUGGED ME.
YOU ARE UNDER ARREST FOR ASSAULT AND BATTERY OF MEMBERS OF THE SECRET SERVICE, THREATENING A U.S. SENATOR, DESTRUCTION OF ABOUT A HUNDRED MILLION DOLLARS OF AIRPLANE, AND KIDNAPPING THE PASSENGERS OF PRIORITY EXEC TRANSPORT FLIGHT 536.
FBI
THAT COULD ADD UP TO A FEW DECADES IN PRISON.
SO WOULD YOU MIND ANSWERING A FEW QUESTIONS?
NOT AT ALL. LET'S WORK TOGETHER, HERE, AGENT ROBERTSON.
TALK TO YOUR FORENSICS PEOPLE. THE PLANE WAS ATTACKED FROM THE OUTSIDE. BY MUNITIONS, NOT LIGHTNING.
MAYBE WAIT FOR THE FIRST QUESTION, MS. MUNROE?
I SAVED THAT PLANE. TALK TO THE PASSENGERS. TALK TO THE PILOT.
THE REAL CRIMINAL IS STILL OUT THERE, RIGHT NOW.
AND HIS NAME IS DAVIS HARMON, C.E.O. OF EAGLESTAR INTERNATIONAL.
ARE YOU CALLING A UNITED STATES SENATOR AND HIS ENTIRE SECRET SERVICE UNIT LIARS?
I'M NOT REALLY THINKING ABOUT THEM RIGHT NOW, AGENT ROBERTSON.
I'M THINKING ABOUT YOU.

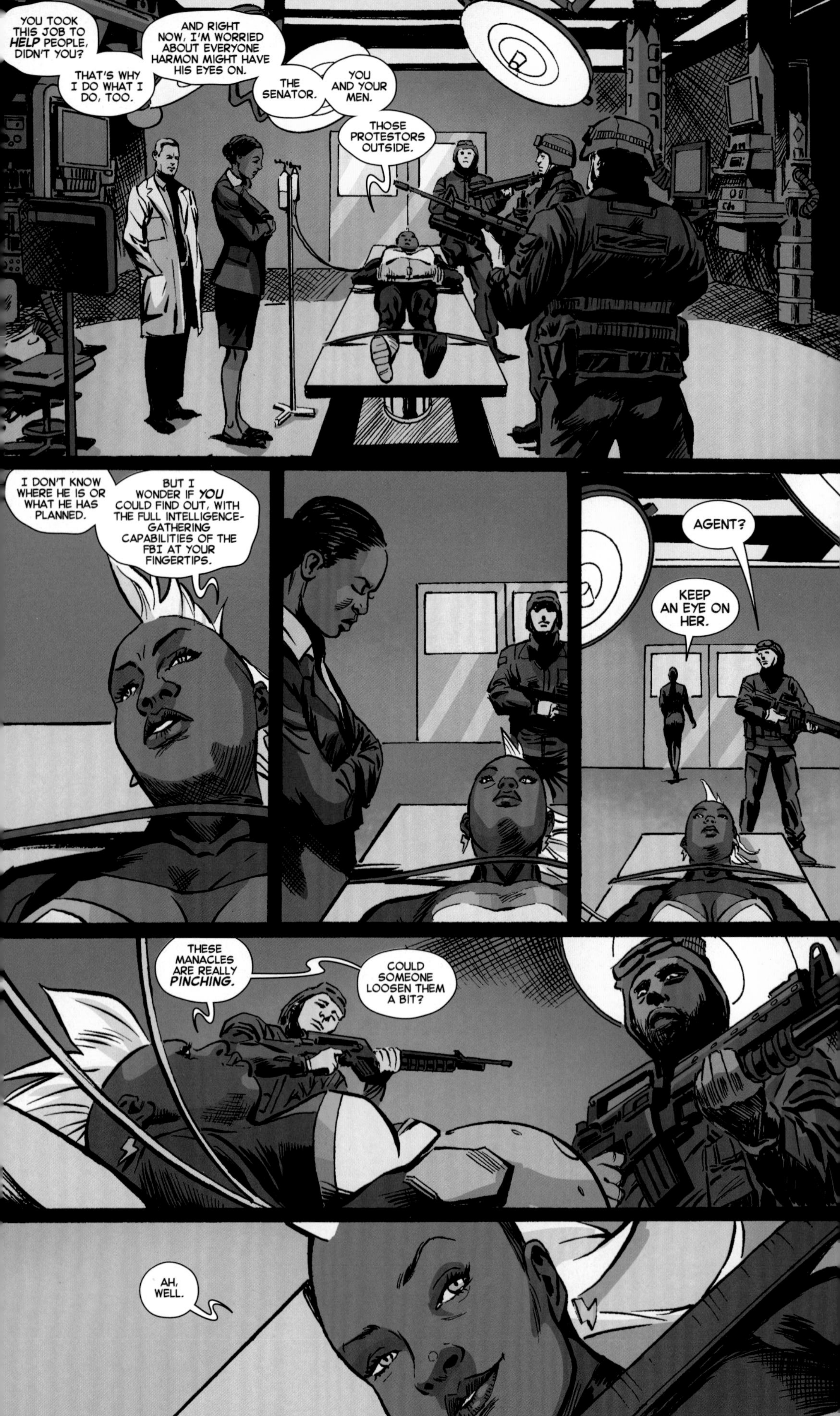
YOU TOOK THIS JOB TO HELP PEOPLE, DIDN'T YOU?
THAT'S WHY I DO WHAT I DO, TOO.
AND RIGHT NOW, I'M WORRIED ABOUT EVERYONE HARMON MIGHT HAVE HIS EYES ON.
THE SENATOR.
YOU AND YOUR MEN.
THOSE PROTESTORS OUTSIDE.
I DON'T KNOW WHERE HE IS OR WHAT HE HAS PLANNED.
BUT I WONDER IF YOU COULD FIND OUT, WITH THE FULL INTELLIGENCE-GATHERING CAPABILITIES OF THE FBI AT YOUR FINGERTIPS.
AGENT?
KEEP AN EYE ON HER.
THESE MANACLES ARE REALLY PINCHING.
COULD SOMEONE LOOSEN THEM A BIT?
AH, WELL.

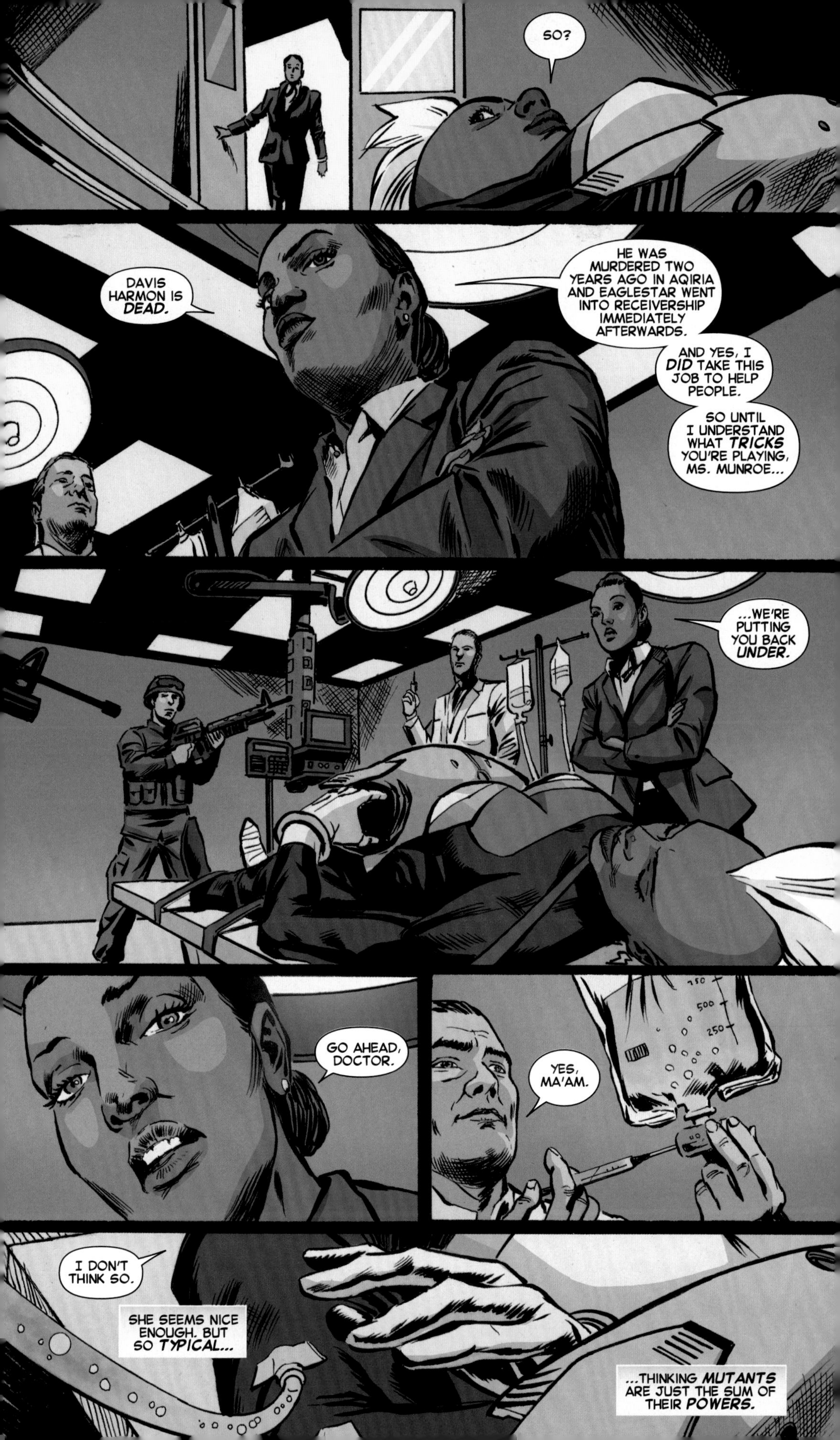
SO?
DAVIS HARMON IS *DEAD.*
HE WAS MURDERED TWO YEARS AGO IN AQIRIA AND EAGLESTAR WENT INTO RECEIVERSHIP IMMEDIATELY AFTERWARDS.
AND YES, I *DID* TAKE THIS JOB TO HELP PEOPLE.
SO UNTIL I UNDERSTAND WHAT *TRICKS* YOU'RE PLAYING, MS. MUNROE...
...WE'RE PUTTING YOU BACK *UNDER.*
GO AHEAD, DOCTOR.
YES, MA'AM.
750
500
250
I DON'T THINK SO.
SHE SEEMS NICE ENOUGH. BUT SO *TYPICAL...*
...THINKING *MUTANTS* ARE JUST THE SUM OF THEIR *POWERS.*

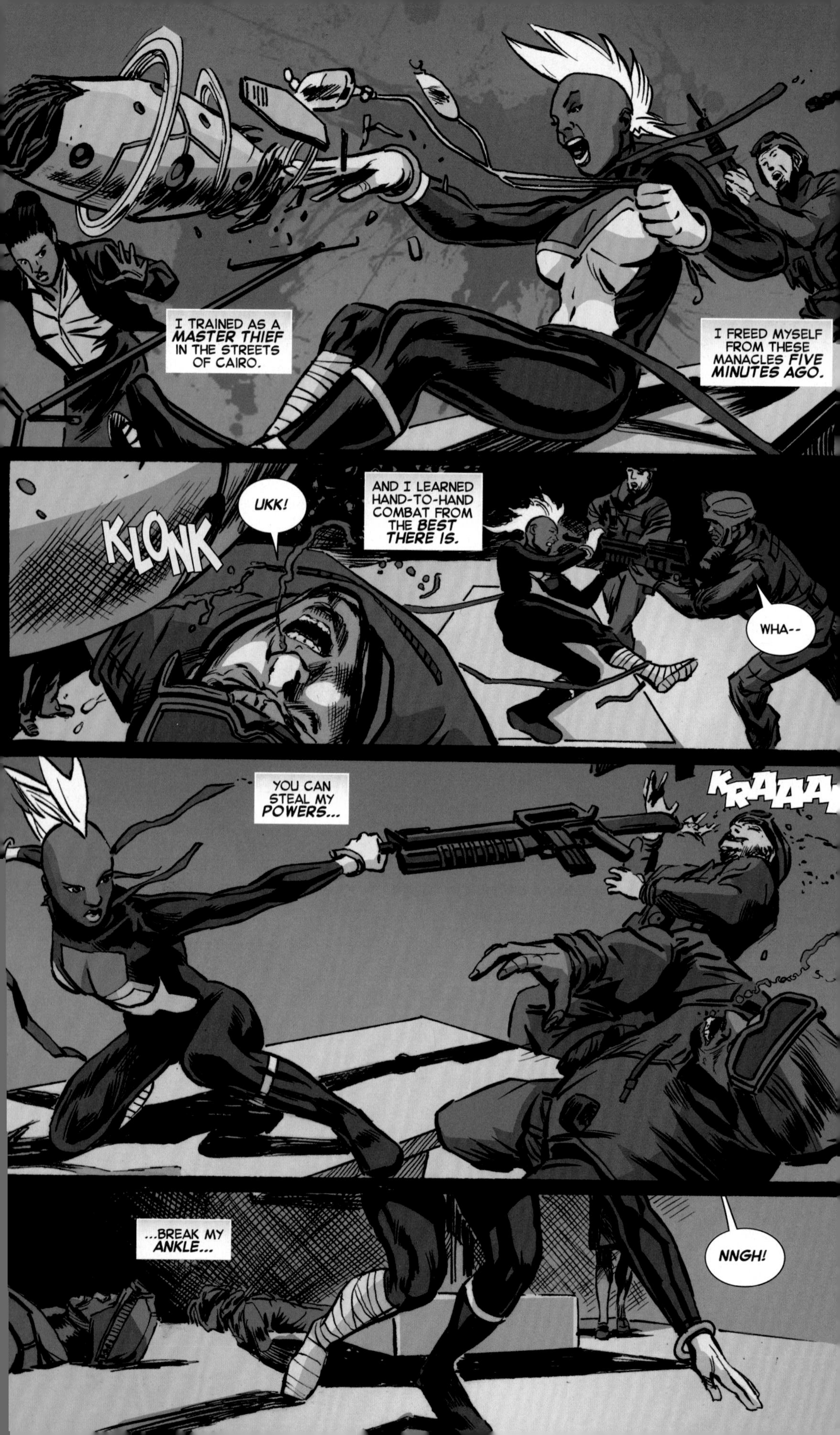

I TRAINED AS A MASTER THIEF IN THE STREETS OF CAIRO.
I FREED MYSELF FROM THESE MANACLES FIVE MINUTES AGO.
KLONK
UKK!
AND I LEARNED HAND-TO-HAND COMBAT FROM THE BEST THERE IS.
WHA--
YOU CAN STEAL MY POWERS...
KRAAA
...BREAK MY ANKLE...
NNGH!

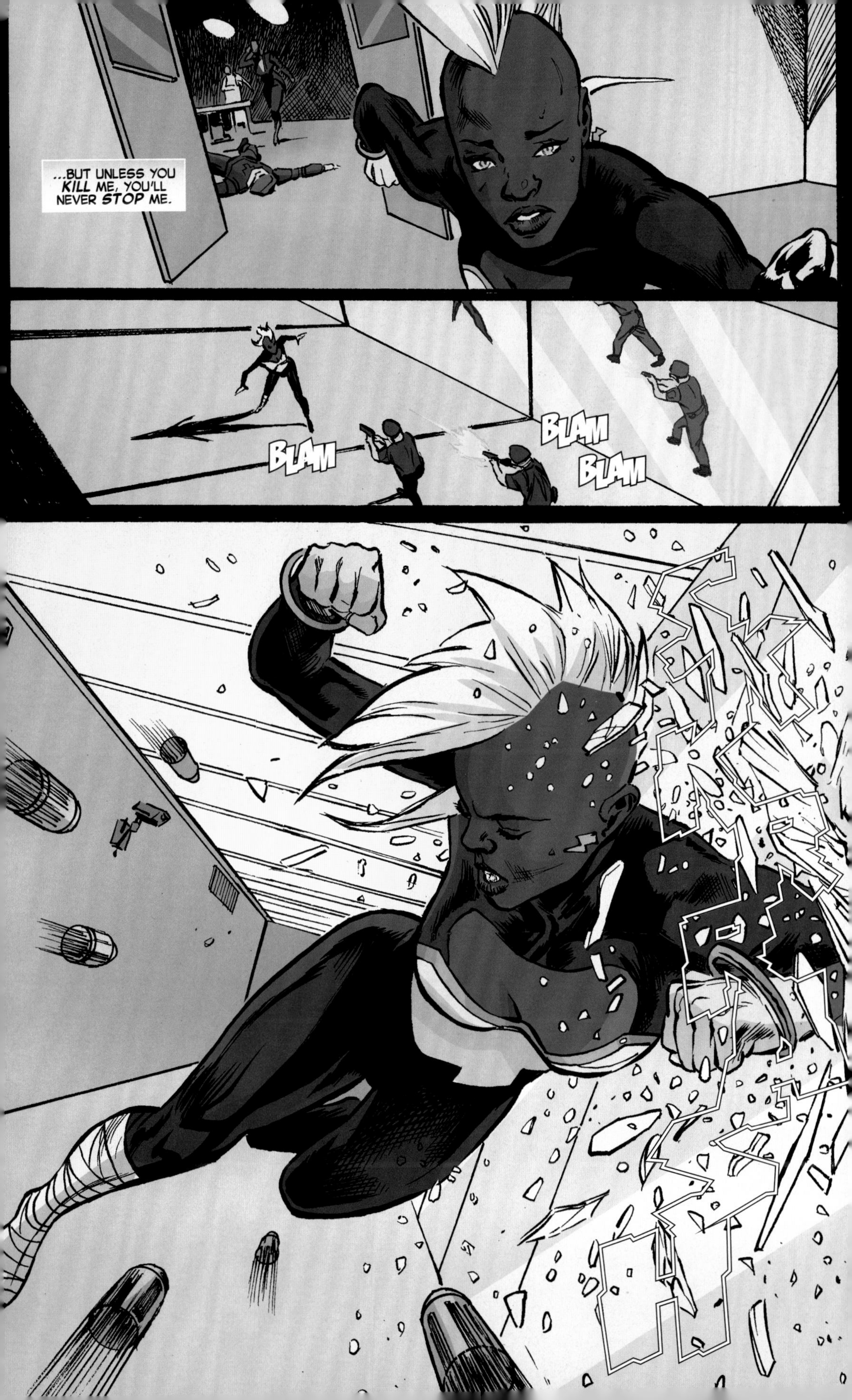
...BUT UNLESS YOU KILL ME, YOU'LL NEVER STOP ME.
BLAM
BLAM
BLAM

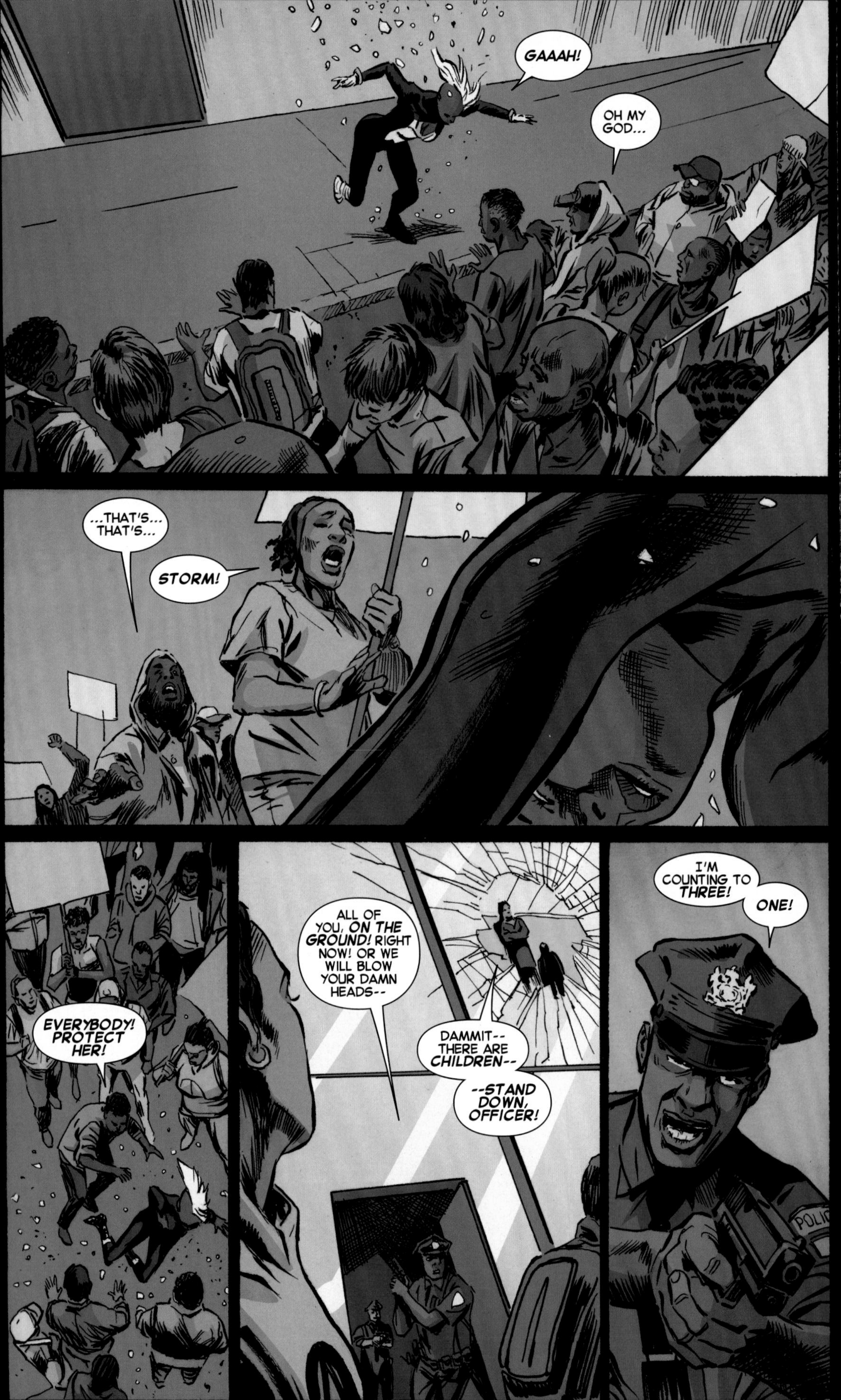
GAAAH!
OH MY GOD...
...THAT'S... THAT'S...
STORM!
EVERYBODY! PROTECT HER!
ALL OF YOU, ON THE GROUND! RIGHT NOW! OR WE WILL BLOW YOUR DAMN HEADS--
DAMMIT-- THERE ARE CHILDREN--
--STAND DOWN, OFFICER!
I'M COUNTING TO THREE!
ONE!

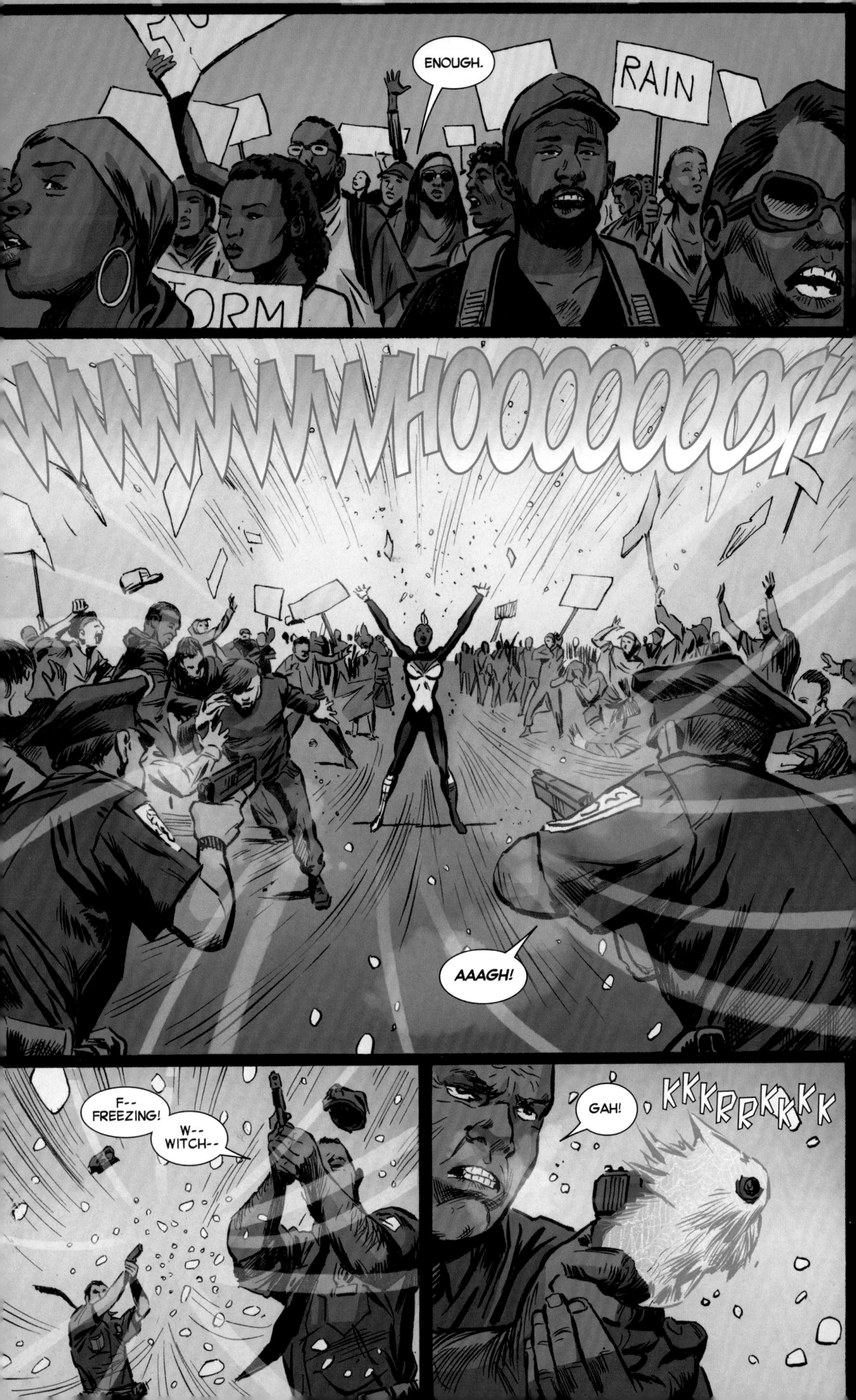

ENOUGH.
RAIN
TORM
WWWWWWWHOOOOOOOSH
AAAGH!
F-- FREEZING!
W-- WITCH--
GAH!
KKKRRRKKKK

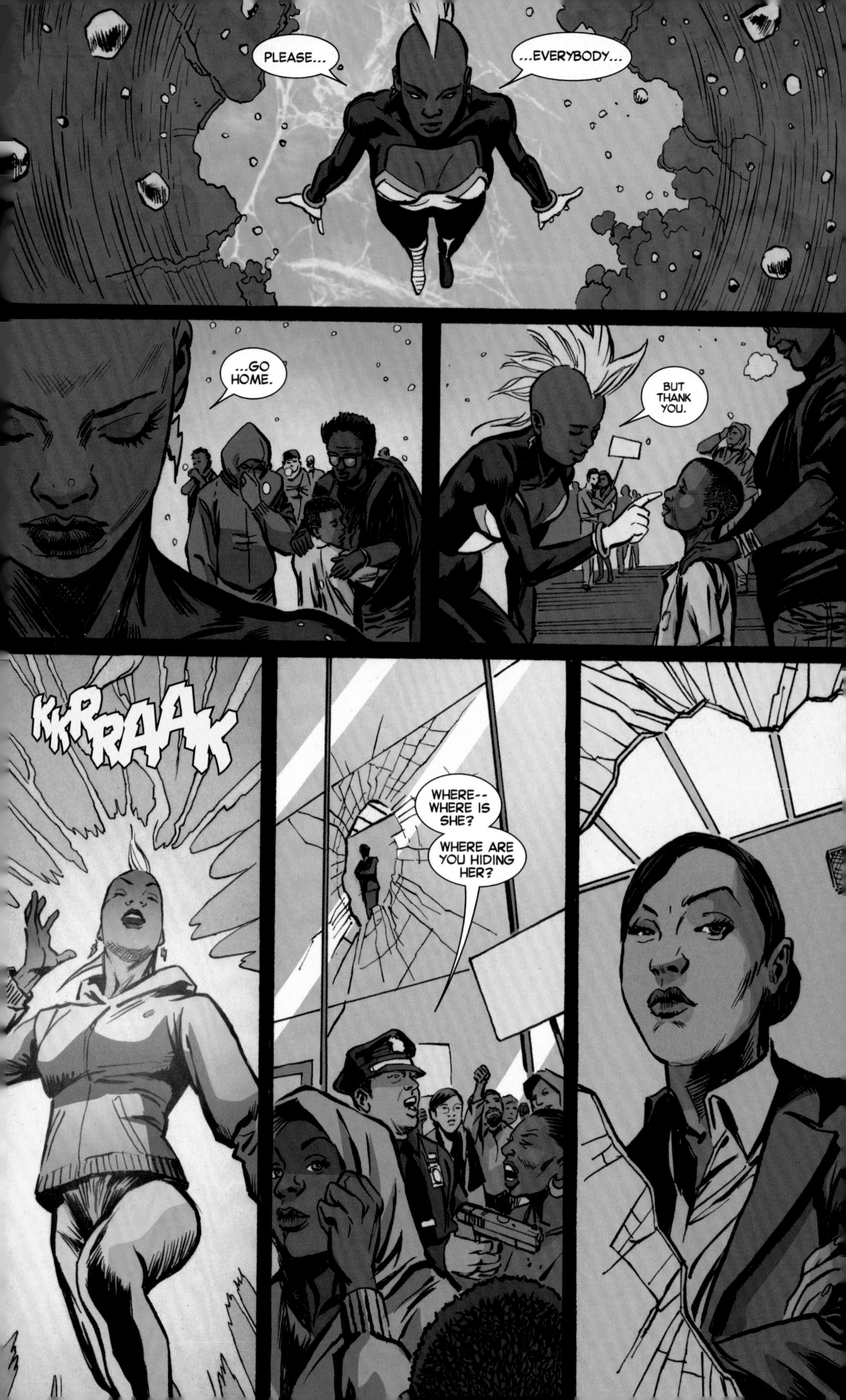
PLEASE...
...EVERYBODY...
...GO HOME.
BUT THANK YOU.
KKRRAAK
WHERE-- WHERE IS SHE?
WHERE ARE YOU HIDING HER?

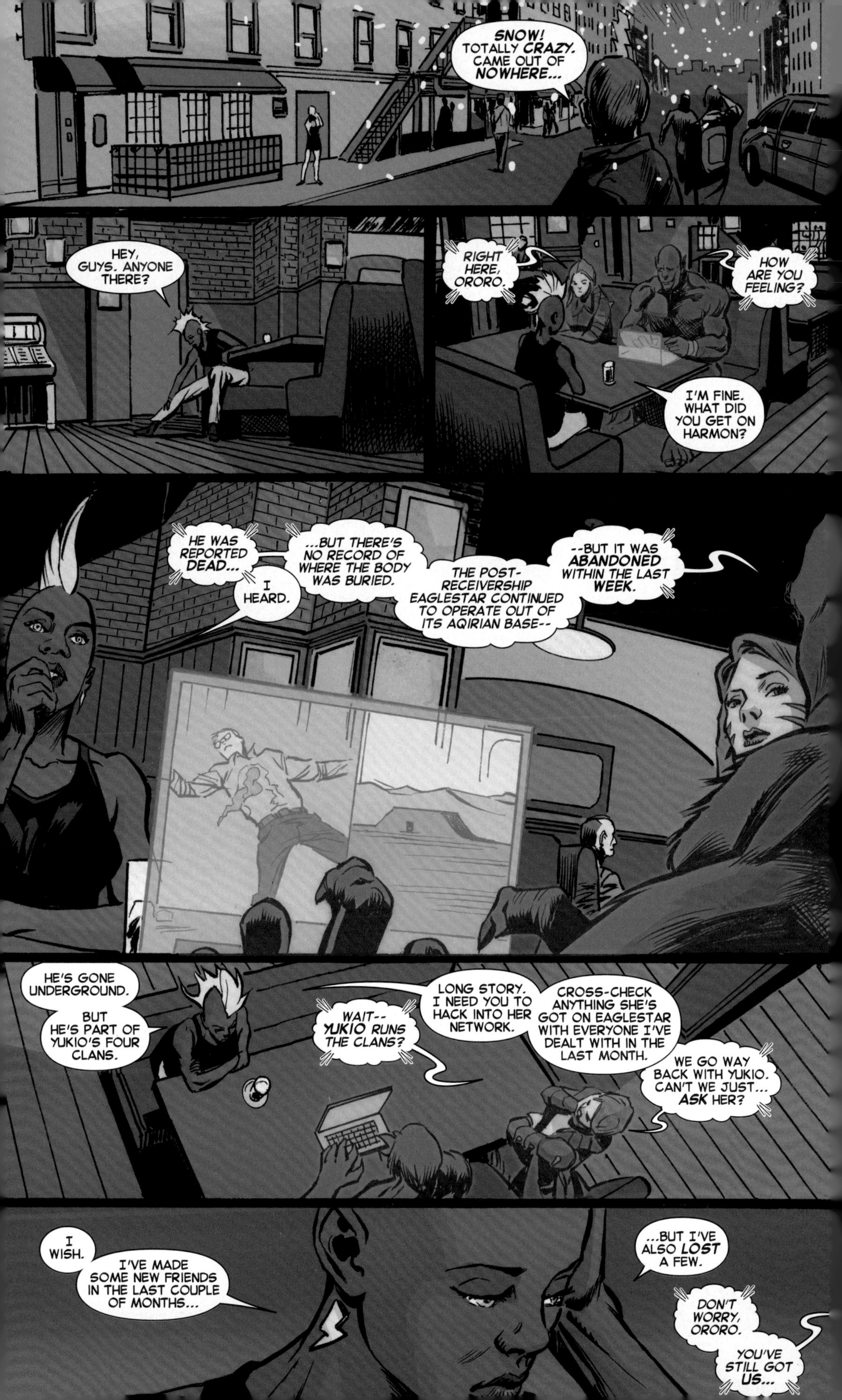

SNOW! TOTALLY CRAZY. CAME OUT OF NOWHERE...
HEY, GUYS. ANYONE THERE?
RIGHT HERE, ORORO.
HOW ARE YOU FEELING?
I'M FINE. WHAT DID YOU GET ON HARMON?
HE WAS REPORTED DEAD...
...BUT THERE'S NO RECORD OF WHERE THE BODY WAS BURIED.
I HEARD.
THE POST-RECEIVERSHIP EAGLESTAR CONTINUED TO OPERATE OUT OF ITS AQIRIAN BASE--
--BUT IT WAS ABANDONED WITHIN THE LAST WEEK.
HE'S GONE UNDERGROUND.
BUT HE'S PART OF YUKIO'S FOUR CLANS.
WAIT-- YUKIO RUNS THE CLANS?
LONG STORY. I NEED YOU TO HACK INTO HER NETWORK.
CROSS-CHECK ANYTHING SHE'S GOT ON EAGLESTAR WITH EVERYONE I'VE DEALT WITH IN THE LAST MONTH.
WE GO WAY BACK WITH YUKIO. CAN'T WE JUST... ASK HER?
I WISH.
I'VE MADE SOME NEW FRIENDS IN THE LAST COUPLE OF MONTHS...
...BUT I'VE ALSO LOST A FEW.
DON'T WORRY, ORORO.
YOU'VE STILL GOT US...

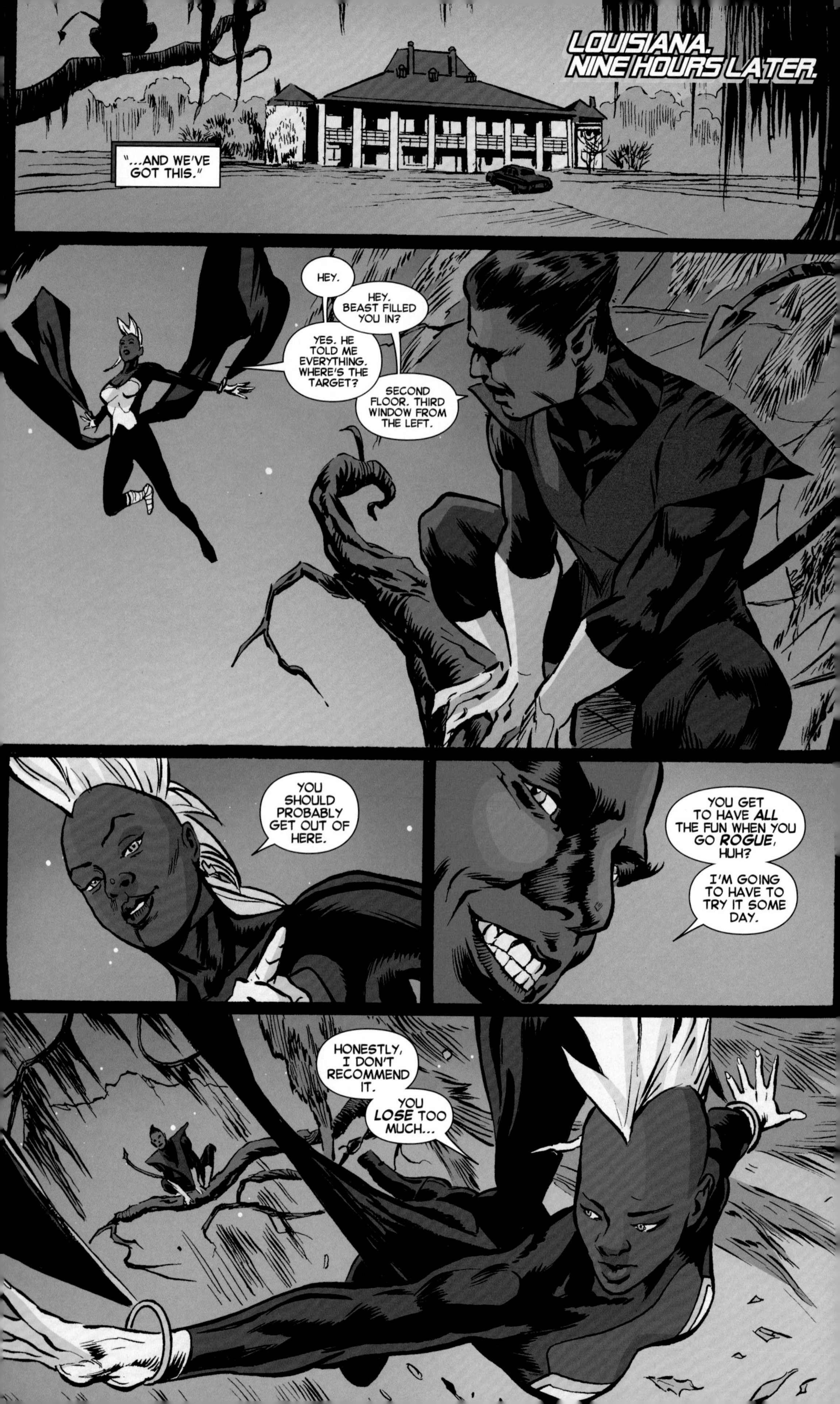
LOUISIANA. NINE HOURS LATER.
"...AND WE'VE GOT THIS."
HEY.
HEY. BEAST FILLED YOU IN?
YES. HE TOLD ME EVERYTHING. WHERE'S THE TARGET?
SECOND FLOOR. THIRD WINDOW FROM THE LEFT.
YOU SHOULD PROBABLY GET OUT OF HERE.
YOU GET TO HAVE ALL THE FUN WHEN YOU GO ROGUE, HUH?
I'M GOING TO HAVE TO TRY IT SOME DAY.
HONESTLY, I DON'T RECOMMEND IT.
YOU LOSE TOO MUCH...

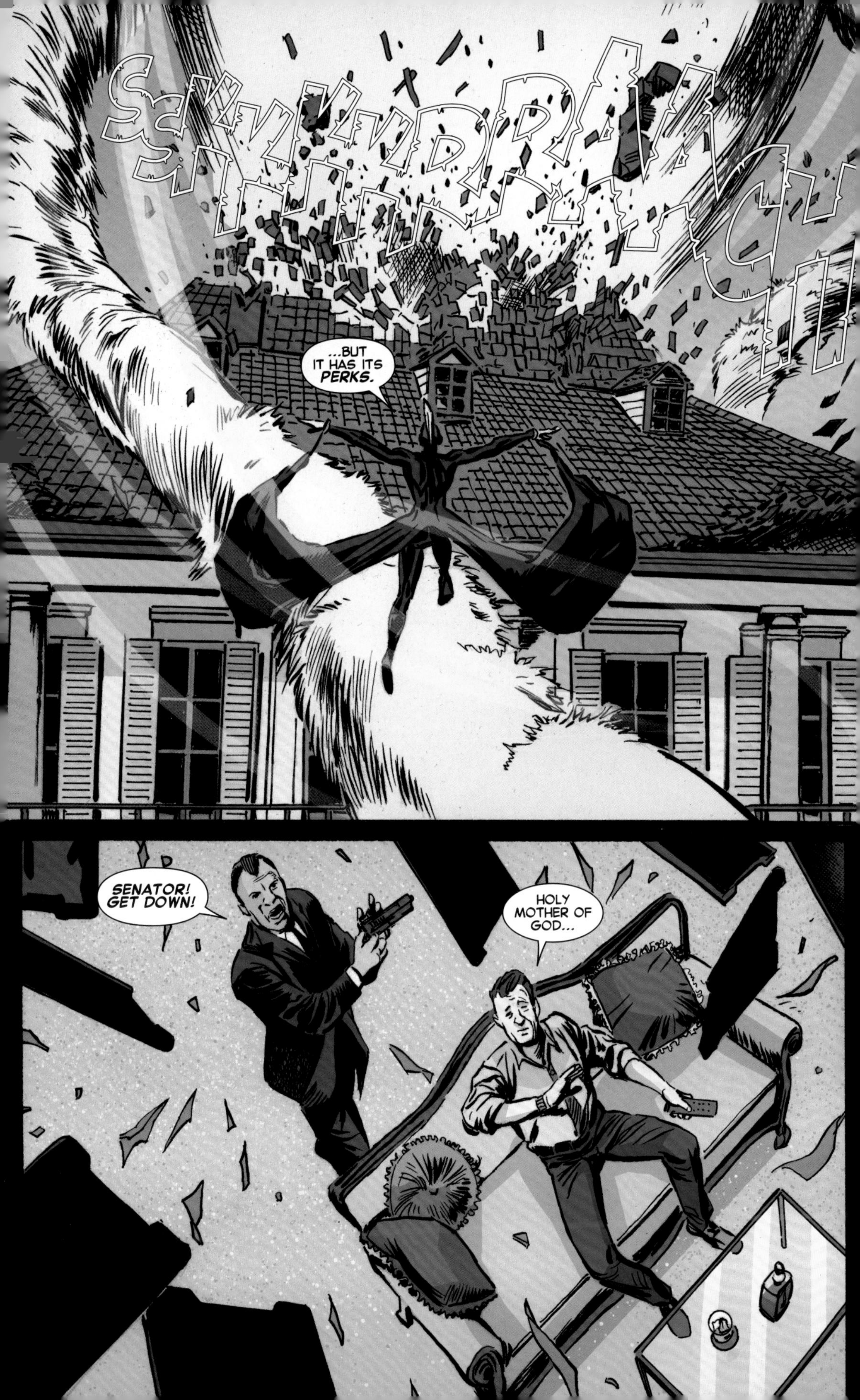
...BUT IT HAS ITS PERKS.
SENATOR! GET DOWN!
HOLY MOTHER OF GOD...

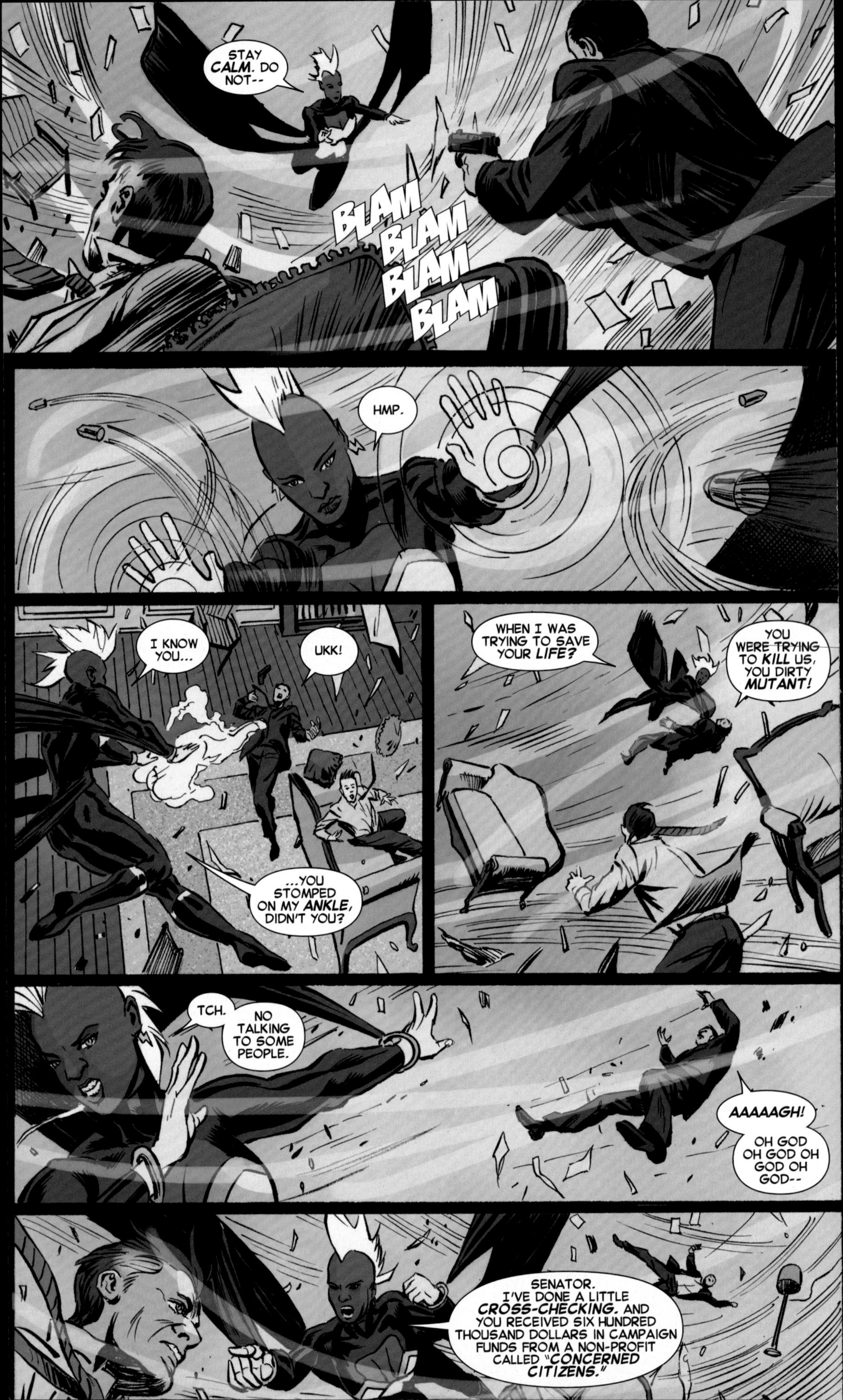

STAY CALM. DO NOT--
BLAM BLAM BLAM BLAM
HMP.
I KNOW YOU...
UKK!
...YOU STOMPED ON MY ANKLE, DIDN'T YOU?
WHEN I WAS TRYING TO SAVE YOUR LIFE?
YOU WERE TRYING TO KILL US, YOU DIRTY MUTANT!
TCH.
NO TALKING TO SOME PEOPLE.
AAAAAGH!
OH GOD OH GOD OH GOD OH GOD--
SENATOR. I'VE DONE A LITTLE CROSS-CHECKING. AND YOU RECEIVED SIX HUNDRED THOUSAND DOLLARS IN CAMPAIGN FUNDS FROM A NON-PROFIT CALLED "CONCERNED CITIZENS."

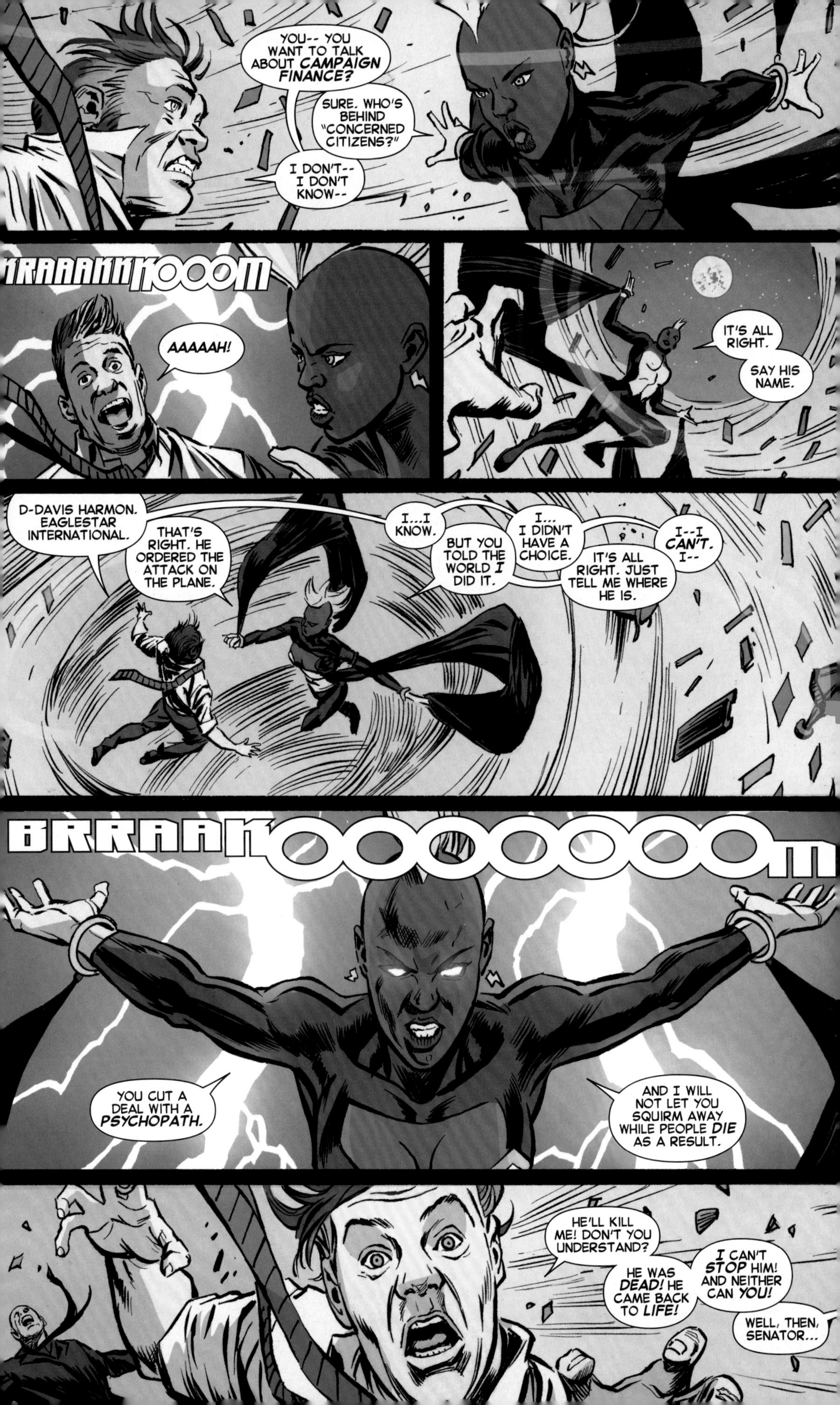
YOU-- YOU WANT TO TALK ABOUT CAMPAIGN FINANCE?
SURE. WHO'S BEHIND "CONCERNED CITIZENS?"
I DON'T-- I DON'T KNOW--
KRAAAKKKOOOM
AAAAAH!
IT'S ALL RIGHT.
SAY HIS NAME.
D-DAVIS HARMON. EAGLESTAR INTERNATIONAL.
THAT'S RIGHT. HE ORDERED THE ATTACK ON THE PLANE.
I...I KNOW.
BUT YOU TOLD THE WORLD I DID IT.
I... I DIDN'T HAVE A CHOICE.
IT'S ALL RIGHT. JUST TELL ME WHERE HE IS.
I--I CAN'T. I--
BRRAAKOOOOOOOOM
YOU CUT A DEAL WITH A PSYCHOPATH.
AND I WILL NOT LET YOU SQUIRM AWAY WHILE PEOPLE DIE AS A RESULT.
HE'LL KILL ME! DON'T YOU UNDERSTAND?
HE WAS DEAD! HE CAME BACK TO LIFE!
I CAN'T STOP HIM! AND NEITHER CAN YOU!
WELL, THEN, SENATOR...

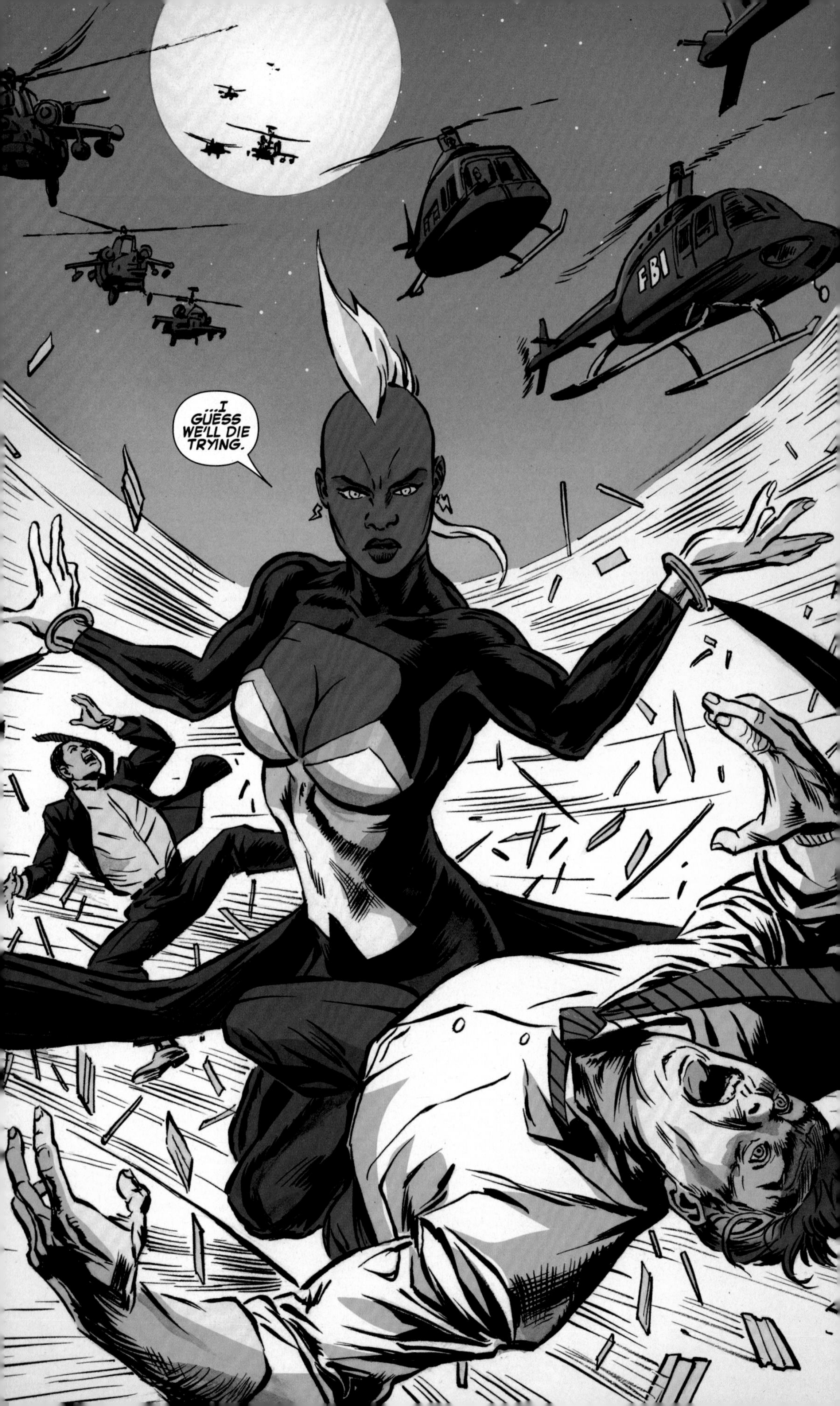
...I GUESS WE'LL DIE TRYING.

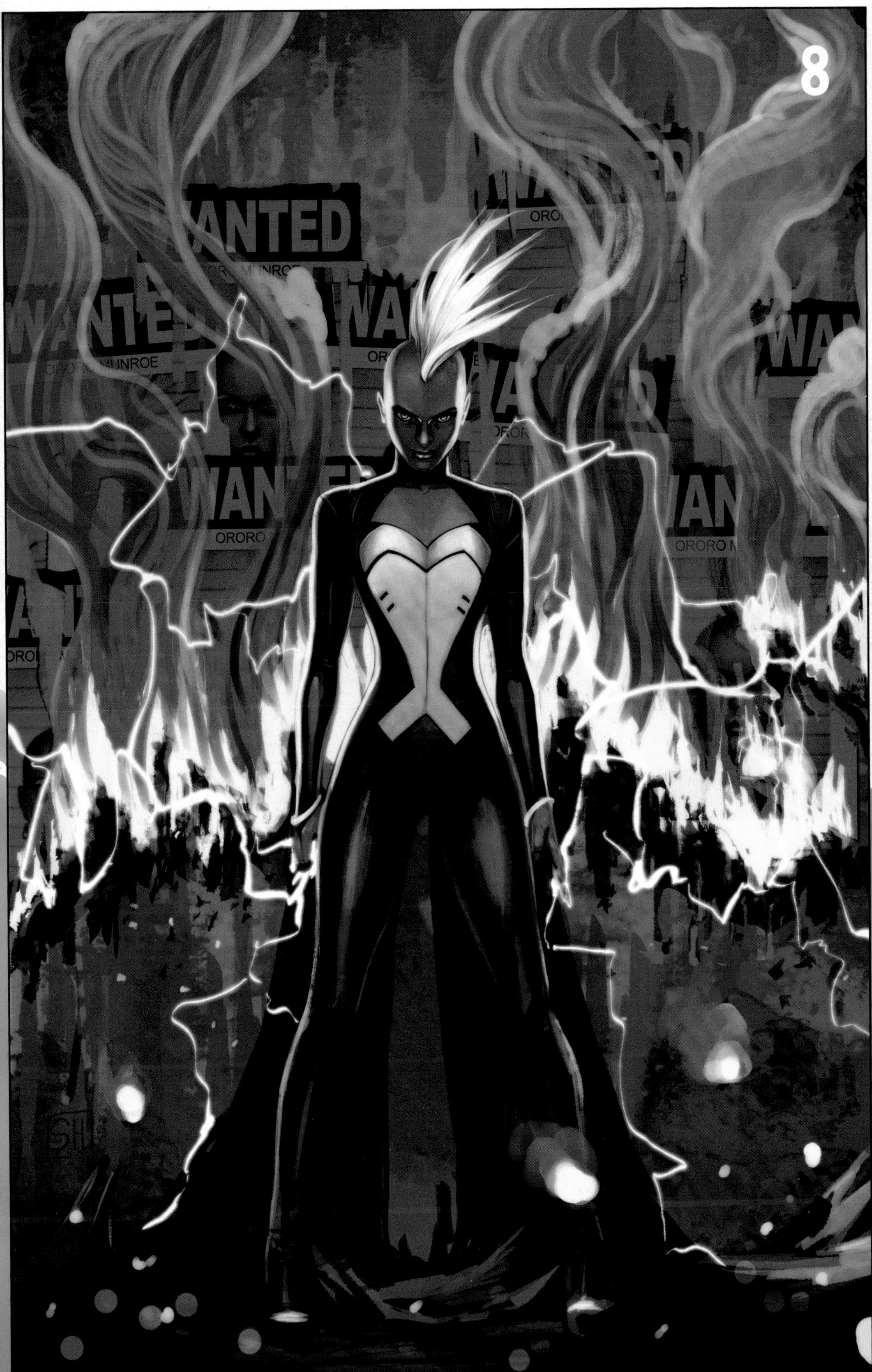
8
ANTED
ORORO

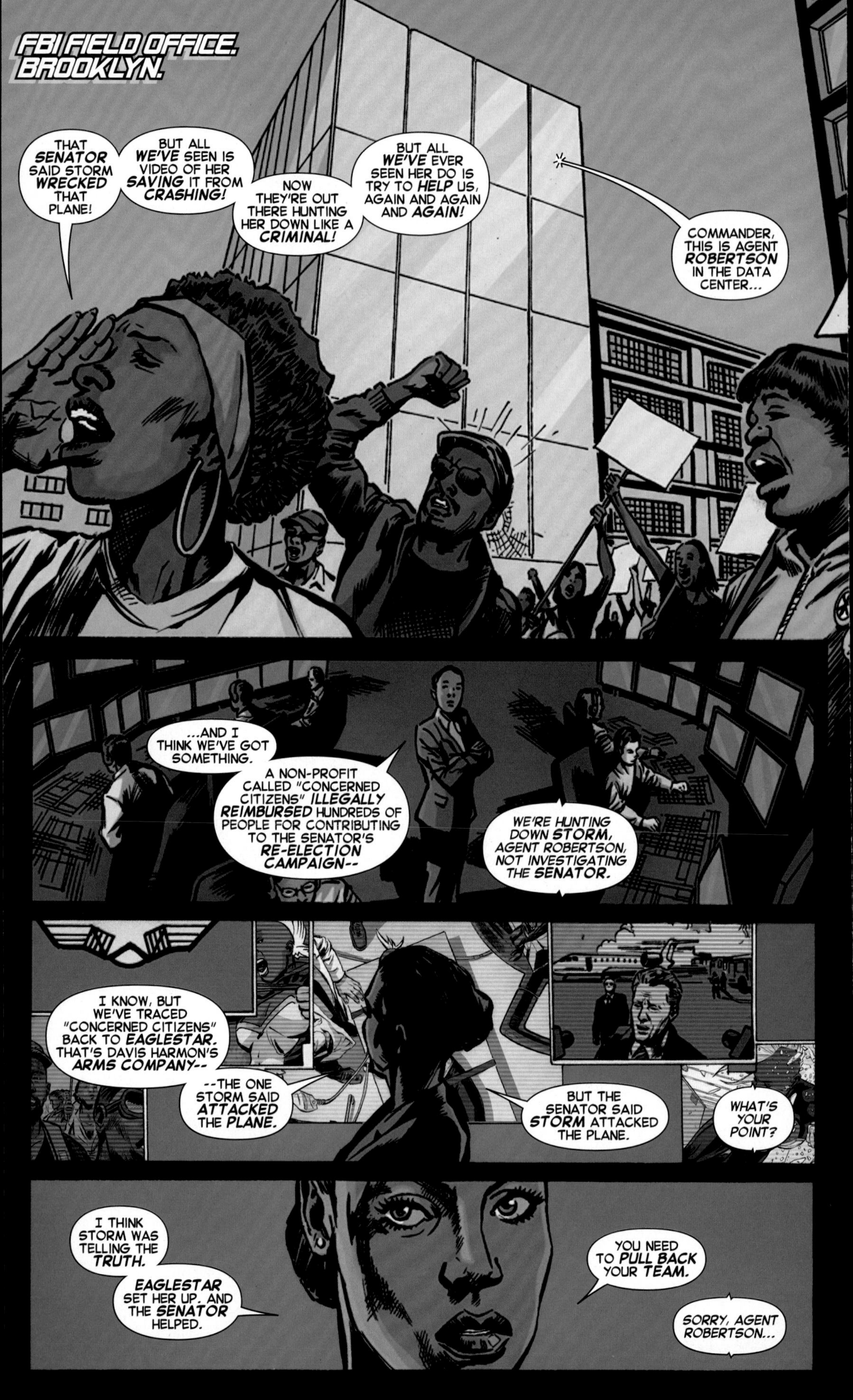
FBI FIELD OFFICE. BROOKLYN.
THAT SENATOR SAID STORM WRECKED THAT PLANE!
BUT ALL WE'VE SEEN IS VIDEO OF HER SAVING IT FROM CRASHING!
NOW THEY'RE OUT THERE HUNTING HER DOWN LIKE A CRIMINAL!
BUT ALL WE'VE EVER SEEN HER DO IS TRY TO HELP US, AGAIN AND AGAIN AND AGAIN!
COMMANDER, THIS IS AGENT ROBERTSON IN THE DATA CENTER...
...AND I THINK WE'VE GOT SOMETHING.
A NON-PROFIT CALLED "CONCERNED CITIZENS" ILLEGALLY REIMBURSED HUNDREDS OF PEOPLE FOR CONTRIBUTING TO THE SENATOR'S RE-ELECTION CAMPAIGN--
WE'RE HUNTING DOWN STORM, AGENT ROBERTSON, NOT INVESTIGATING THE SENATOR.
I KNOW, BUT WE'VE TRACED "CONCERNED CITIZENS" BACK TO EAGLESTAR. THAT'S DAVIS HARMON'S ARMS COMPANY--
--THE ONE STORM SAID ATTACKED THE PLANE.
BUT THE SENATOR SAID STORM ATTACKED THE PLANE.
WHAT'S YOUR POINT?
I THINK STORM WAS TELLING THE TRUTH.
EAGLESTAR SET HER UP. AND THE SENATOR HELPED.
YOU NEED TO PULL BACK YOUR TEAM.
SORRY, AGENT ROBERTSON...

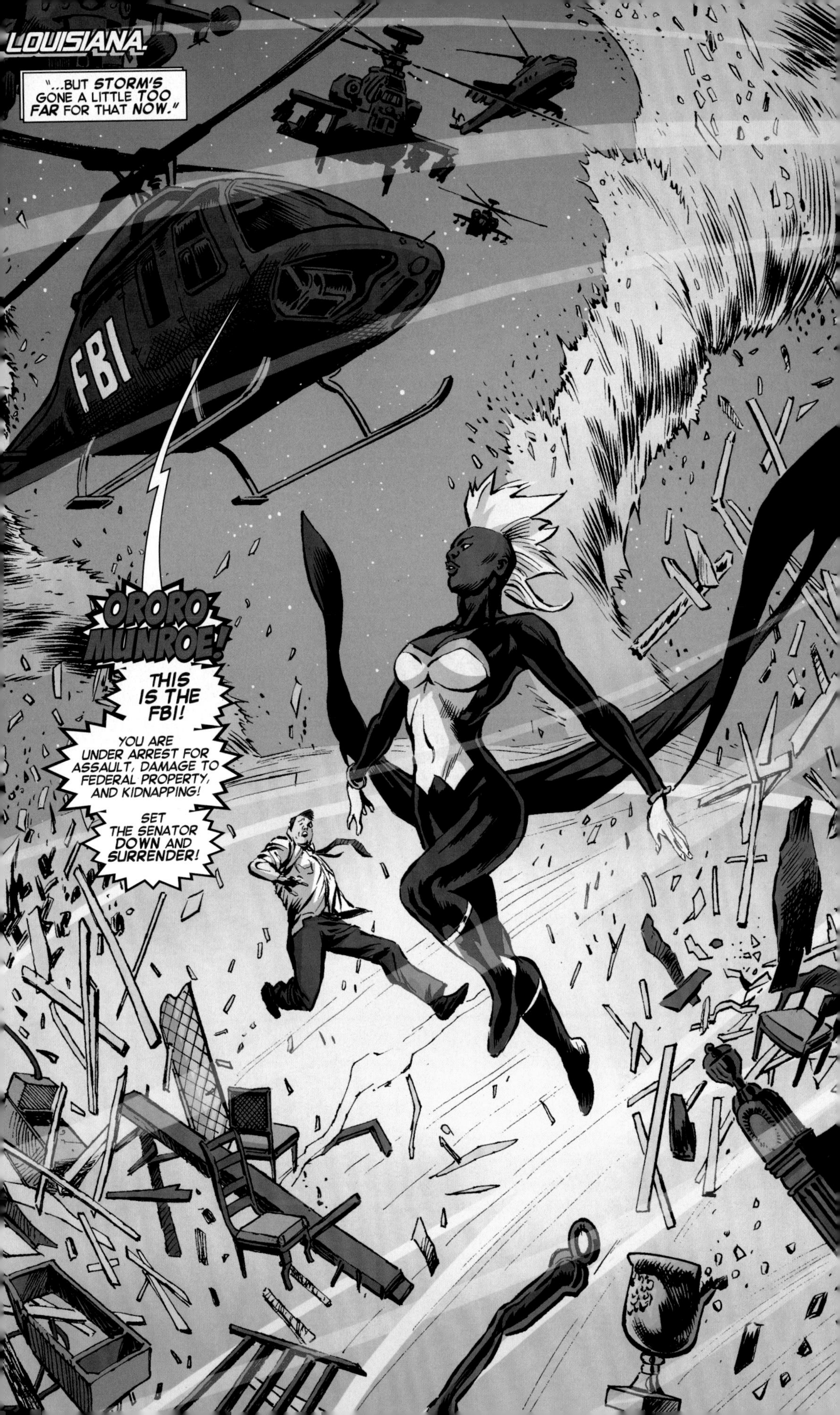
LOUISIANA.
"...BUT STORM'S GONE A LITTLE TOO FAR FOR THAT NOW."
ORORO MUNROE!
THIS IS THE FBI!
YOU ARE UNDER ARREST FOR ASSAULT, DAMAGE TO FEDERAL PROPERTY, AND KIDNAPPING!
SET THE SENATOR DOWN AND SURRENDER!
FBI

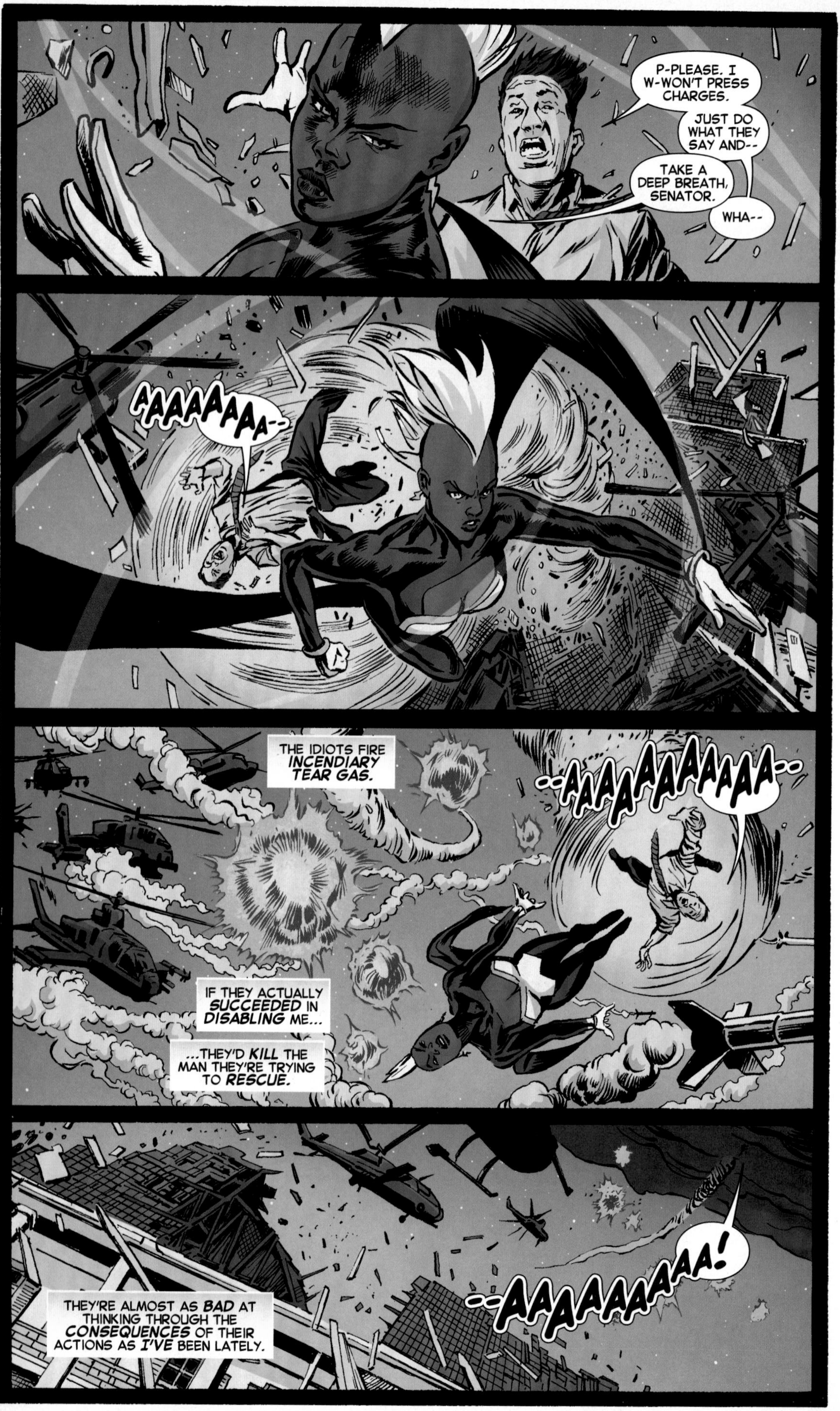

P-PLEASE. I W-WON'T PRESS CHARGES.
JUST DO WHAT THEY SAY AND--
TAKE A DEEP BREATH, SENATOR.
WHA--
AAAAAAAA--
THE IDIOTS FIRE INCENDIARY TEAR GAS.
--AAAAAAAAAAAA--
IF THEY ACTUALLY SUCCEEDED IN DISABLING ME...
...THEY'D KILL THE MAN THEY'RE TRYING TO RESCUE.
--AAAAAAAAAA!
THEY'RE ALMOST AS BAD AT THINKING THROUGH THE CONSEQUENCES OF THEIR ACTIONS AS I'VE BEEN LATELY.

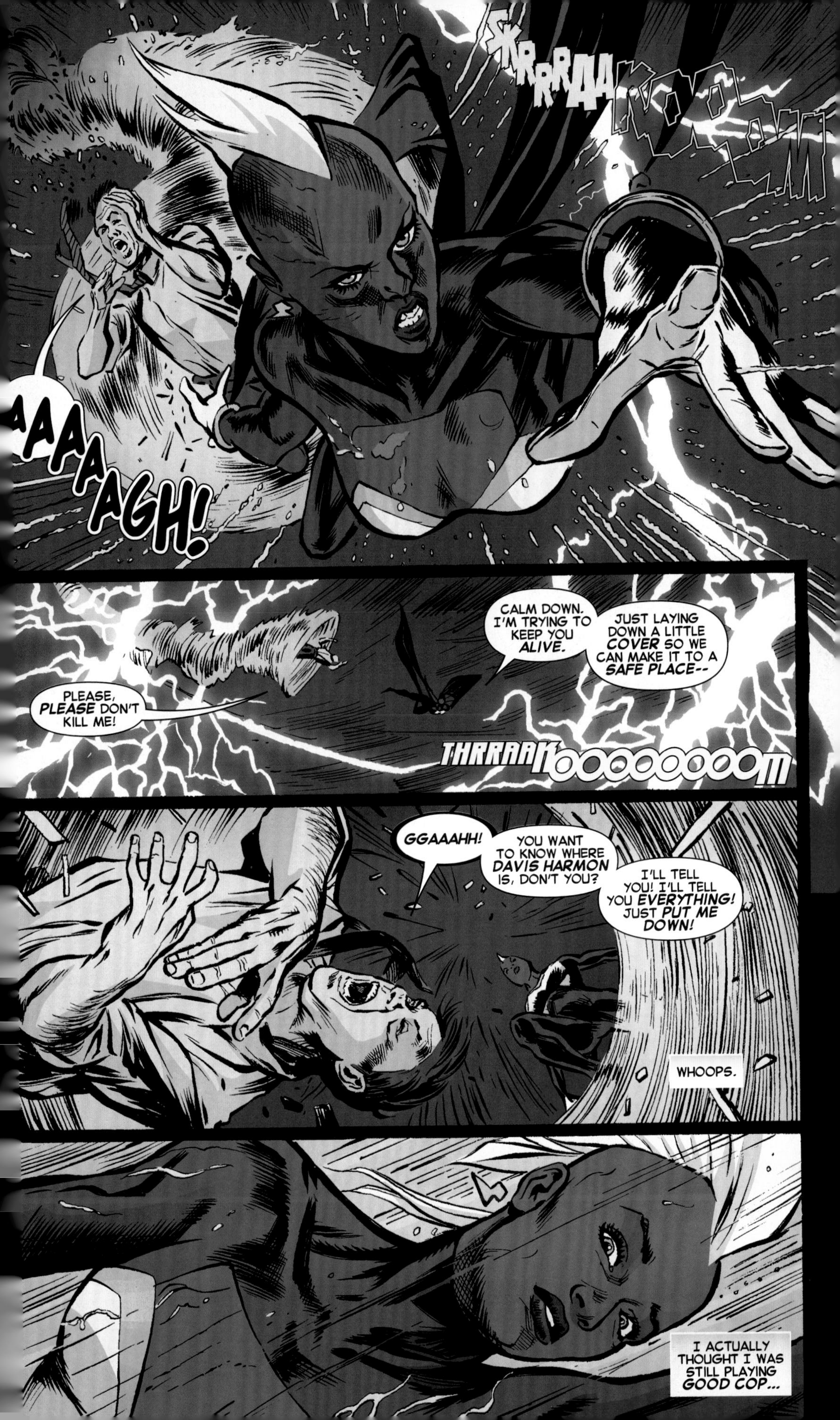
SKRRRAAKOOOOM
AAAAAAGH!
PLEASE, PLEASE DON'T KILL ME!
CALM DOWN. I'M TRYING TO KEEP YOU ALIVE.
JUST LAYING DOWN A LITTLE COVER SO WE CAN MAKE IT TO A SAFE PLACE--
THRRAAKOOOOOOOOOM
GGAAAHH!
YOU WANT TO KNOW WHERE DAVIS HARMON IS, DON'T YOU?
I'LL TELL YOU! I'LL TELL YOU EVERYTHING! JUST PUT ME DOWN!
WHOOPS.
I ACTUALLY THOUGHT I WAS STILL PLAYING GOOD COP...

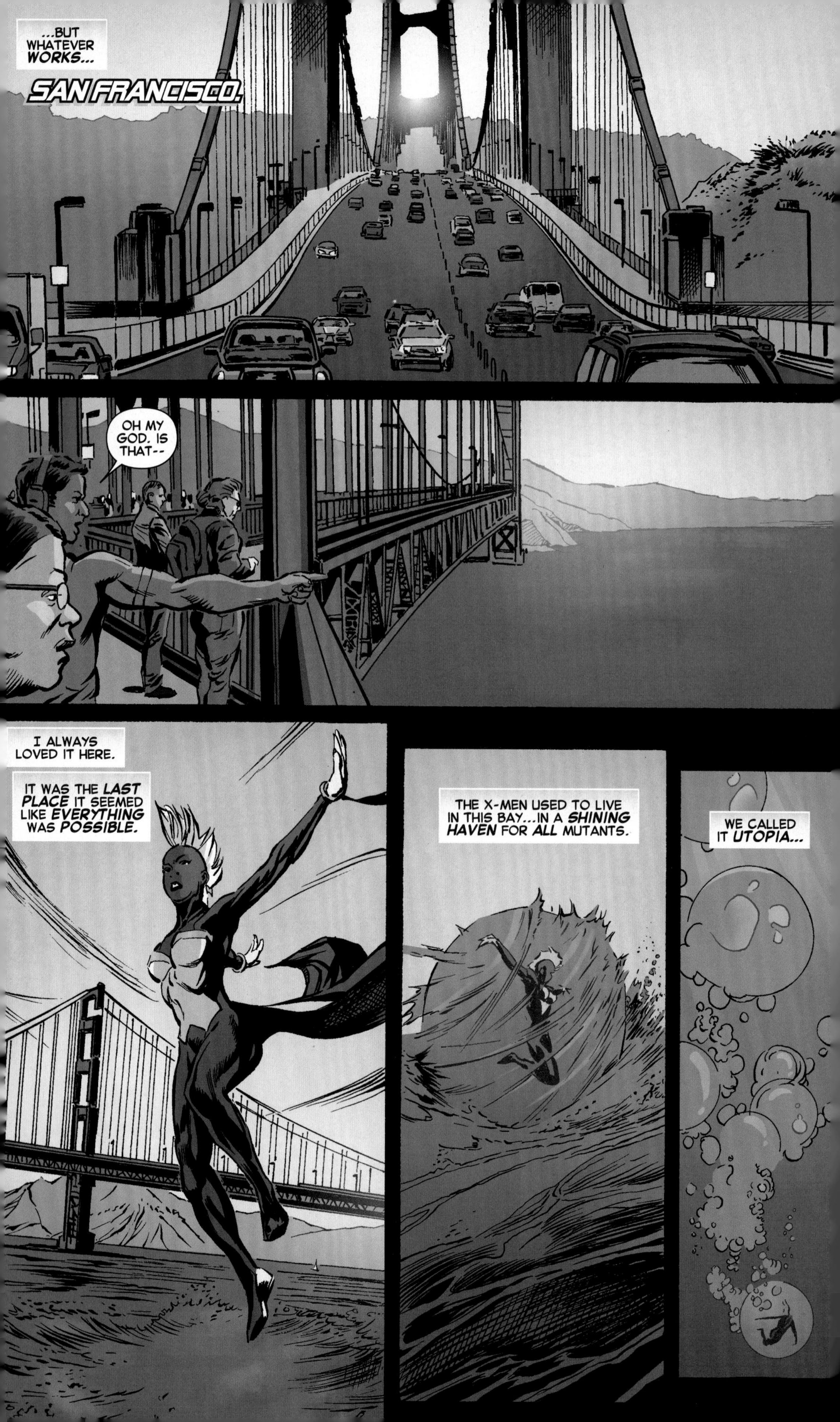
...BUT WHATEVER WORKS...
SAN FRANCISCO.
OH MY GOD. IS THAT--
I ALWAYS LOVED IT HERE.
IT WAS THE LAST PLACE IT SEEMED LIKE EVERYTHING WAS POSSIBLE.
THE X-MEN USED TO LIVE IN THIS BAY...IN A SHINING HAVEN FOR ALL MUTANTS.
WE CALLED IT UTOPIA...

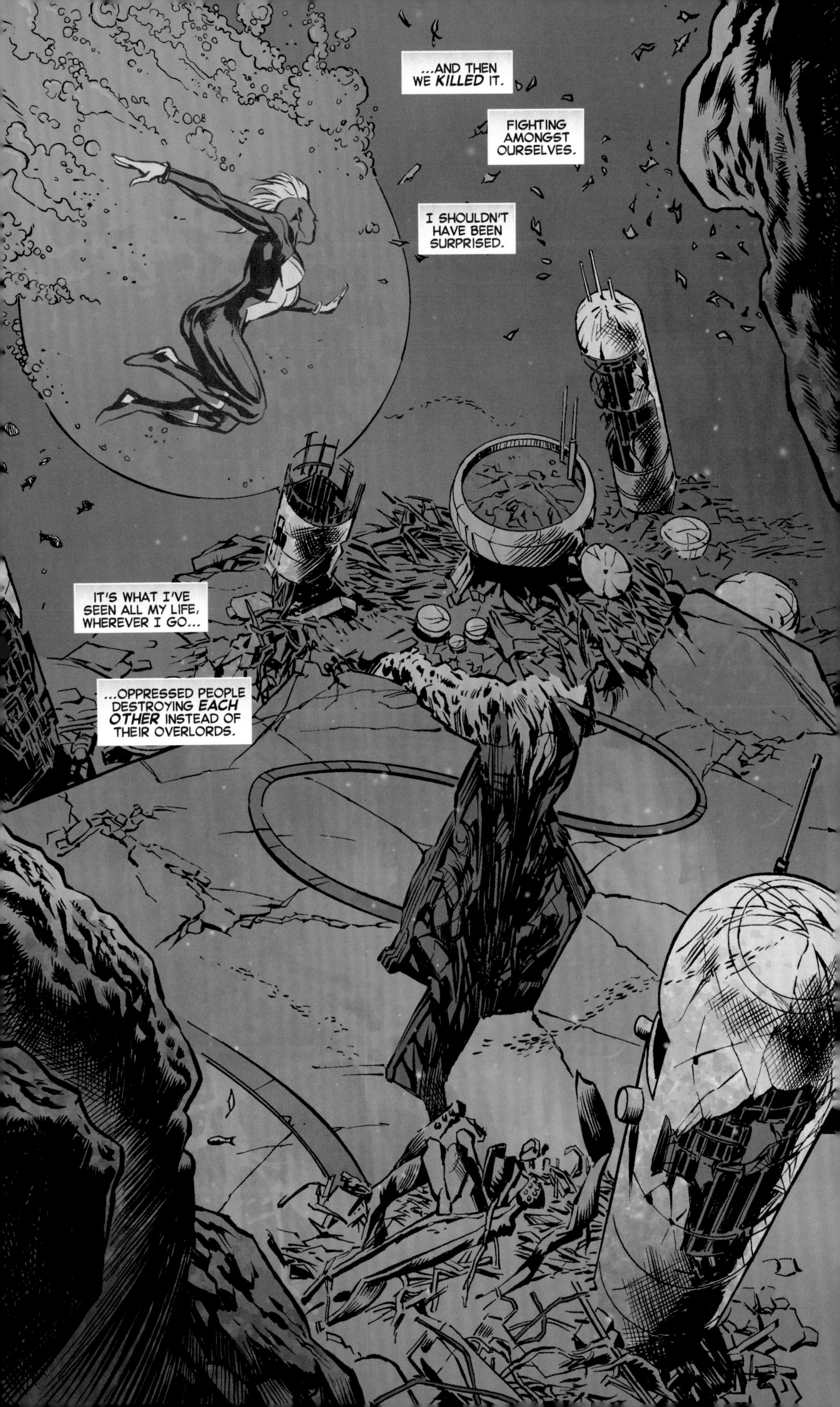
...AND THEN WE KILLED IT.
FIGHTING AMONGST OURSELVES.
I SHOULDN'T HAVE BEEN SURPRISED.
IT'S WHAT I'VE SEEN ALL MY LIFE, WHEREVER I GO...
...OPPRESSED PEOPLE DESTROYING EACH OTHER INSTEAD OF THEIR OVERLORDS.

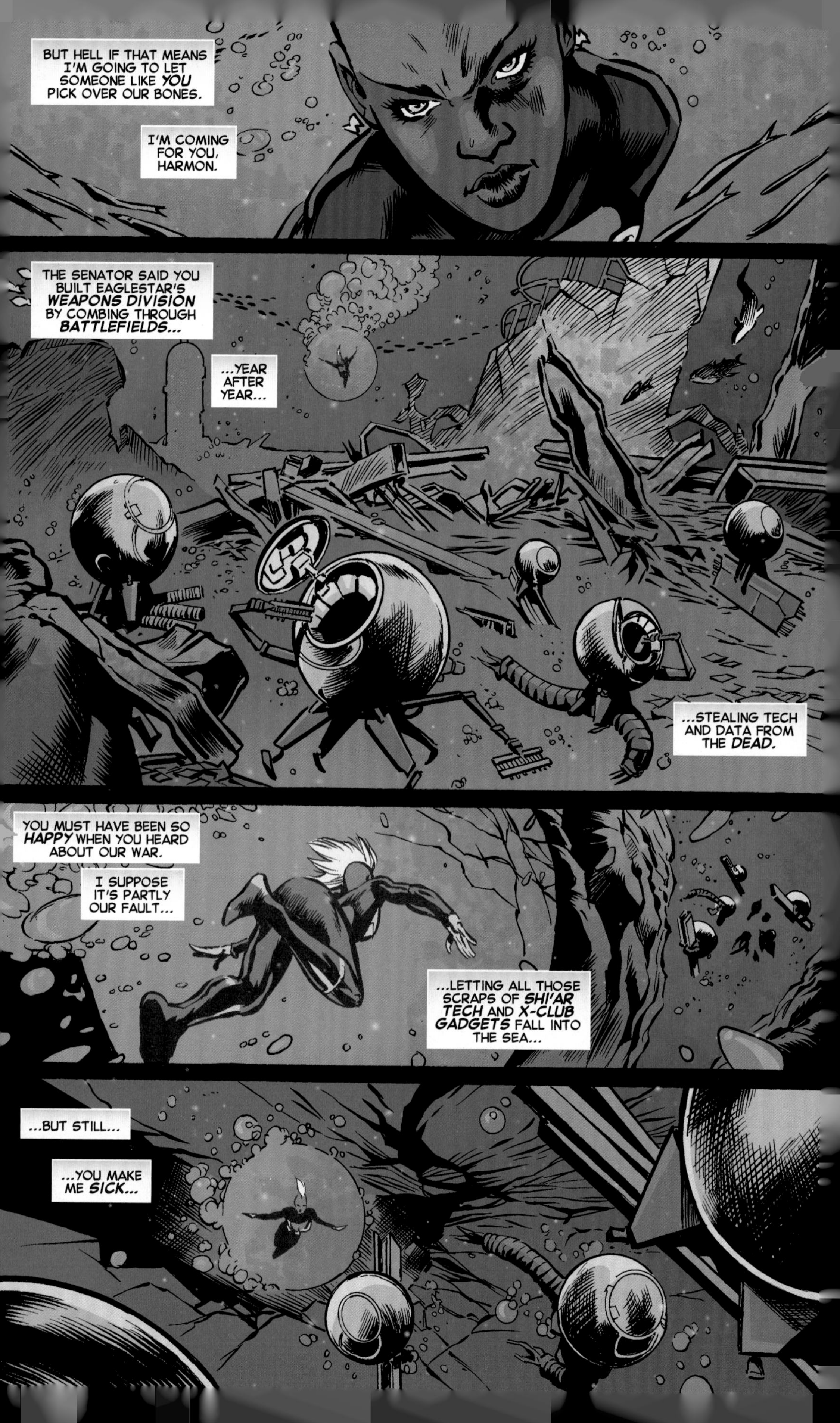

BUT HELL IF THAT MEANS I'M GOING TO LET SOMEONE LIKE *YOU* PICK OVER OUR BONES.
I'M COMING FOR YOU, HARMON.
THE SENATOR SAID YOU BUILT EAGLESTAR'S *WEAPONS DIVISION* BY COMBING THROUGH *BATTLEFIELDS...*
...YEAR AFTER YEAR...
...STEALING TECH AND DATA FROM THE *DEAD.*
YOU MUST HAVE BEEN SO *HAPPY* WHEN YOU HEARD ABOUT OUR WAR.
I SUPPOSE IT'S PARTLY OUR FAULT...
...LETTING ALL THOSE SCRAPS OF *SHI'AR TECH* AND *X-CLUB GADGETS* FALL INTO THE SEA...
...BUT STILL...
...YOU MAKE ME *SICK...*

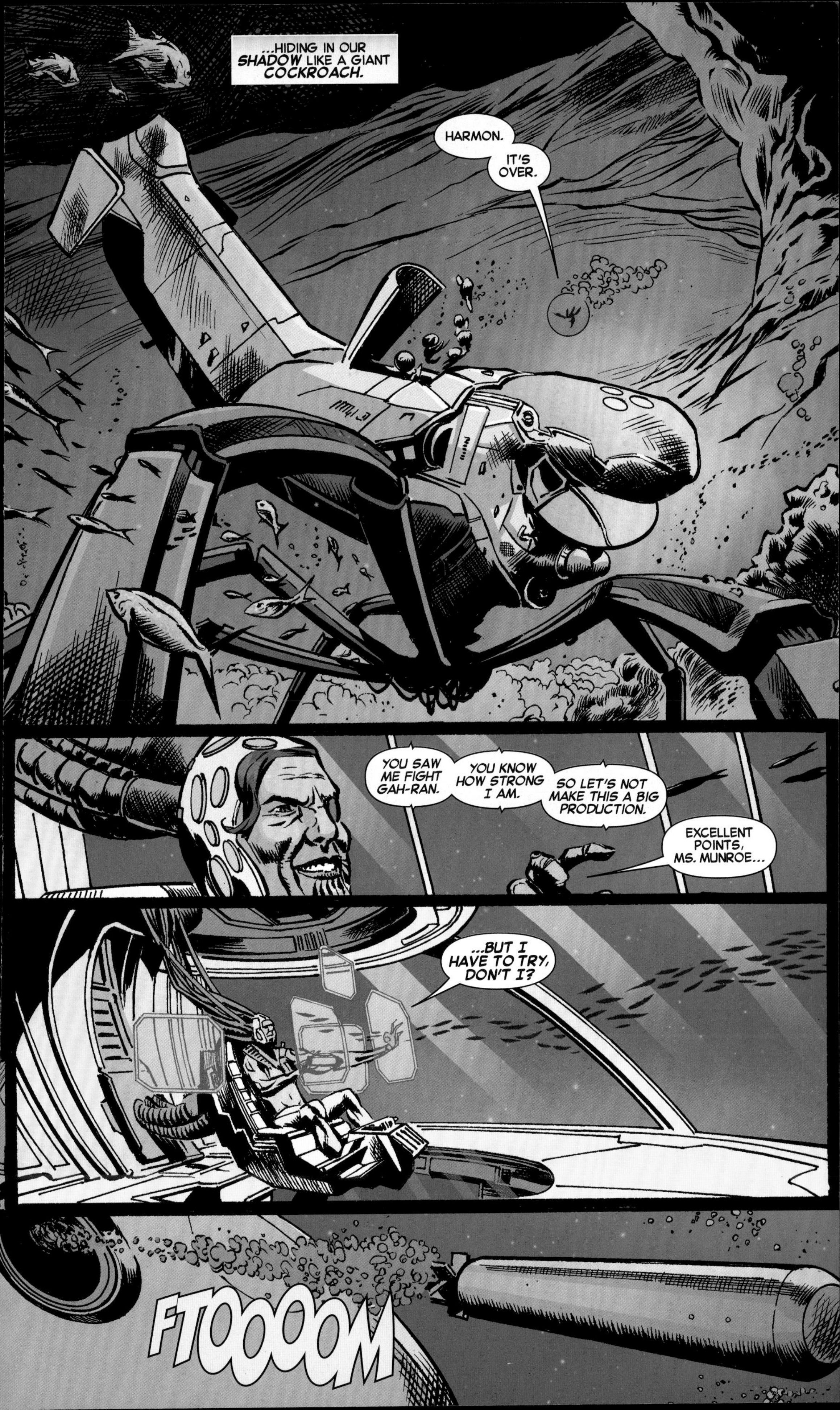
...HIDING IN OUR SHADOW LIKE A GIANT COCKROACH.
HARMON.
IT'S OVER.
YOU SAW ME FIGHT GAH-RAN.
YOU KNOW HOW STRONG I AM.
SO LET'S NOT MAKE THIS A BIG PRODUCTION.
EXCELLENT POINTS, MS. MUNROE...
...BUT I HAVE TO TRY, DON'T I?
FTOOOOM

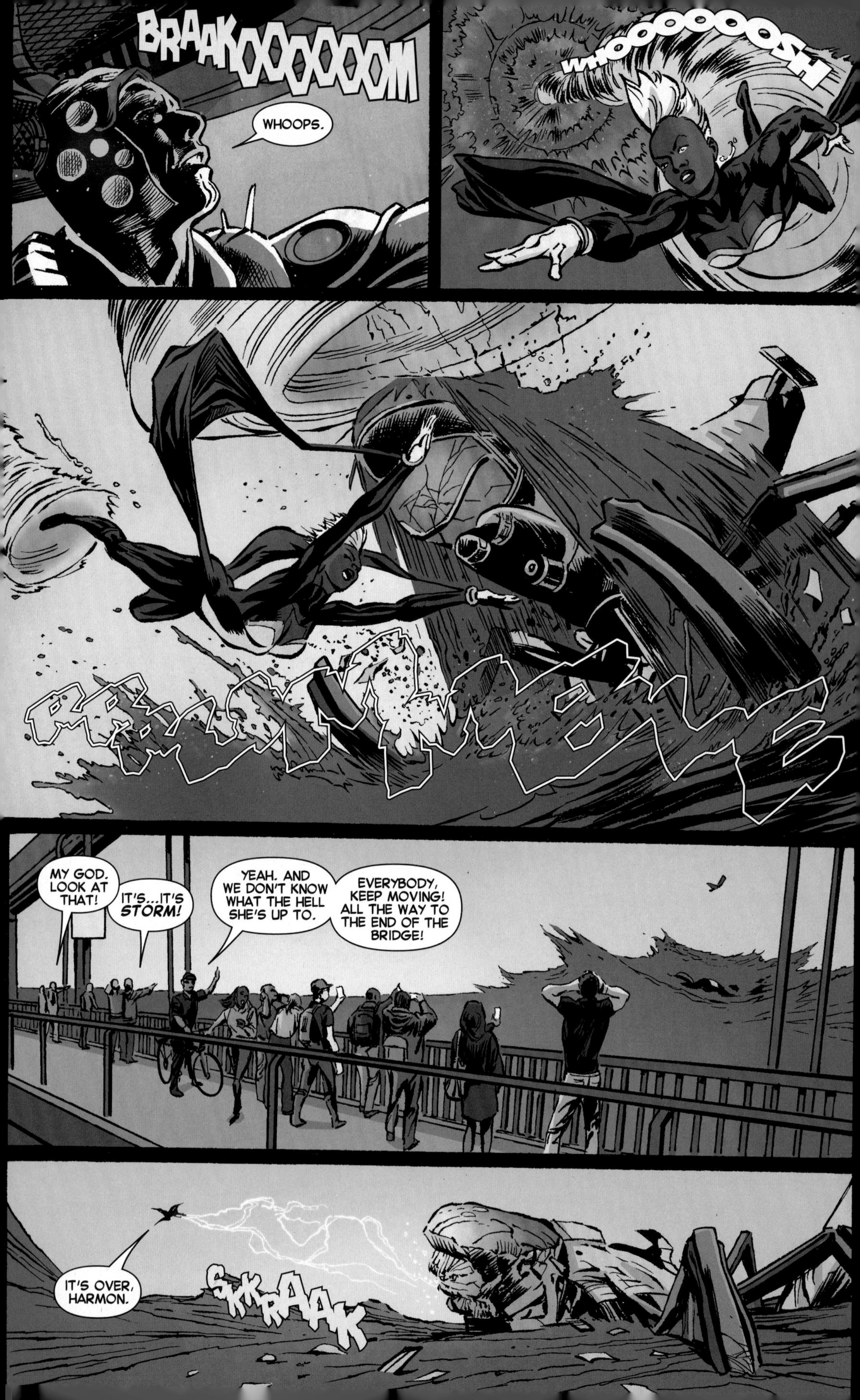
BRAAKOOOOOOM
WHOOPS.
WHOOOOOOOOSH
MY GOD. LOOK AT THAT!
IT'S...IT'S *STORM!*
YEAH. AND WE DON'T KNOW WHAT THE HELL SHE'S UP TO.
EVERYBODY, KEEP MOVING! ALL THE WAY TO THE END OF THE BRIDGE!
IT'S OVER, HARMON.
SKKRAAAK

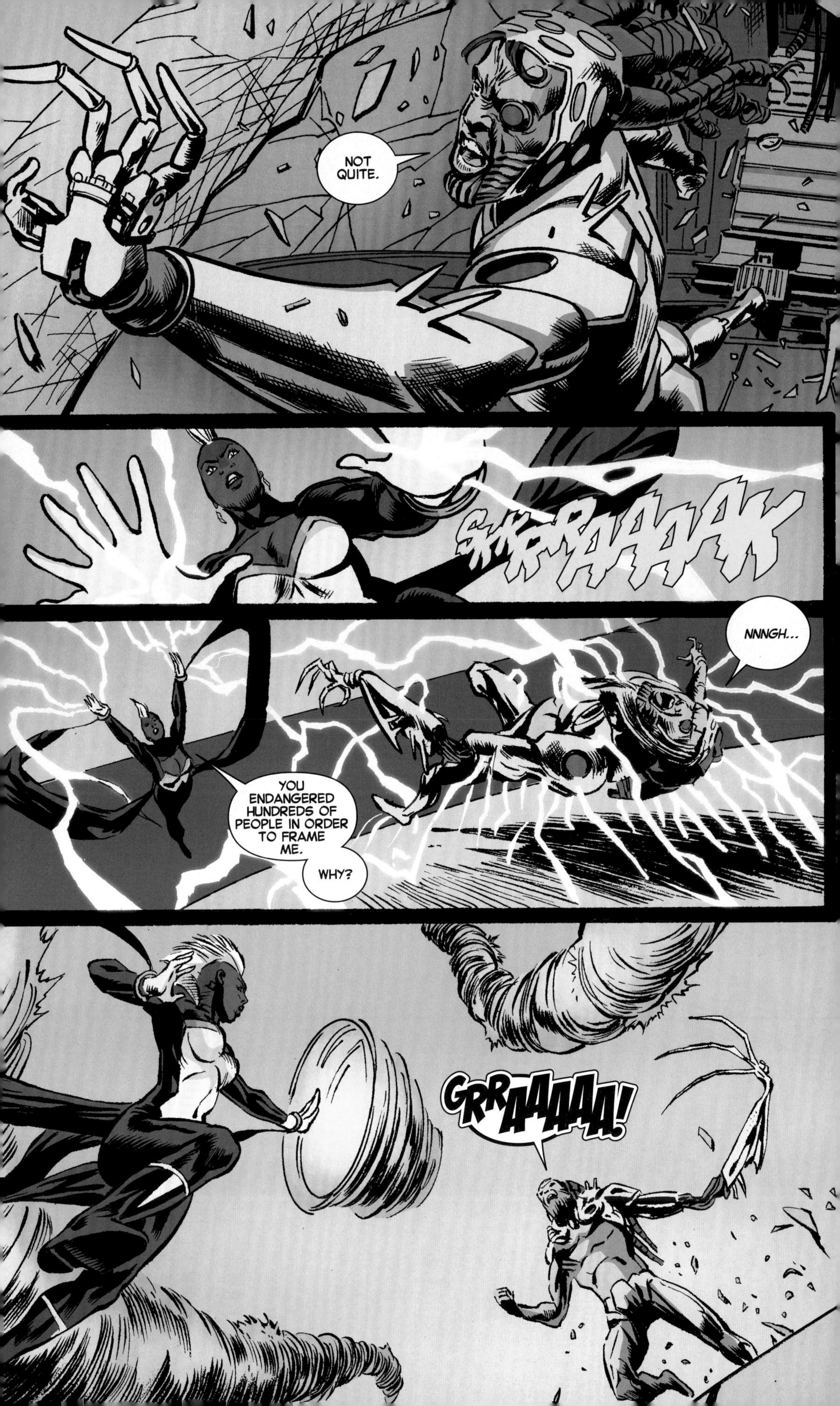
NOT QUITE.
SHKRRAAAAK
NNNGH...
YOU ENDANGERED HUNDREDS OF PEOPLE IN ORDER TO FRAME ME.
WHY?
GRRAAAAAA!

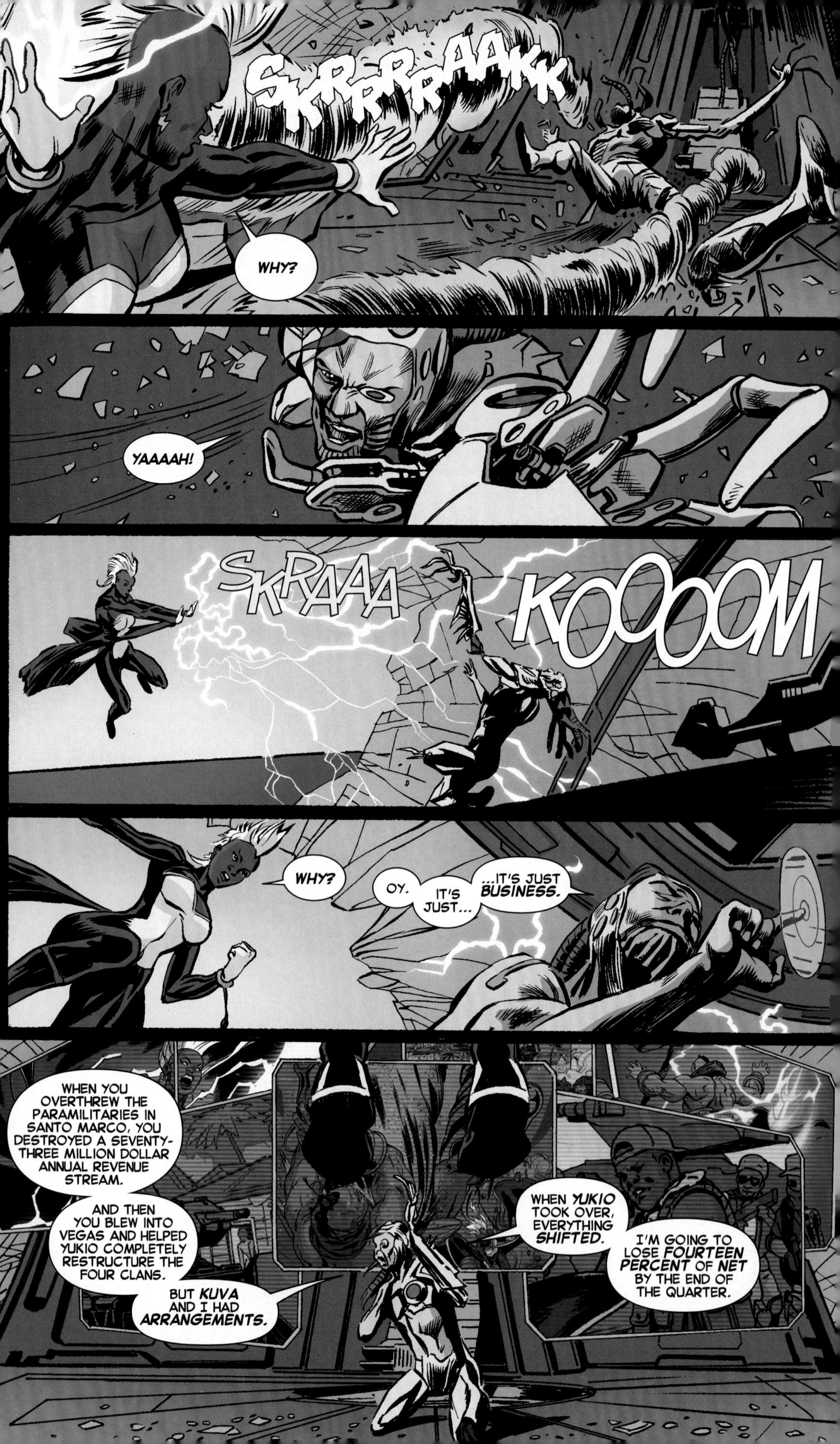
SKRRRRAAKK
WHY?
YAAAAH!
SKRAAA
KOOOOOM
WHY?
OY.
IT'S JUST...
...IT'S JUST BUSINESS.
WHEN YOU OVERTHREW THE PARAMILITARIES IN SANTO MARCO, YOU DESTROYED A SEVENTY-THREE MILLION DOLLAR ANNUAL REVENUE STREAM.
AND THEN YOU BLEW INTO VEGAS AND HELPED YUKIO COMPLETELY RESTRUCTURE THE FOUR CLANS.
BUT KUVA AND I HAD ARRANGEMENTS.
WHEN YUKIO TOOK OVER, EVERYTHING SHIFTED.
I'M GOING TO LOSE FOURTEEN PERCENT OF NET BY THE END OF THE QUARTER.

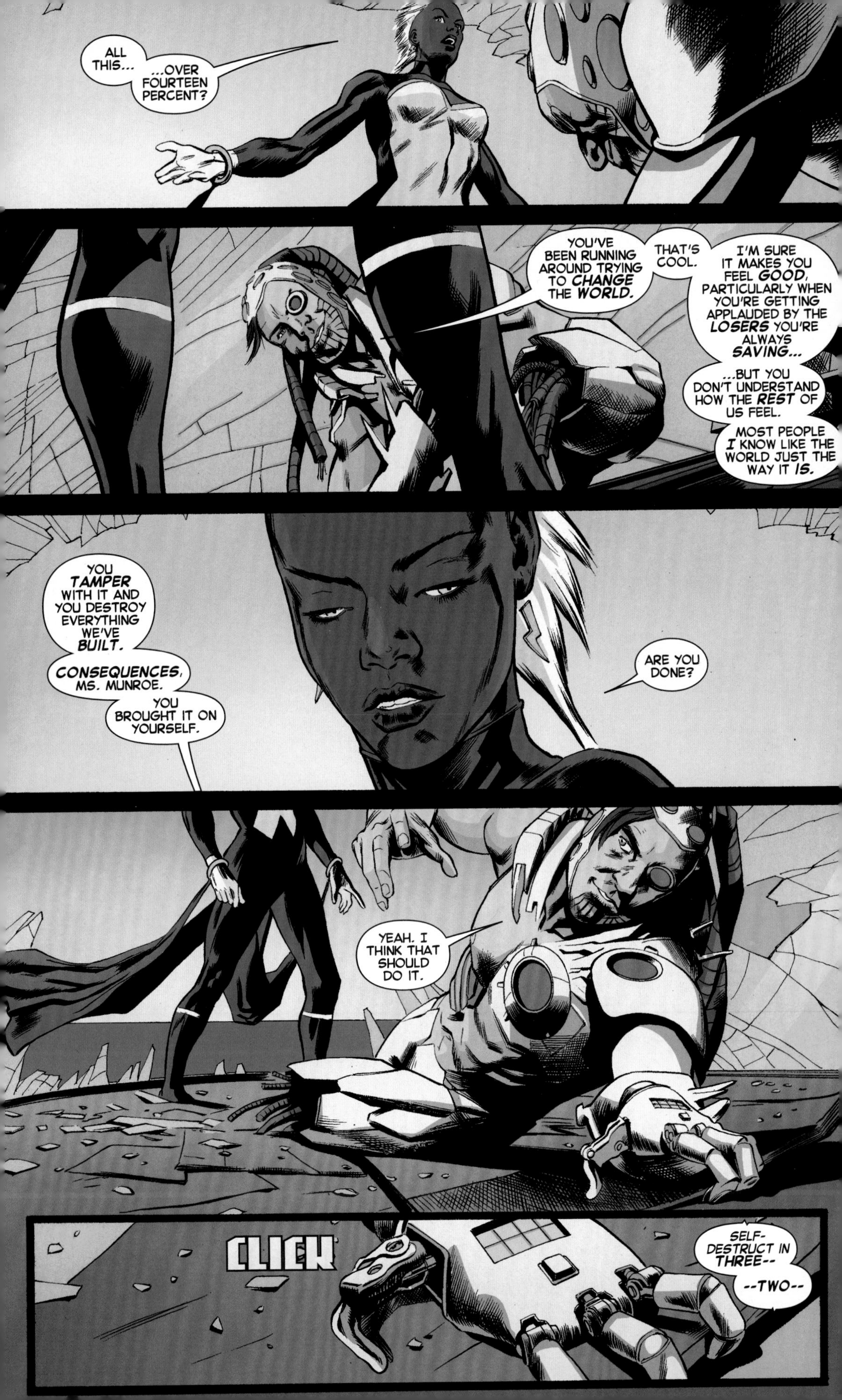
ALL THIS...
...OVER FOURTEEN PERCENT?
YOU'VE BEEN RUNNING AROUND TRYING TO CHANGE THE WORLD.
THAT'S COOL.
I'M SURE IT MAKES YOU FEEL GOOD, PARTICULARLY WHEN YOU'RE GETTING APPLAUDED BY THE LOSERS YOU'RE ALWAYS SAVING...
...BUT YOU DON'T UNDERSTAND HOW THE REST OF US FEEL.
MOST PEOPLE I KNOW LIKE THE WORLD JUST THE WAY IT IS.
YOU TAMPER WITH IT AND YOU DESTROY EVERYTHING WE'VE BUILT.
CONSEQUENCES, MS. MUNROE.
YOU BROUGHT IT ON YOURSELF.
ARE YOU DONE?
YEAH. I THINK THAT SHOULD DO IT.
CLICK
SELF-DESTRUCT IN THREE--
--TWO--

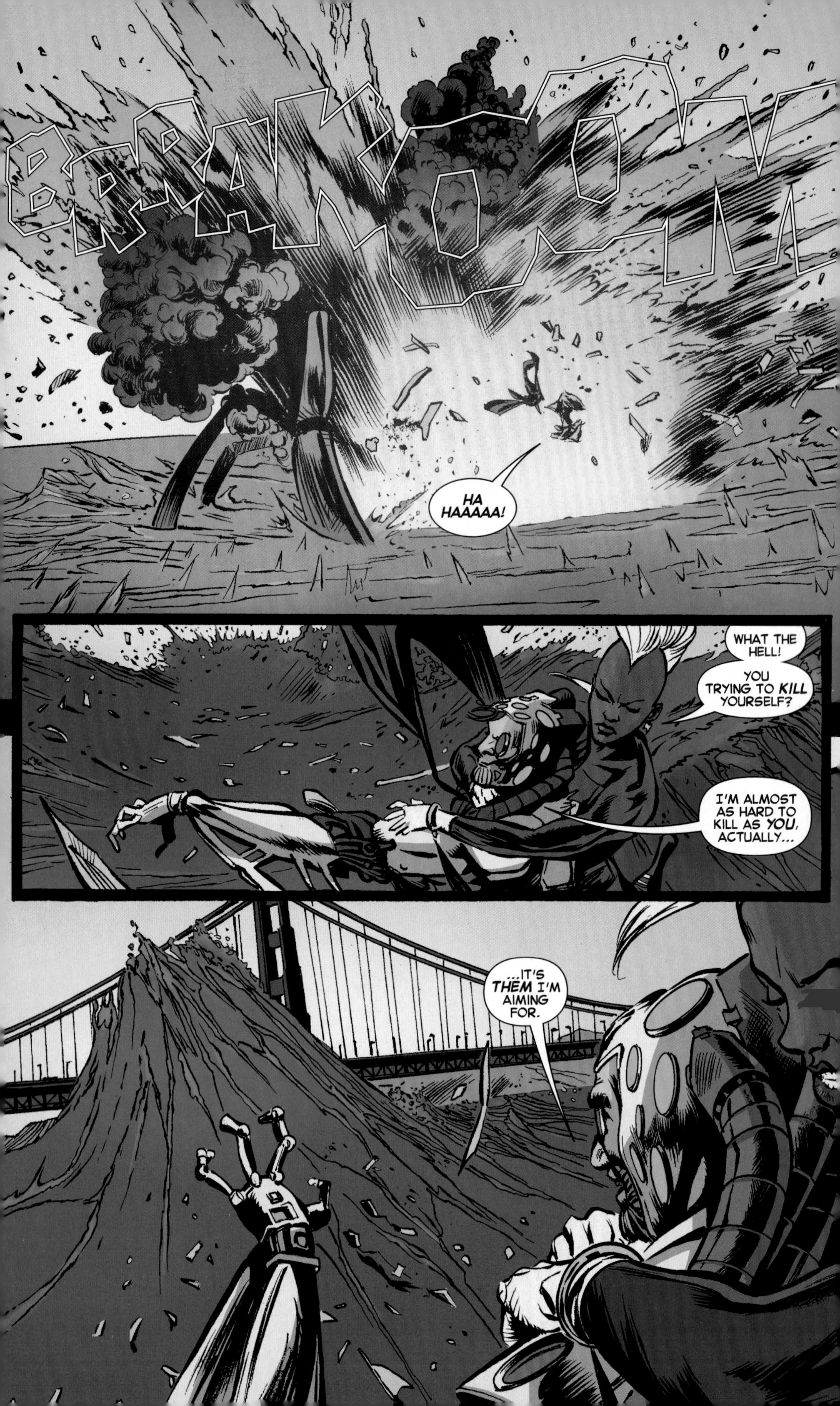
HA HAAAAA!
WHAT THE HELL!
YOU TRYING TO *KILL* YOURSELF?
I'M ALMOST AS HARD TO KILL AS *YOU*, ACTUALLY...
...IT'S *THEM* I'M AIMING FOR.

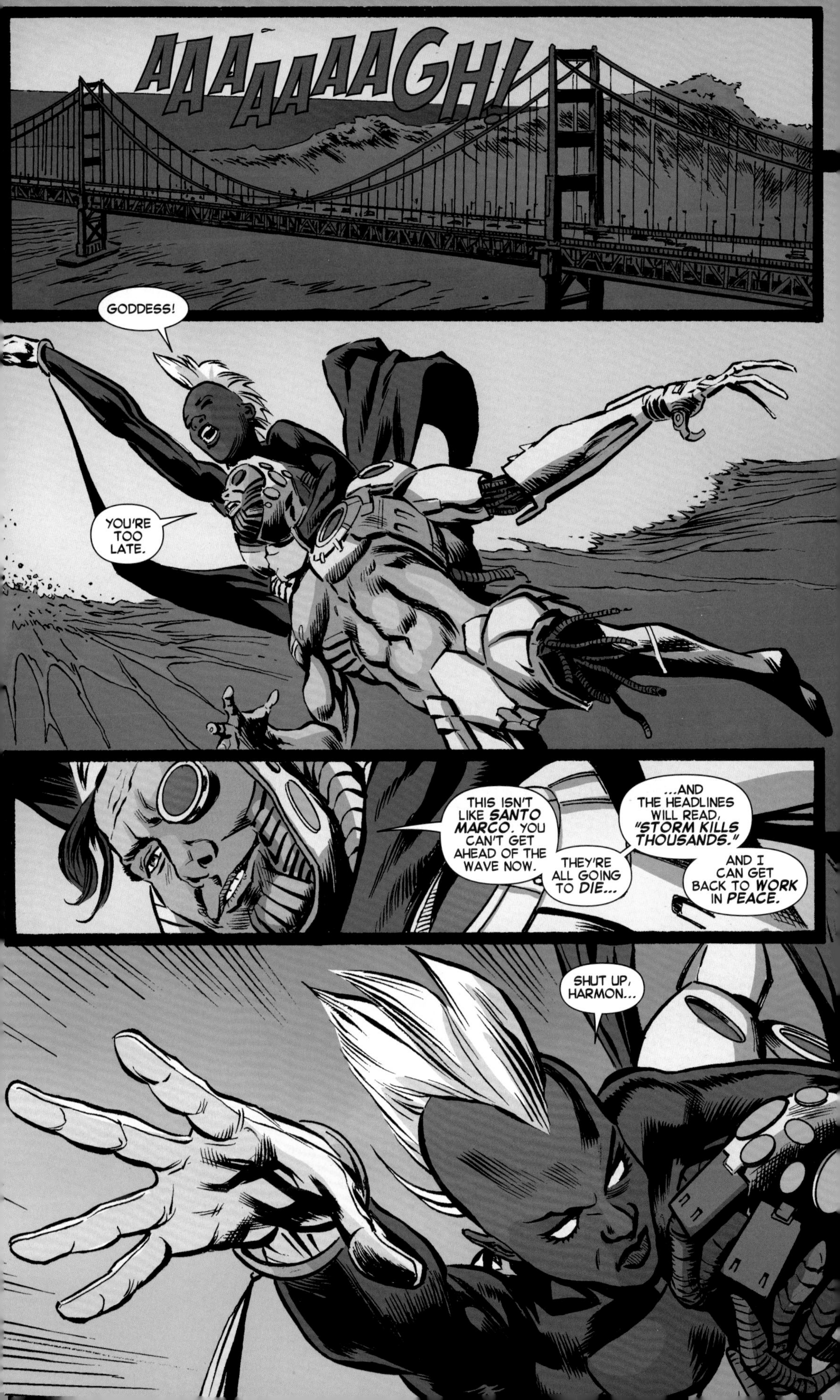
AAAAAAAGH!
GODDESS!
YOU'RE TOO LATE.
THIS ISN'T LIKE SANTO MARCO. YOU CAN'T GET AHEAD OF THE WAVE NOW.
THEY'RE ALL GOING TO DIE...
...AND THE HEADLINES WILL READ, "STORM KILLS THOUSANDS."
AND I CAN GET BACK TO WORK IN PEACE.
SHUT UP, HARMON...

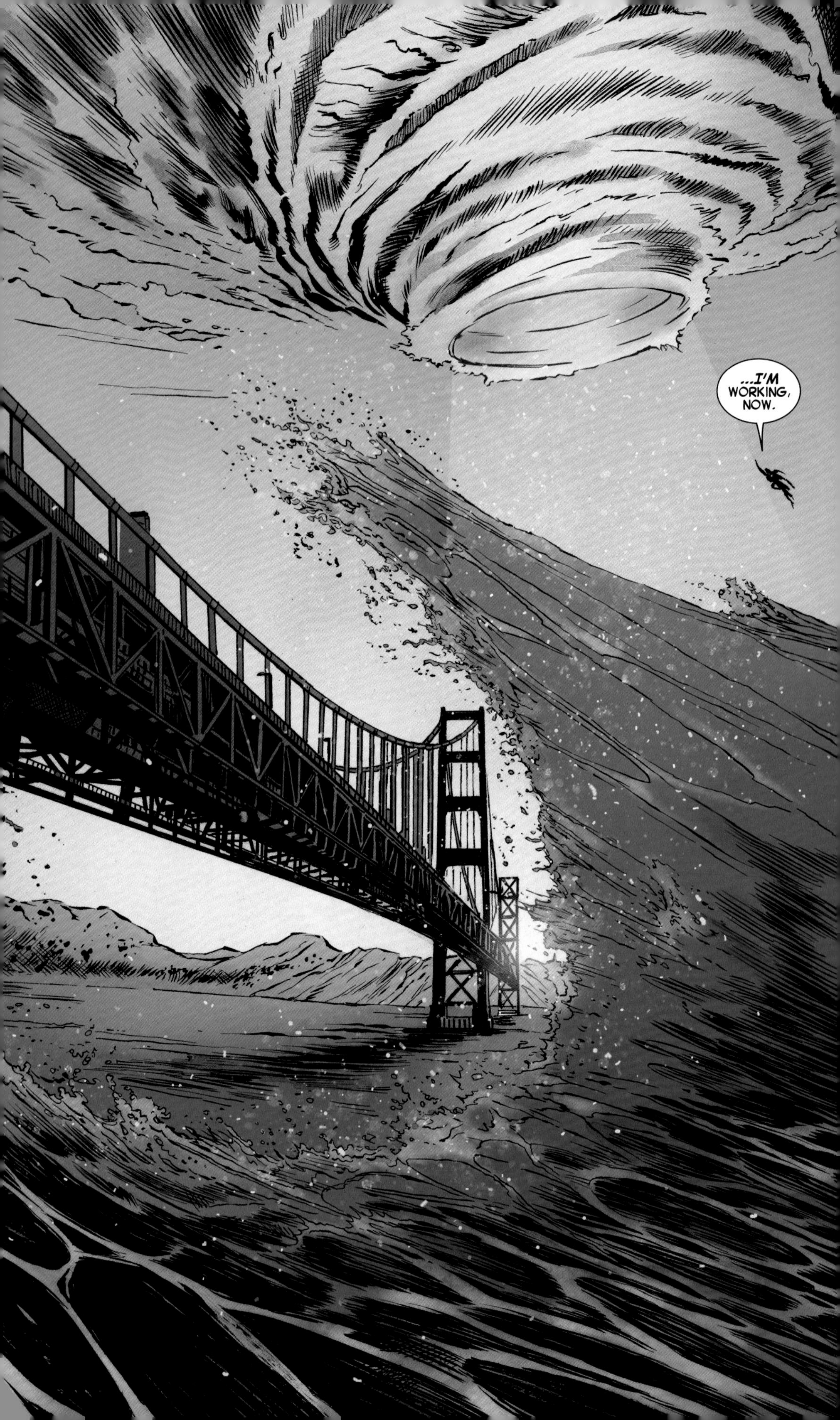
...I'M WORKING, NOW.

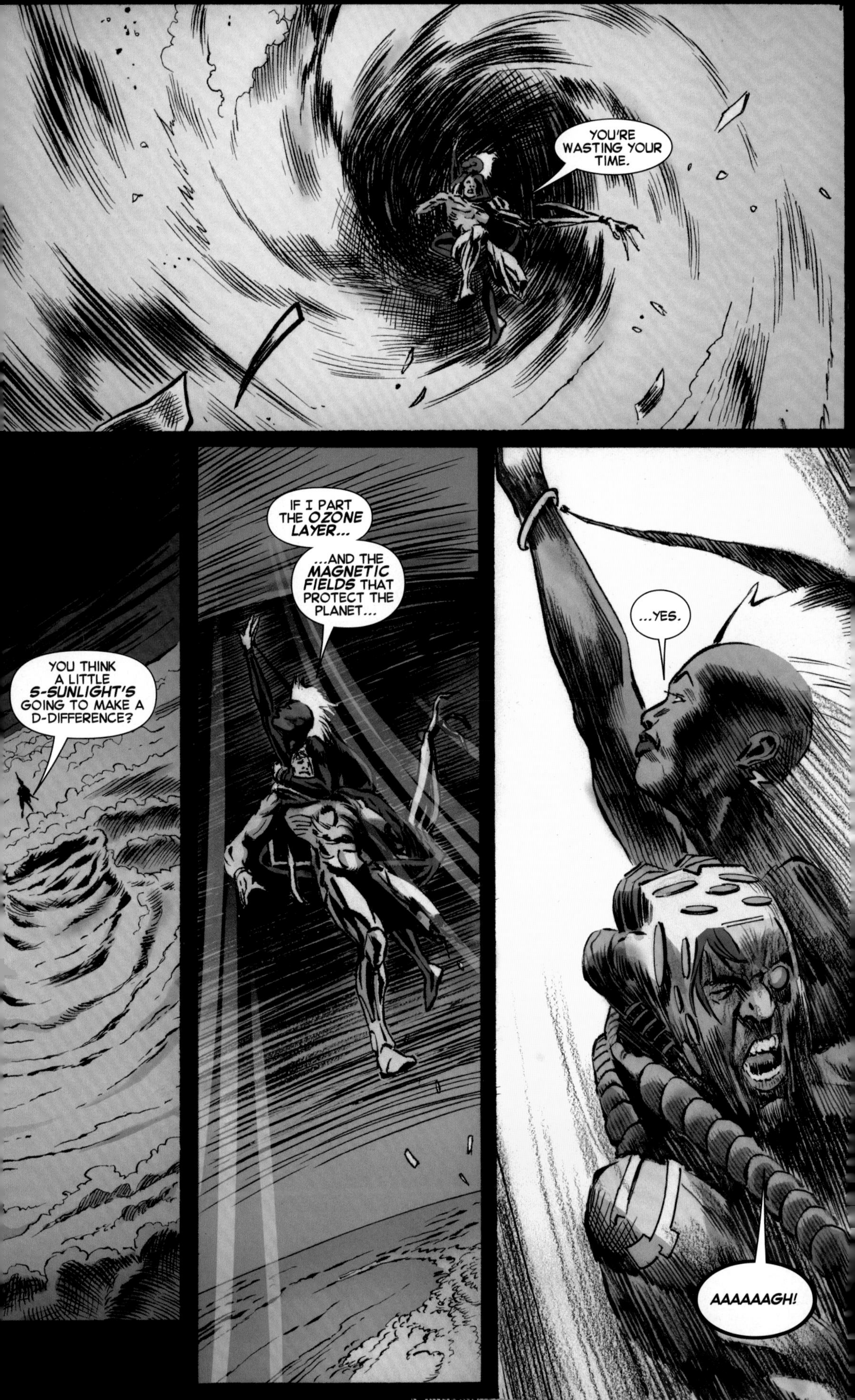
YOU'RE WASTING YOUR TIME.
YOU THINK A LITTLE S-SUNLIGHT'S GOING TO MAKE A D-DIFFERENCE?
IF I PART THE OZONE LAYER...
...AND THE MAGNETIC FIELDS THAT PROTECT THE PLANET...
...YES.
AAAAAAGH!

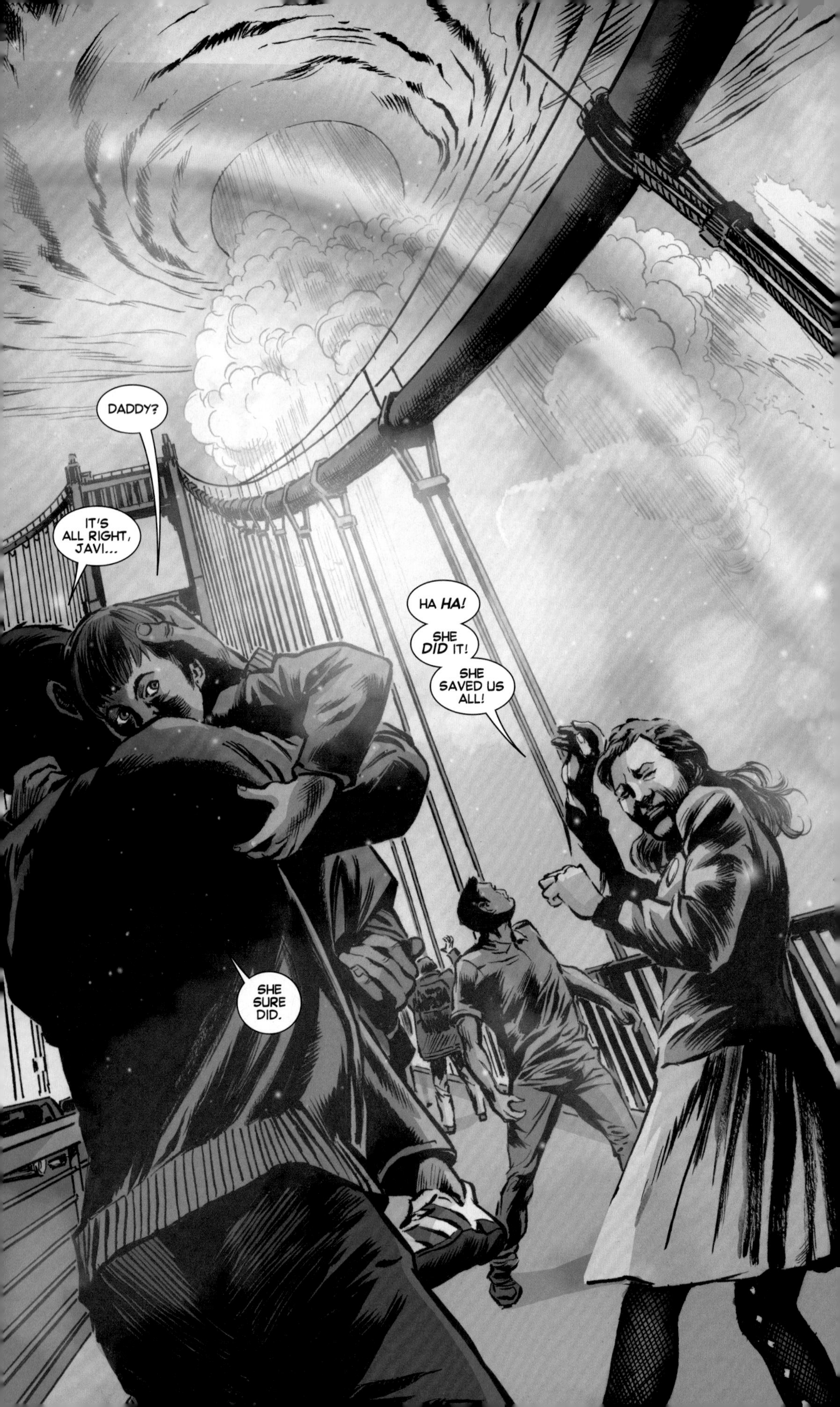
DADDY?
IT'S ALL RIGHT, JAVI...
HA HA!
SHE DID IT!
SHE SAVED US ALL!
SHE SURE DID.

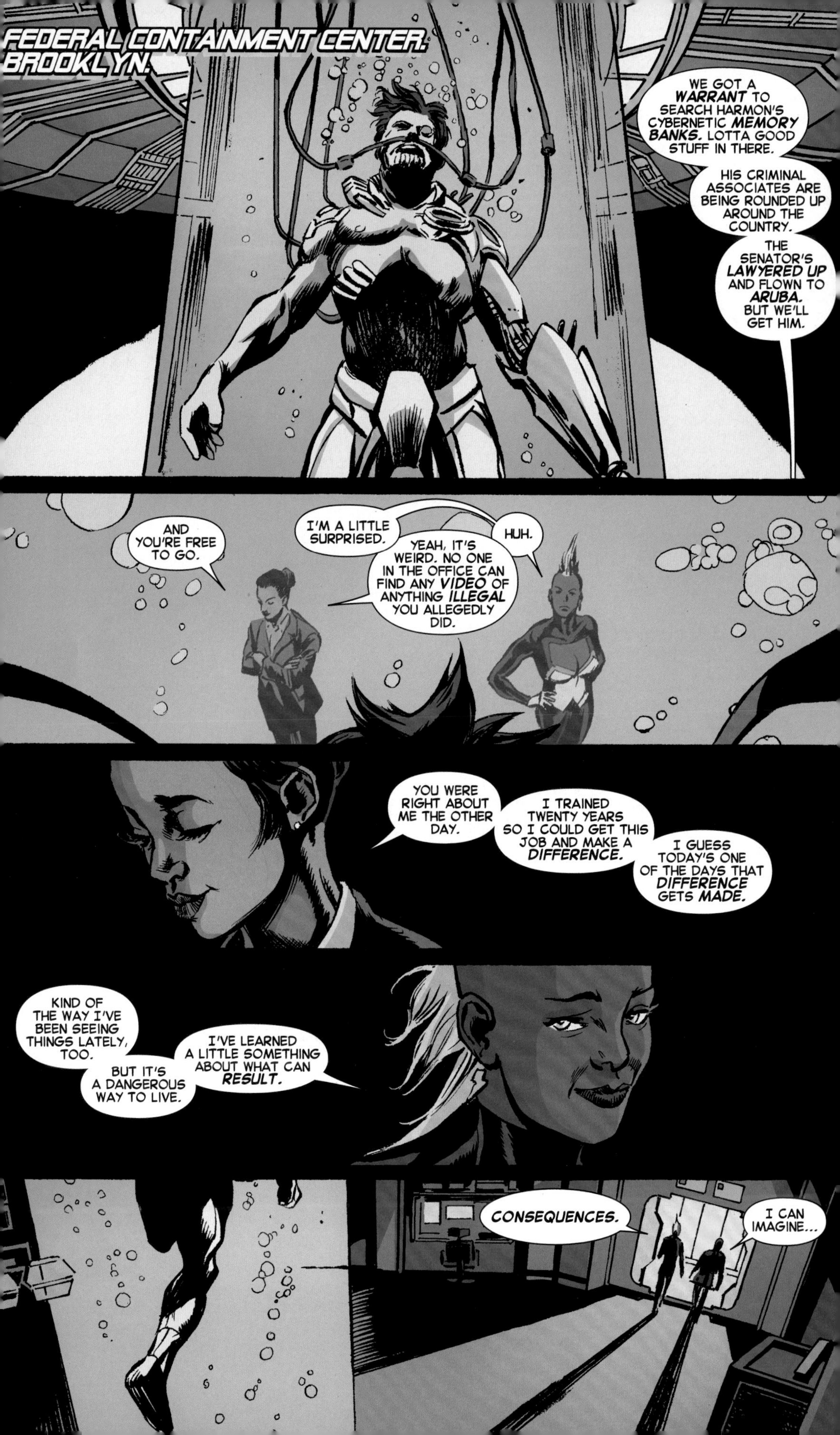
FEDERAL CONTAINMENT CENTER. BROOKLYN.
WE GOT A WARRANT TO SEARCH HARMON'S CYBERNETIC MEMORY BANKS. LOTTA GOOD STUFF IN THERE.
HIS CRIMINAL ASSOCIATES ARE BEING ROUNDED UP AROUND THE COUNTRY.
THE SENATOR'S LAWYERED UP AND FLOWN TO ARUBA. BUT WE'LL GET HIM.
AND YOU'RE FREE TO GO.
I'M A LITTLE SURPRISED.
HUH.
YEAH, IT'S WEIRD. NO ONE IN THE OFFICE CAN FIND ANY VIDEO OF ANYTHING ILLEGAL YOU ALLEGEDLY DID.
YOU WERE RIGHT ABOUT ME THE OTHER DAY.
I TRAINED TWENTY YEARS SO I COULD GET THIS JOB AND MAKE A DIFFERENCE.
I GUESS TODAY'S ONE OF THE DAYS THAT DIFFERENCE GETS MADE.
KIND OF THE WAY I'VE BEEN SEEING THINGS LATELY, TOO.
BUT IT'S A DANGEROUS WAY TO LIVE.
I'VE LEARNED A LITTLE SOMETHING ABOUT WHAT CAN RESULT.
CONSEQUENCES.
I CAN IMAGINE...

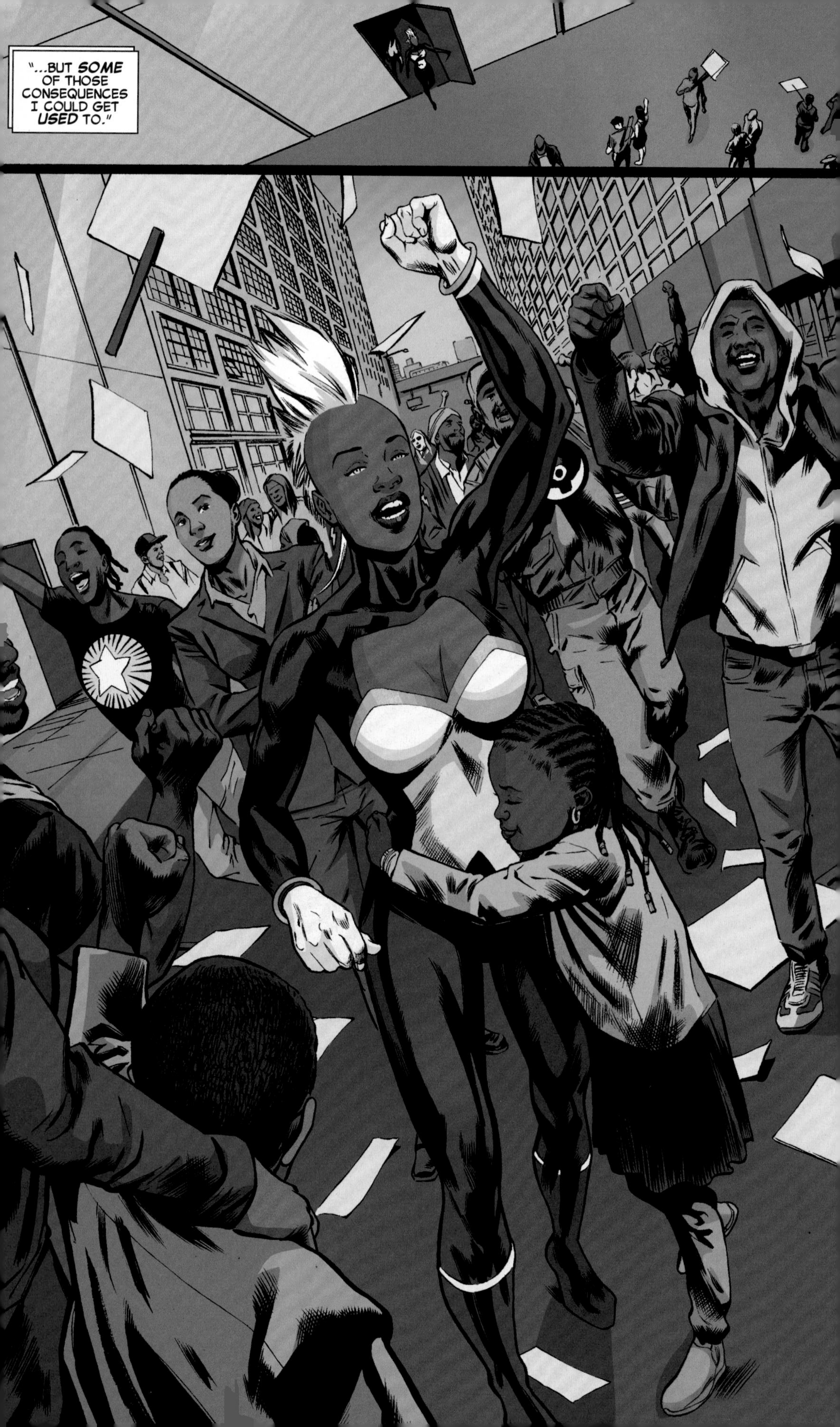
"...BUT **SOME** OF THOSE CONSEQUENCES I COULD GET **USED** TO."

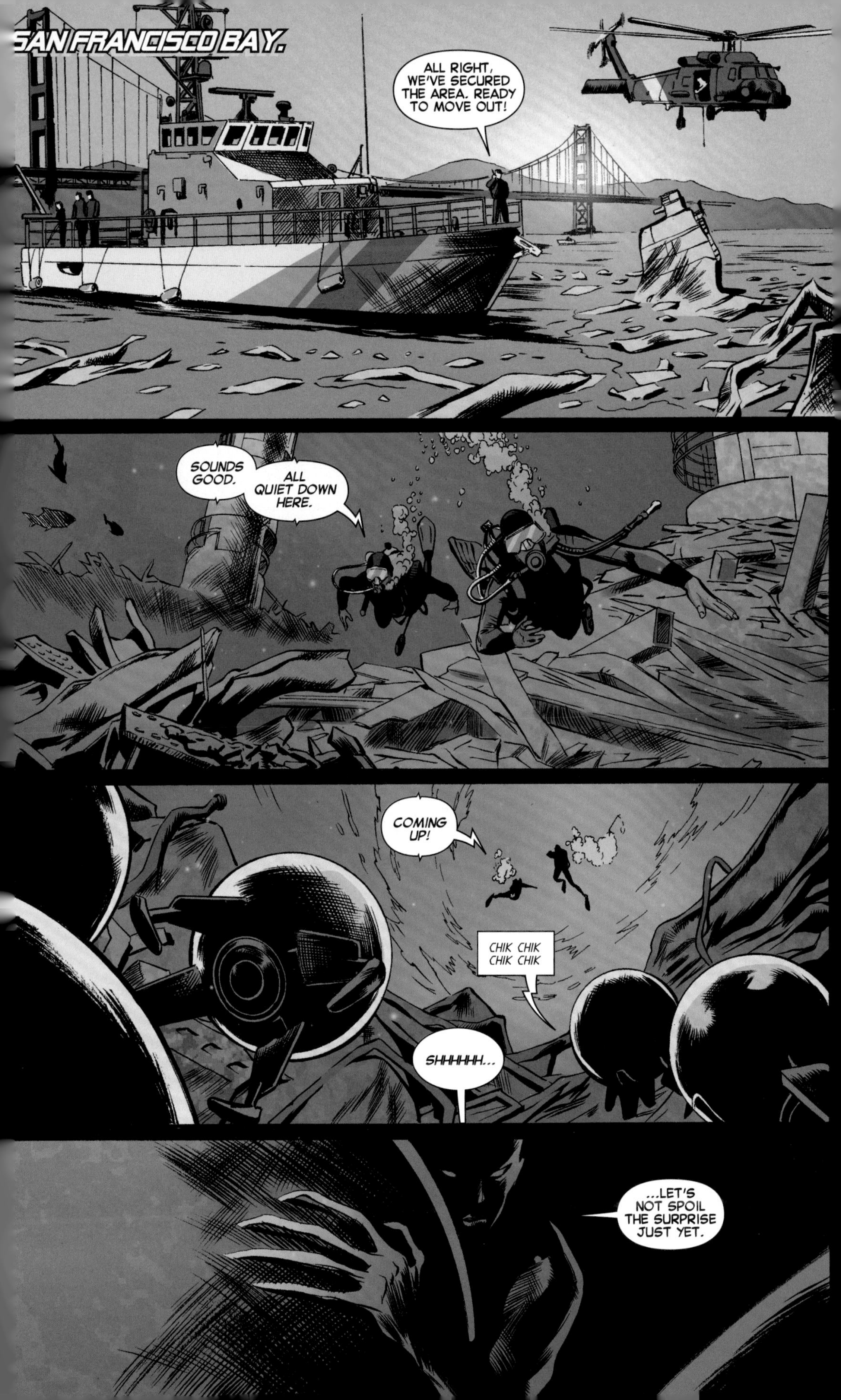
SAN FRANCISCO BAY.
ALL RIGHT, WE'VE SECURED THE AREA. READY TO MOVE OUT!
SOUNDS GOOD.
ALL QUIET DOWN HERE.
COMING UP!
CHIK CHIK CHIK CHIK
SHHHHHH...
...LET'S NOT SPOIL THE SURPRISE JUST YET.

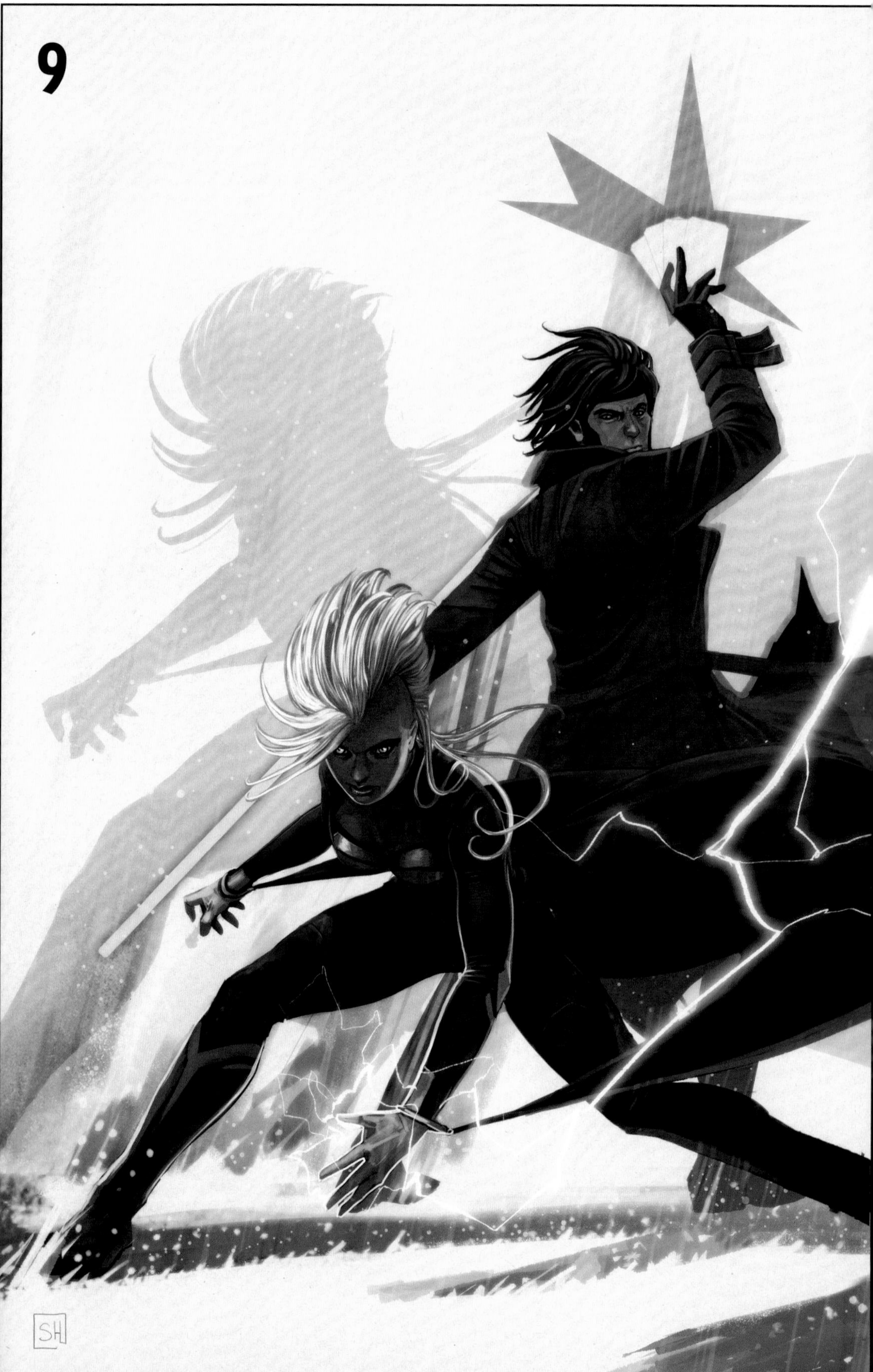
9
SH

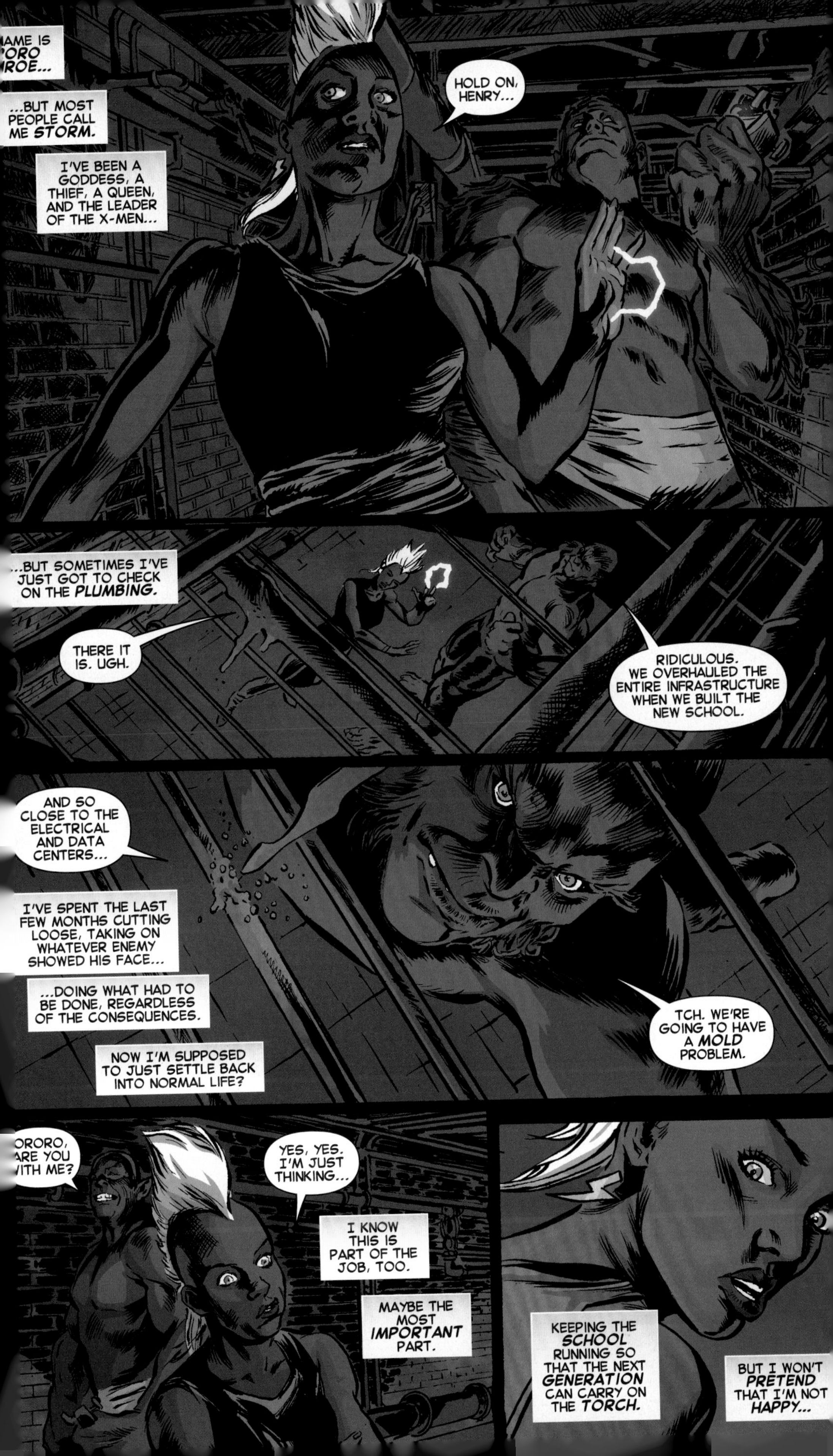

...AME IS ...ORO ...ROE...
...BUT MOST PEOPLE CALL ME STORM.
I'VE BEEN A GODDESS, A THIEF, A QUEEN, AND THE LEADER OF THE X-MEN...
HOLD ON, HENRY...
...BUT SOMETIMES I'VE JUST GOT TO CHECK ON THE PLUMBING.
THERE IT IS. UGH.
RIDICULOUS. WE OVERHAULED THE ENTIRE INFRASTRUCTURE WHEN WE BUILT THE NEW SCHOOL.
AND SO CLOSE TO THE ELECTRICAL AND DATA CENTERS...
I'VE SPENT THE LAST FEW MONTHS CUTTING LOOSE, TAKING ON WHATEVER ENEMY SHOWED HIS FACE...
...DOING WHAT HAD TO BE DONE, REGARDLESS OF THE CONSEQUENCES.
NOW I'M SUPPOSED TO JUST SETTLE BACK INTO NORMAL LIFE?
TCH. WE'RE GOING TO HAVE A MOLD PROBLEM.
ORORO, ARE YOU WITH ME?
YES, YES. I'M JUST THINKING...
I KNOW THIS IS PART OF THE JOB, TOO.
MAYBE THE MOST IMPORTANT PART.
KEEPING THE SCHOOL RUNNING SO THAT THE NEXT GENERATION CAN CARRY ON THE TORCH.
BUT I WON'T PRETEND THAT I'M NOT HAPPY...

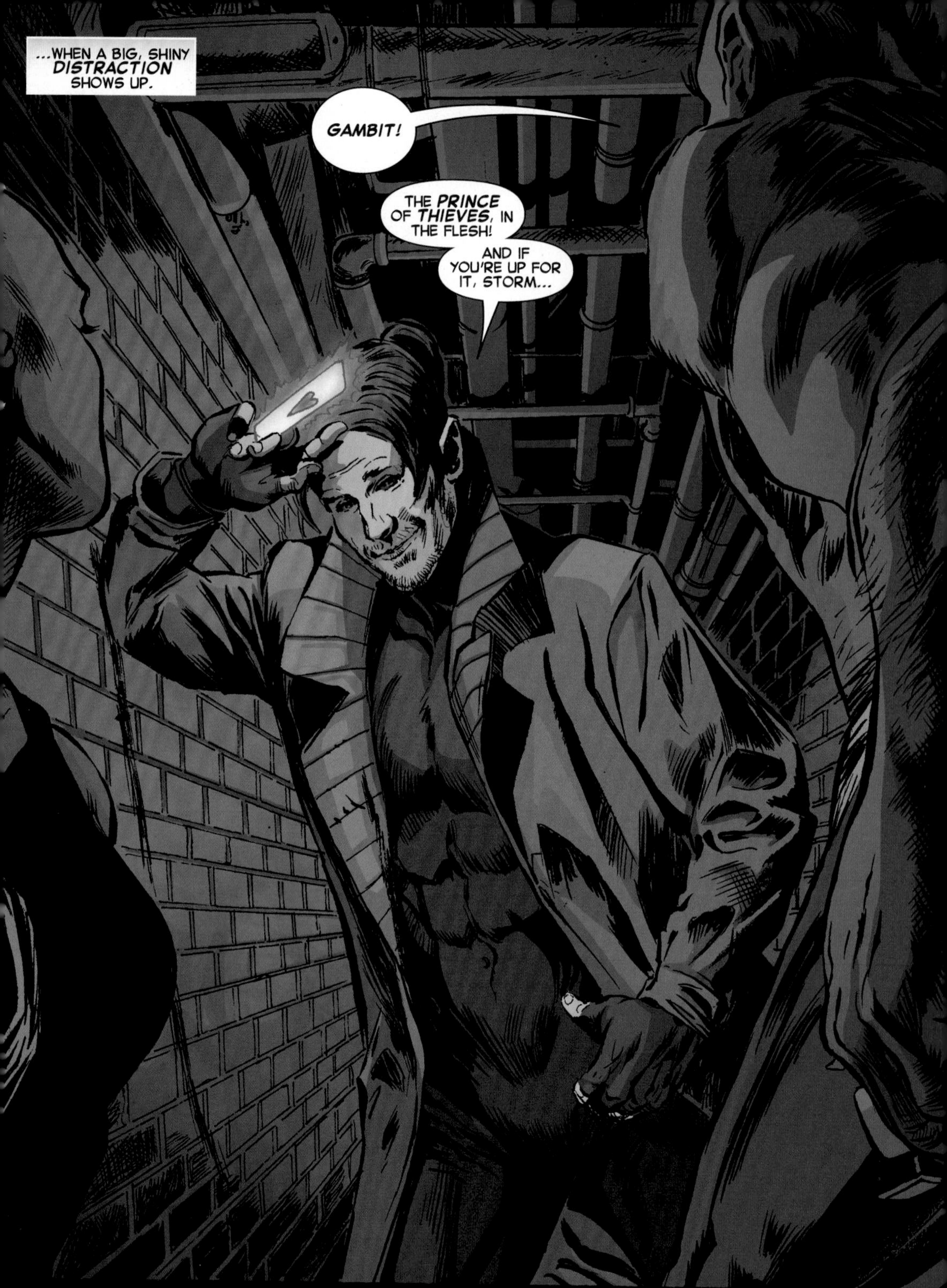
...WHEN A BIG, SHINY DISTRACTION SHOWS UP.
GAMBIT!
THE PRINCE OF THIEVES, IN THE FLESH!
AND IF YOU'RE UP FOR IT, STORM...

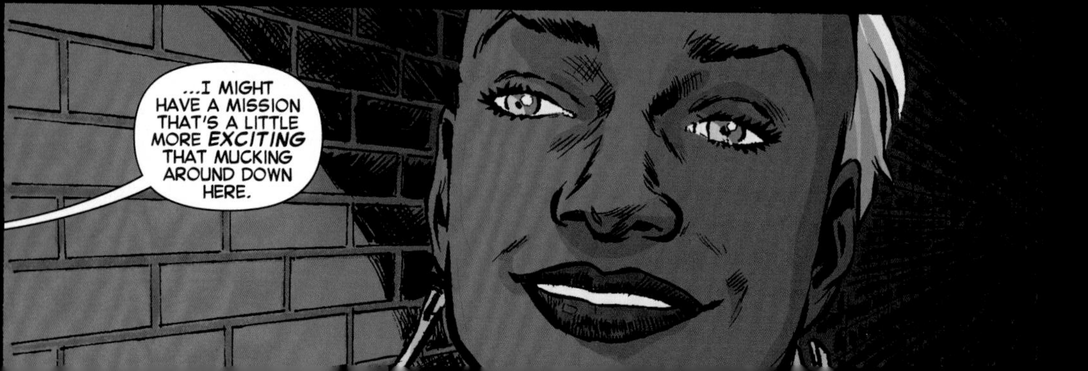
...I MIGHT HAVE A MISSION THAT'S A LITTLE MORE EXCITING THAT MUCKING AROUND DOWN HERE.

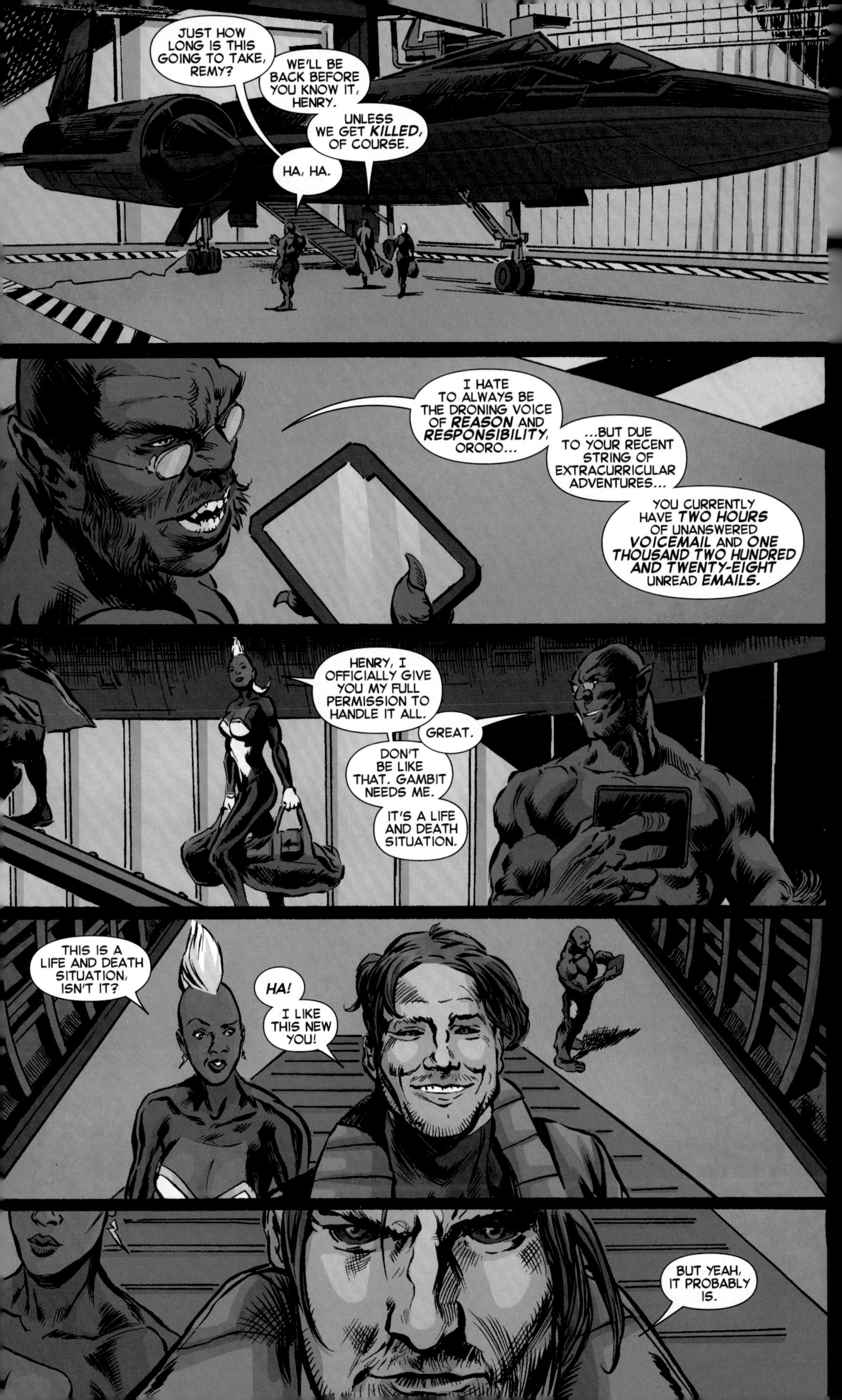
JUST HOW LONG IS THIS GOING TO TAKE, REMY?
WE'LL BE BACK BEFORE YOU KNOW IT, HENRY.
UNLESS WE GET KILLED, OF COURSE.
HA, HA.
I HATE TO ALWAYS BE THE DRONING VOICE OF REASON AND RESPONSIBILITY, ORORO...
...BUT DUE TO YOUR RECENT STRING OF EXTRACURRICULAR ADVENTURES...
YOU CURRENTLY HAVE TWO HOURS OF UNANSWERED VOICEMAIL AND ONE THOUSAND TWO HUNDRED AND TWENTY-EIGHT UNREAD EMAILS.
HENRY, I OFFICIALLY GIVE YOU MY FULL PERMISSION TO HANDLE IT ALL.
GREAT.
DON'T BE LIKE THAT. GAMBIT NEEDS ME.
IT'S A LIFE AND DEATH SITUATION.
THIS IS A LIFE AND DEATH SITUATION, ISN'T IT?
HA!
I LIKE THIS NEW YOU!
BUT YEAH, IT PROBABLY IS.

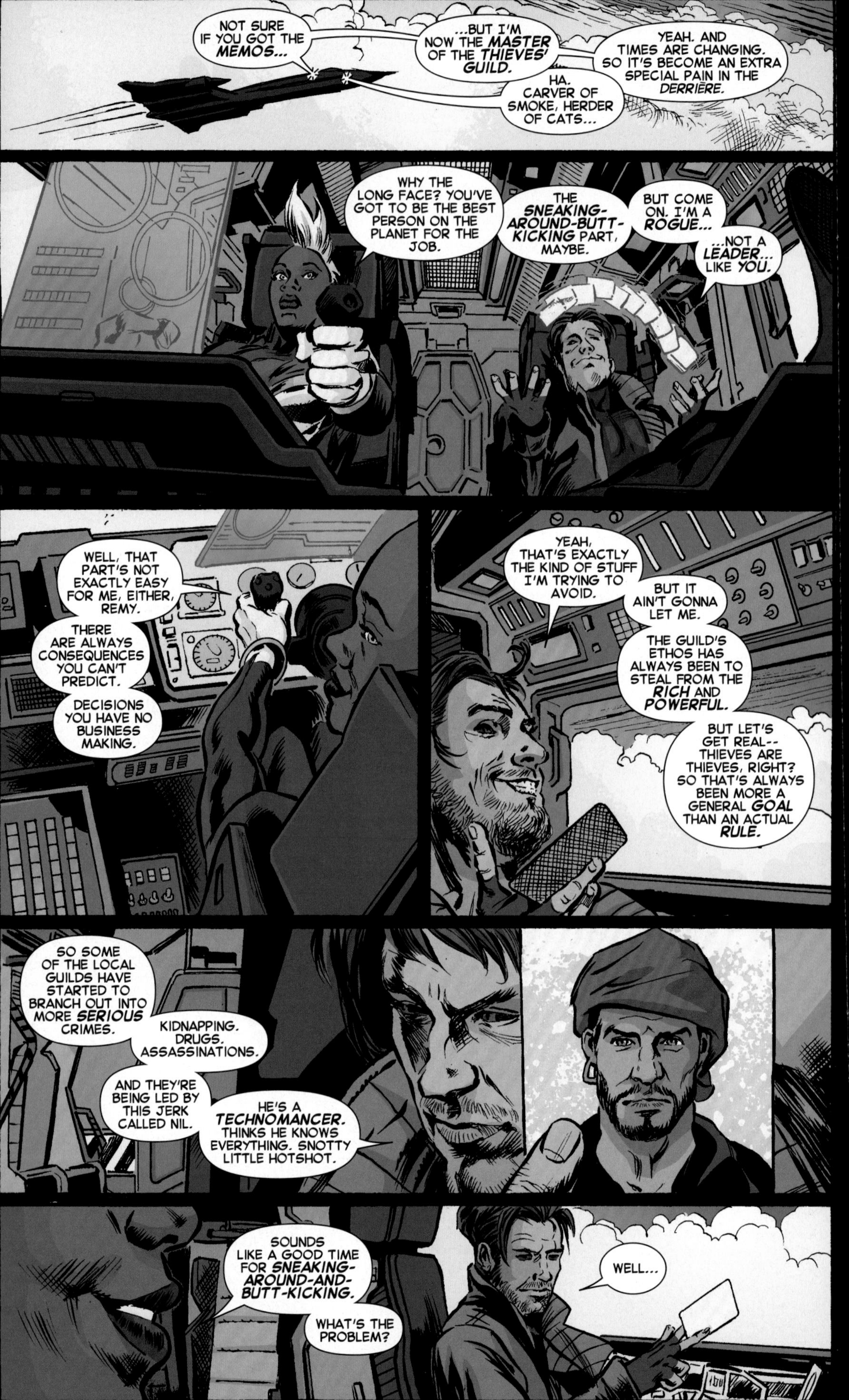
NOT SURE IF YOU GOT THE MEMOS...
...BUT I'M NOW THE MASTER OF THE THIEVES' GUILD.
HA. CARVER OF SMOKE, HERDER OF CATS...
YEAH. AND TIMES ARE CHANGING. SO IT'S BECOME AN EXTRA SPECIAL PAIN IN THE DERRIÈRE.
WHY THE LONG FACE? YOU'VE GOT TO BE THE BEST PERSON ON THE PLANET FOR THE JOB.
THE SNEAKING-AROUND-BUTT-KICKING PART, MAYBE.
BUT COME ON. I'M A ROGUE...
...NOT A LEADER... LIKE YOU.
WELL, THAT PART'S NOT EXACTLY EASY FOR ME, EITHER, REMY.
THERE ARE ALWAYS CONSEQUENCES YOU CAN'T PREDICT.
DECISIONS YOU HAVE NO BUSINESS MAKING.
YEAH, THAT'S EXACTLY THE KIND OF STUFF I'M TRYING TO AVOID.
BUT IT AIN'T GONNA LET ME.
THE GUILD'S ETHOS HAS ALWAYS BEEN TO STEAL FROM THE RICH AND POWERFUL.
BUT LET'S GET REAL-- THIEVES ARE THIEVES, RIGHT? SO THAT'S ALWAYS BEEN MORE A GENERAL GOAL THAN AN ACTUAL RULE.
SO SOME OF THE LOCAL GUILDS HAVE STARTED TO BRANCH OUT INTO MORE SERIOUS CRIMES.
KIDNAPPING. DRUGS. ASSASSINATIONS.
AND THEY'RE BEING LED BY THIS JERK CALLED NIL.
HE'S A TECHNOMANCER. THINKS HE KNOWS EVERYTHING. SNOTTY LITTLE HOTSHOT.
SOUNDS LIKE A GOOD TIME FOR SNEAKING-AROUND-AND-BUTT-KICKING.
WHAT'S THE PROBLEM?
WELL...

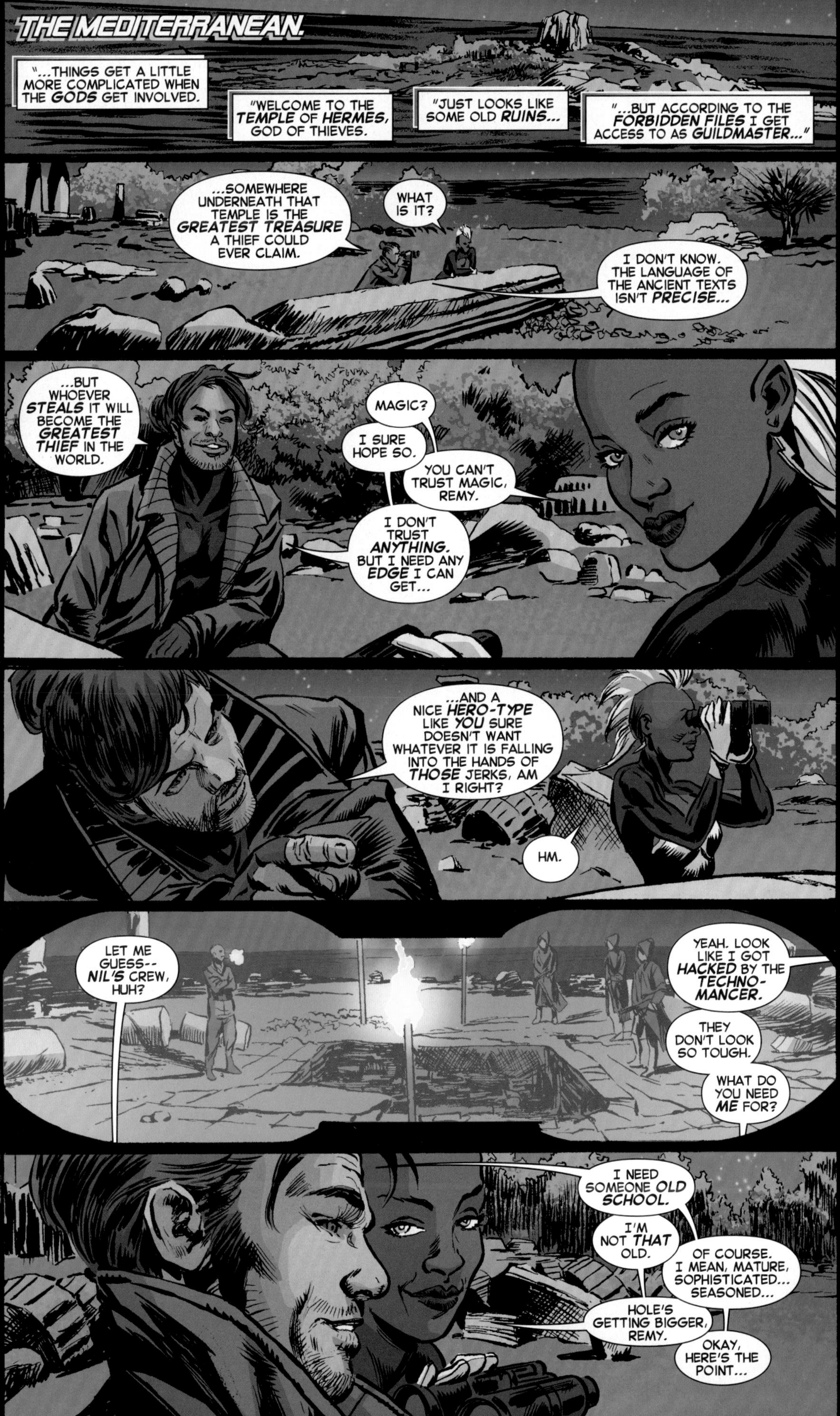
THE MEDITERRANEAN.
"...THINGS GET A LITTLE MORE COMPLICATED WHEN THE GODS GET INVOLVED.
"WELCOME TO THE TEMPLE OF HERMES, GOD OF THIEVES.
"JUST LOOKS LIKE SOME OLD RUINS...
"...BUT ACCORDING TO THE FORBIDDEN FILES I GET ACCESS TO AS GUILDMASTER..."
...SOMEWHERE UNDERNEATH THAT TEMPLE IS THE GREATEST TREASURE A THIEF COULD EVER CLAIM.
WHAT IS IT?
I DON'T KNOW. THE LANGUAGE OF THE ANCIENT TEXTS ISN'T PRECISE...
...BUT WHOEVER STEALS IT WILL BECOME THE GREATEST THIEF IN THE WORLD.
MAGIC?
I SURE HOPE SO.
YOU CAN'T TRUST MAGIC, REMY.
I DON'T TRUST ANYTHING. BUT I NEED ANY EDGE I CAN GET...
...AND A NICE HERO-TYPE LIKE YOU SURE DOESN'T WANT WHATEVER IT IS FALLING INTO THE HANDS OF THOSE JERKS, AM I RIGHT?
HM.
LET ME GUESS-- NIL'S CREW, HUH?
YEAH. LOOK LIKE I GOT HACKED BY THE TECHNO-MANCER.
THEY DON'T LOOK SO TOUGH.
WHAT DO YOU NEED ME FOR?
I NEED SOMEONE OLD SCHOOL.
I'M NOT THAT OLD.
OF COURSE. I MEAN, MATURE, SOPHISTICATED... SEASONED...
HOLE'S GETTING BIGGER, REMY.
OKAY, HERE'S THE POINT...

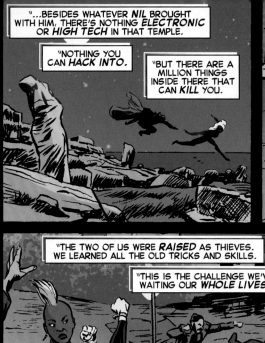

"...BESIDES WHATEVER **NIL** BROUGHT WITH HIM, THERE'S NOTHING **ELECTRONIC** OR **HIGH TECH** IN THAT TEMPLE.

"NOTHING YOU CAN **HACK INTO.**

"BUT THERE ARE A MILLION THINGS INSIDE THERE THAT CAN **KILL YOU.**

"YOUNG THIEVES RELY TOO MUCH ON THEIR **TECH.**

"THIS JOB NEEDS SOMEONE WITH **REAL** TALENTS.

"THE TWO OF US WERE **RAISED** AS THIEVES. WE LEARNED ALL THE OLD TRICKS AND SKILLS.

"THIS IS THE CHALLENGE WE'VE BEEN WAITING OUR **WHOLE LIVES** FOR."

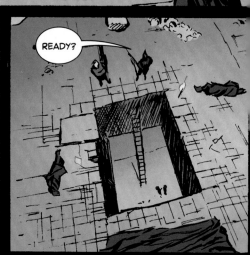

READY?

HELL YEAH.

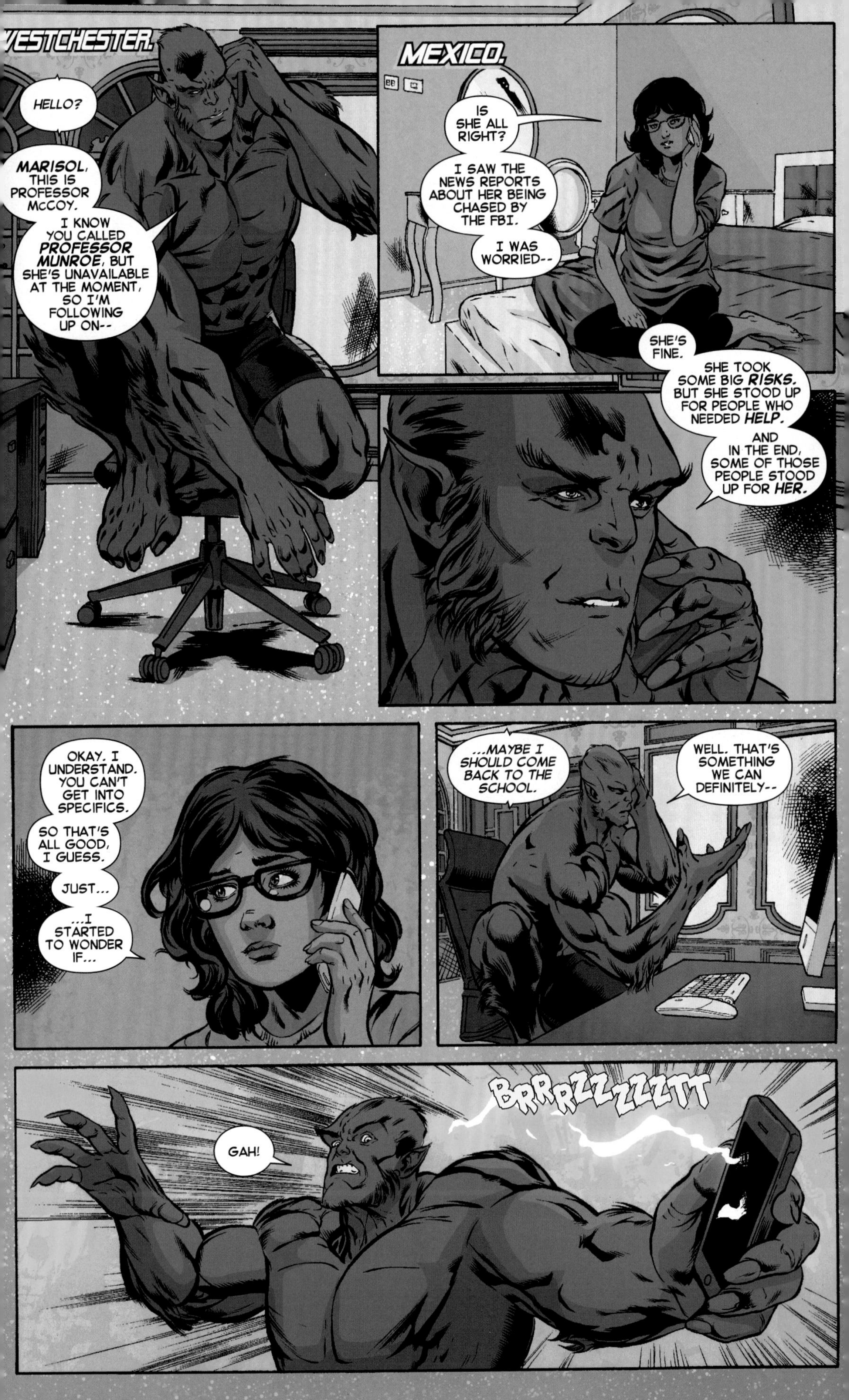
WESTCHESTER.
HELLO?
MARISOL, THIS IS PROFESSOR McCOY.
I KNOW YOU CALLED PROFESSOR MUNROE, BUT SHE'S UNAVAILABLE AT THE MOMENT, SO I'M FOLLOWING UP ON--
MEXICO.
IS SHE ALL RIGHT?
I SAW THE NEWS REPORTS ABOUT HER BEING CHASED BY THE FBI.
I WAS WORRIED--
SHE'S FINE.
SHE TOOK SOME BIG RISKS. BUT SHE STOOD UP FOR PEOPLE WHO NEEDED HELP.
AND IN THE END, SOME OF THOSE PEOPLE STOOD UP FOR HER.
OKAY. I UNDERSTAND. YOU CAN'T GET INTO SPECIFICS.
SO THAT'S ALL GOOD, I GUESS.
JUST...
...I STARTED TO WONDER IF...
...MAYBE I SHOULD COME BACK TO THE SCHOOL.
WELL. THAT'S SOMETHING WE CAN DEFINITELY--
BRRRZZZZZZTT
GAH!

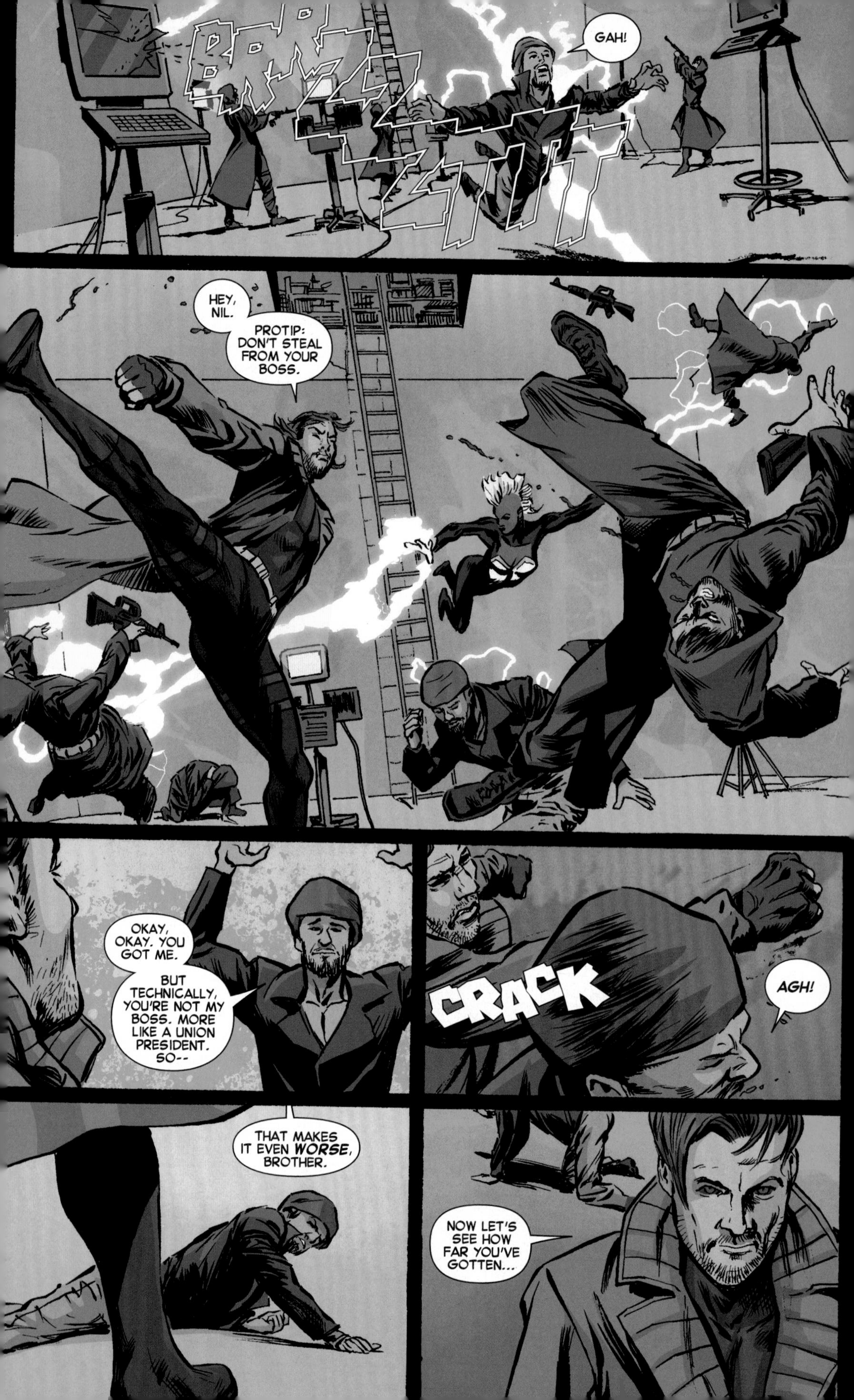
GAH!
HEY, NIL.
PROTIP: DON'T STEAL FROM YOUR BOSS.
OKAY, OKAY. YOU GOT ME.
BUT TECHNICALLY, YOU'RE NOT MY BOSS. MORE LIKE A UNION PRESIDENT. SO--
CRACK
AGH!
THAT MAKES IT EVEN *WORSE*, BROTHER.
NOW LET'S SEE HOW FAR YOU'VE GOTTEN...

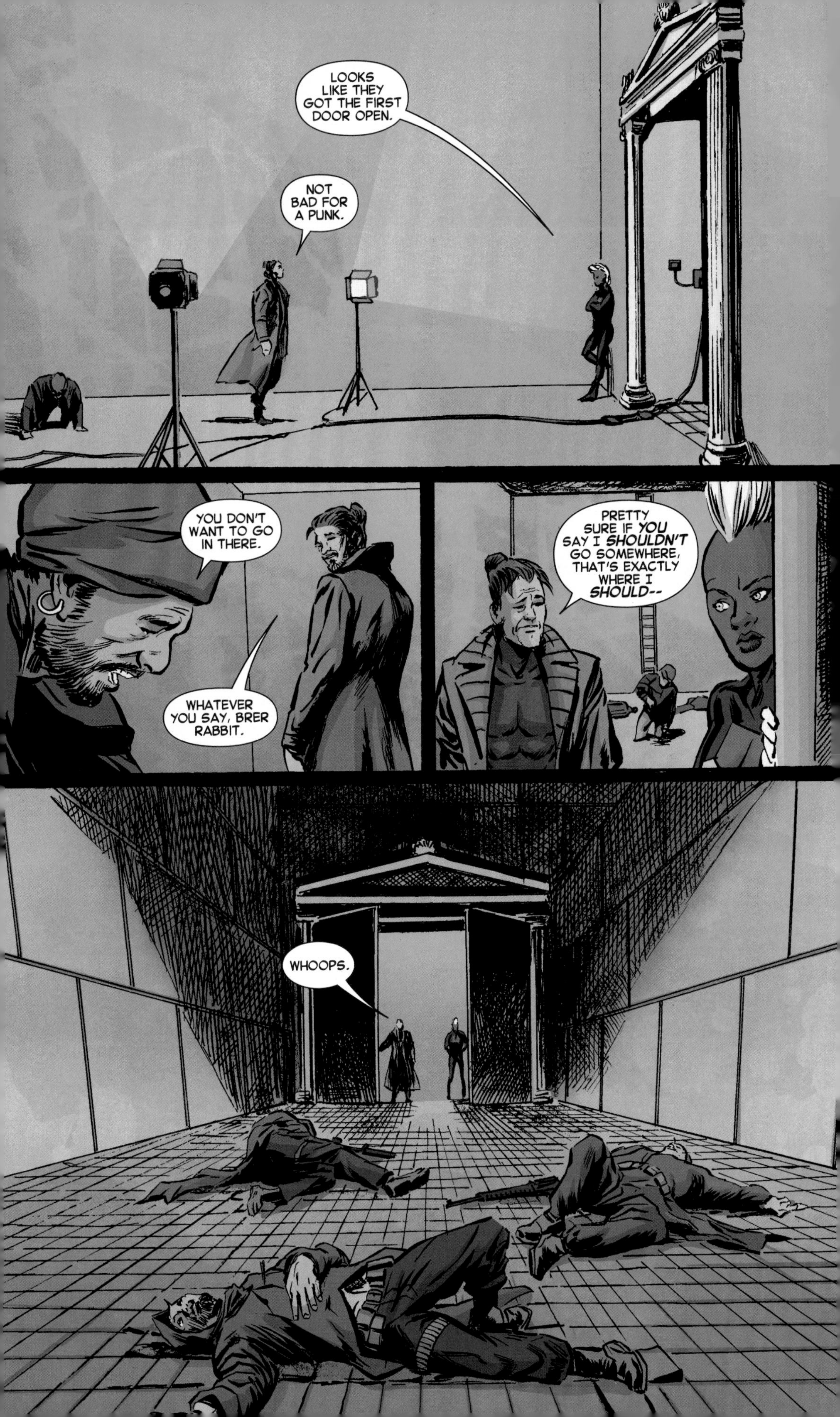
LOOKS LIKE THEY GOT THE FIRST DOOR OPEN.
NOT BAD FOR A PUNK.
YOU DON'T WANT TO GO IN THERE.
WHATEVER YOU SAY, BRER RABBIT.
PRETTY SURE IF YOU SAY I SHOULDN'T GO SOMEWHERE, THAT'S EXACTLY WHERE I SHOULD--
WHOOPS.

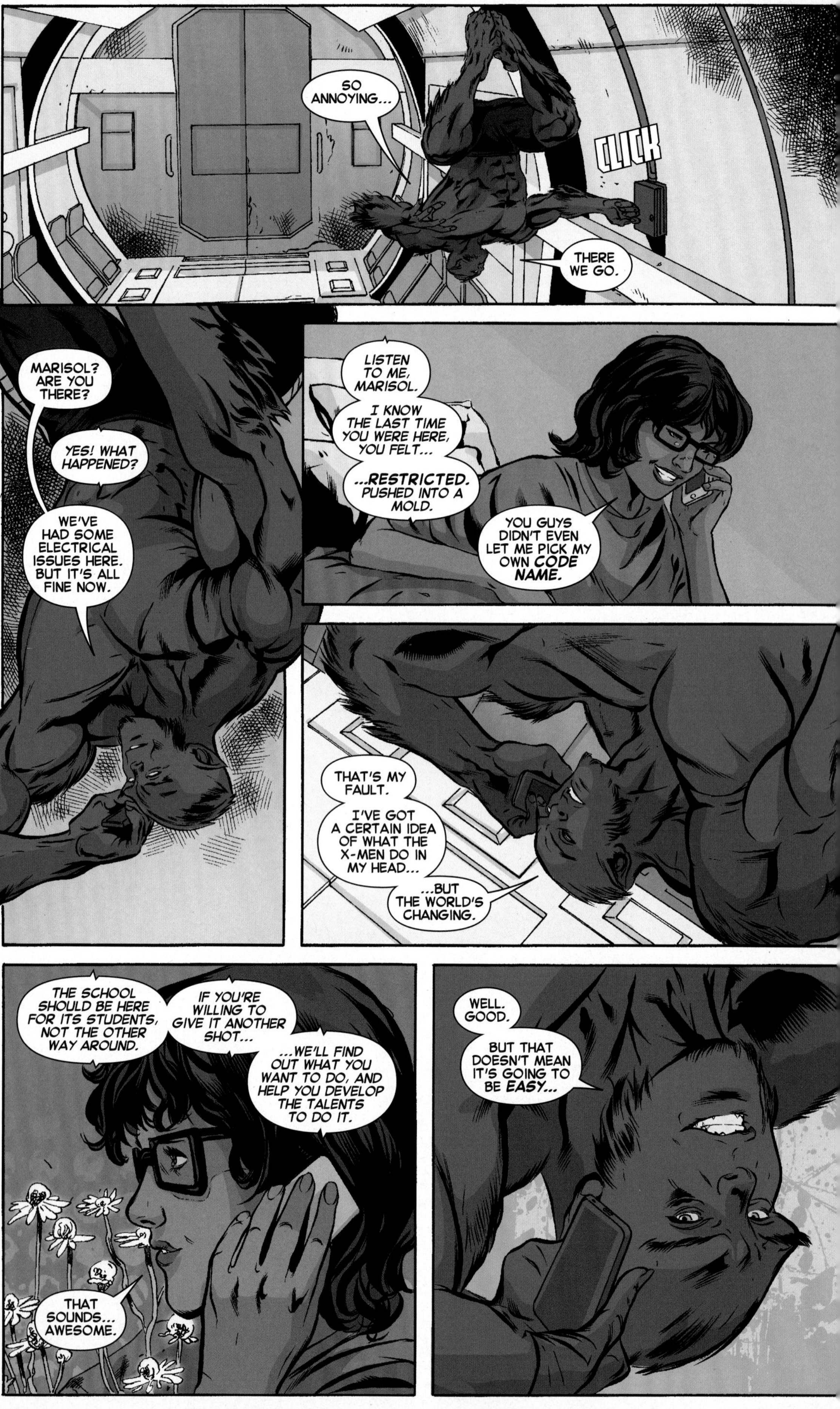
SO ANNOYING...
CLICK
THERE WE GO.
MARISOL? ARE YOU THERE?
YES! WHAT HAPPENED?
WE'VE HAD SOME ELECTRICAL ISSUES HERE. BUT IT'S ALL FINE NOW.
LISTEN TO ME, MARISOL.
I KNOW THE LAST TIME YOU WERE HERE, YOU FELT...
...RESTRICTED. PUSHED INTO A MOLD.
YOU GUYS DIDN'T EVEN LET ME PICK MY OWN CODE NAME.
THAT'S MY FAULT.
I'VE GOT A CERTAIN IDEA OF WHAT THE X-MEN DO IN MY HEAD...
...BUT THE WORLD'S CHANGING.
THE SCHOOL SHOULD BE HERE FOR ITS STUDENTS, NOT THE OTHER WAY AROUND.
IF YOU'RE WILLING TO GIVE IT ANOTHER SHOT...
...WE'LL FIND OUT WHAT YOU WANT TO DO, AND HELP YOU DEVELOP THE TALENTS TO DO IT.
THAT SOUNDS... AWESOME.
WELL. GOOD.
BUT THAT DOESN'T MEAN IT'S GOING TO BE EASY...

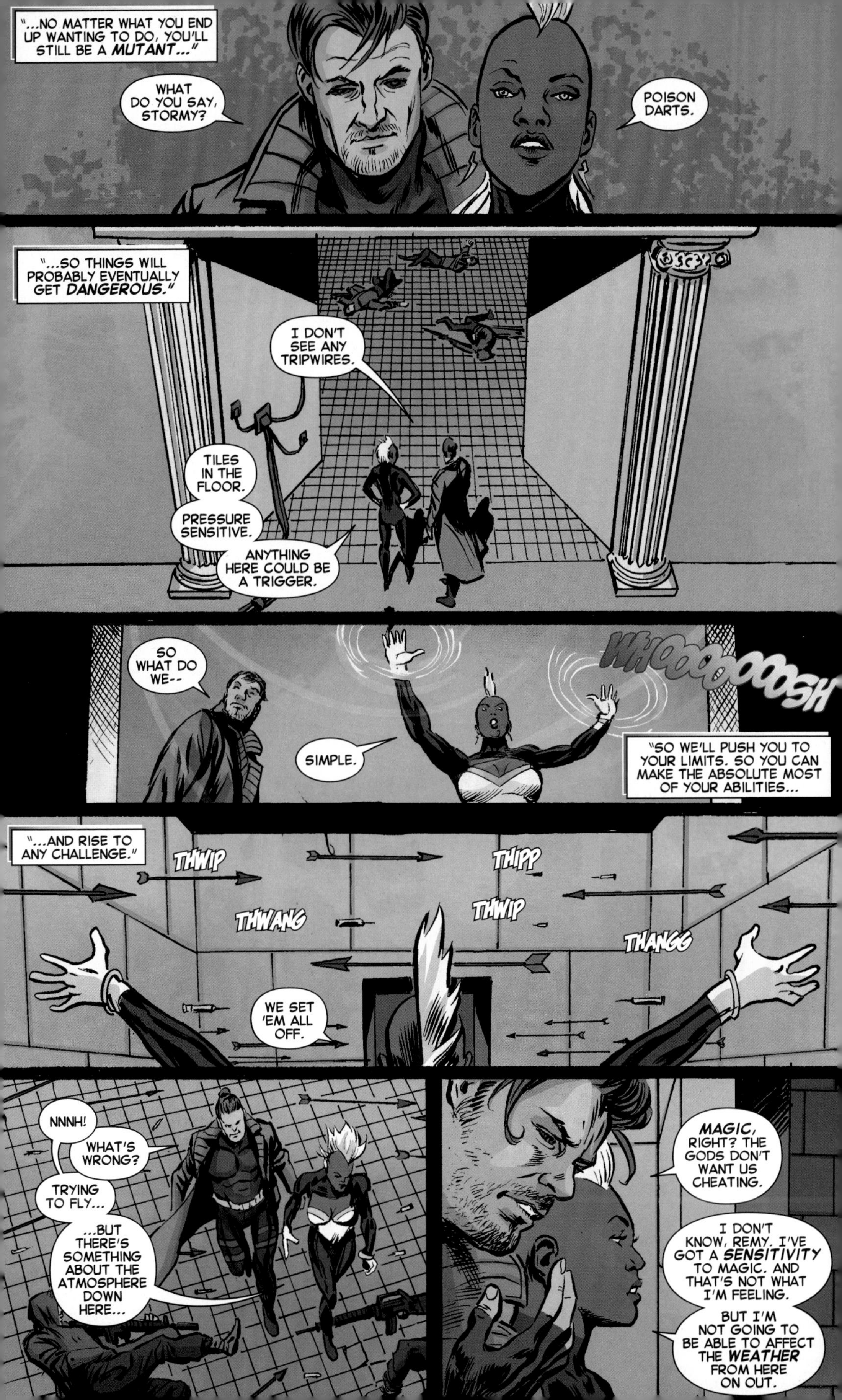
"...NO MATTER WHAT YOU END UP WANTING TO DO, YOU'LL STILL BE A MUTANT..."
WHAT DO YOU SAY, STORMY?
POISON DARTS.
"...SO THINGS WILL PROBABLY EVENTUALLY GET DANGEROUS."
I DON'T SEE ANY TRIPWIRES.
TILES IN THE FLOOR.
PRESSURE SENSITIVE.
ANYTHING HERE COULD BE A TRIGGER.
SO WHAT DO WE--
WHOOOOOOOSH
SIMPLE.
"SO WE'LL PUSH YOU TO YOUR LIMITS. SO YOU CAN MAKE THE ABSOLUTE MOST OF YOUR ABILITIES...
"...AND RISE TO ANY CHALLENGE."
THWIP
THIPP
THWIP
THWANG
THANGG
WE SET 'EM ALL OFF.
NNNH!
WHAT'S WRONG?
TRYING TO FLY...
...BUT THERE'S SOMETHING ABOUT THE ATMOSPHERE DOWN HERE...
MAGIC, RIGHT? THE GODS DON'T WANT US CHEATING.
I DON'T KNOW, REMY. I'VE GOT A SENSITIVITY TO MAGIC. AND THAT'S NOT WHAT I'M FEELING.
BUT I'M NOT GOING TO BE ABLE TO AFFECT THE WEATHER FROM HERE ON OUT.

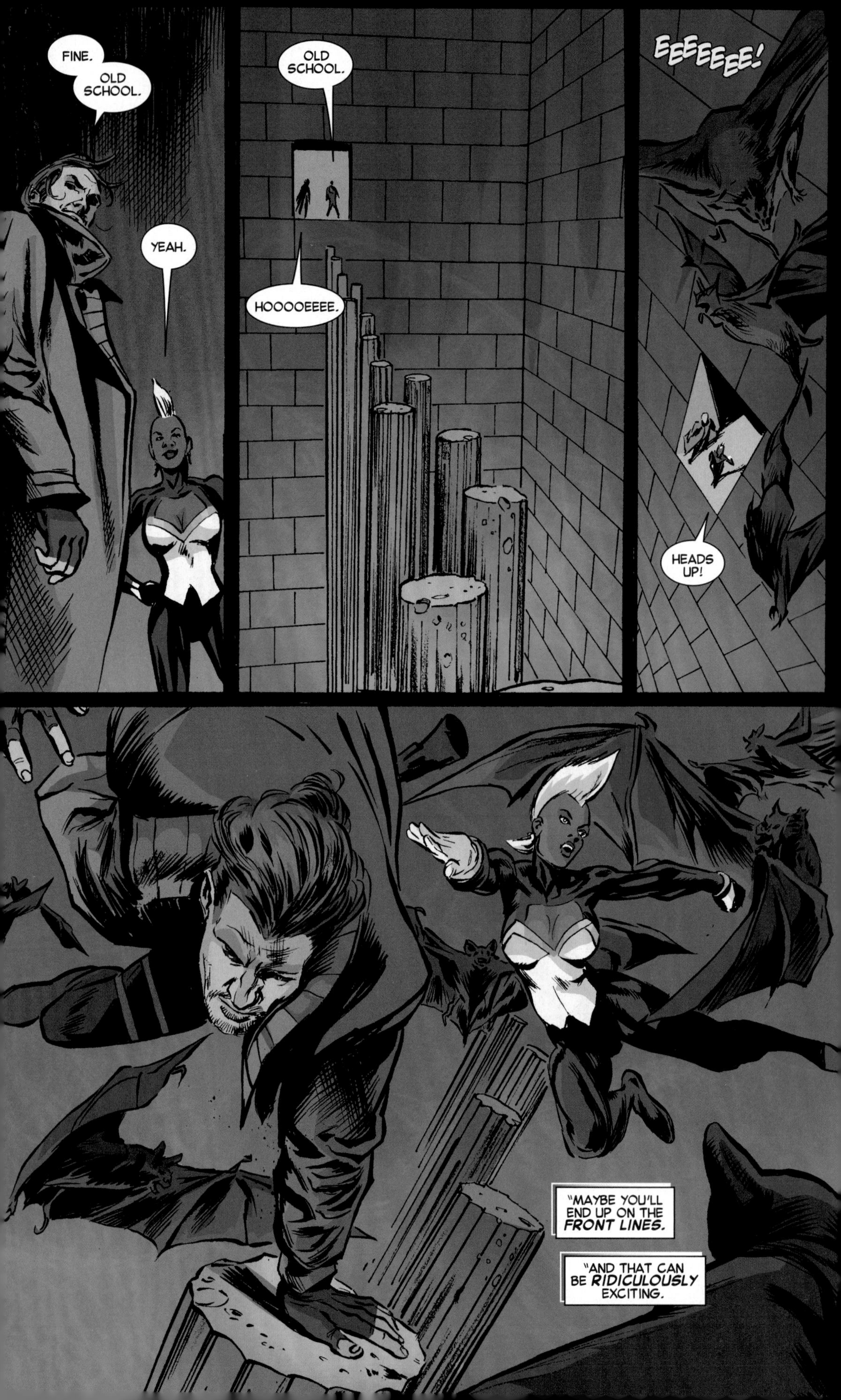
FINE.
OLD SCHOOL.
YEAH.
OLD SCHOOL.
HOOOOEEEE.
EEEEEEE!
HEADS UP!
"MAYBE YOU'LL END UP ON THE FRONT LINES.
"AND THAT CAN BE RIDICULOUSLY EXCITING.

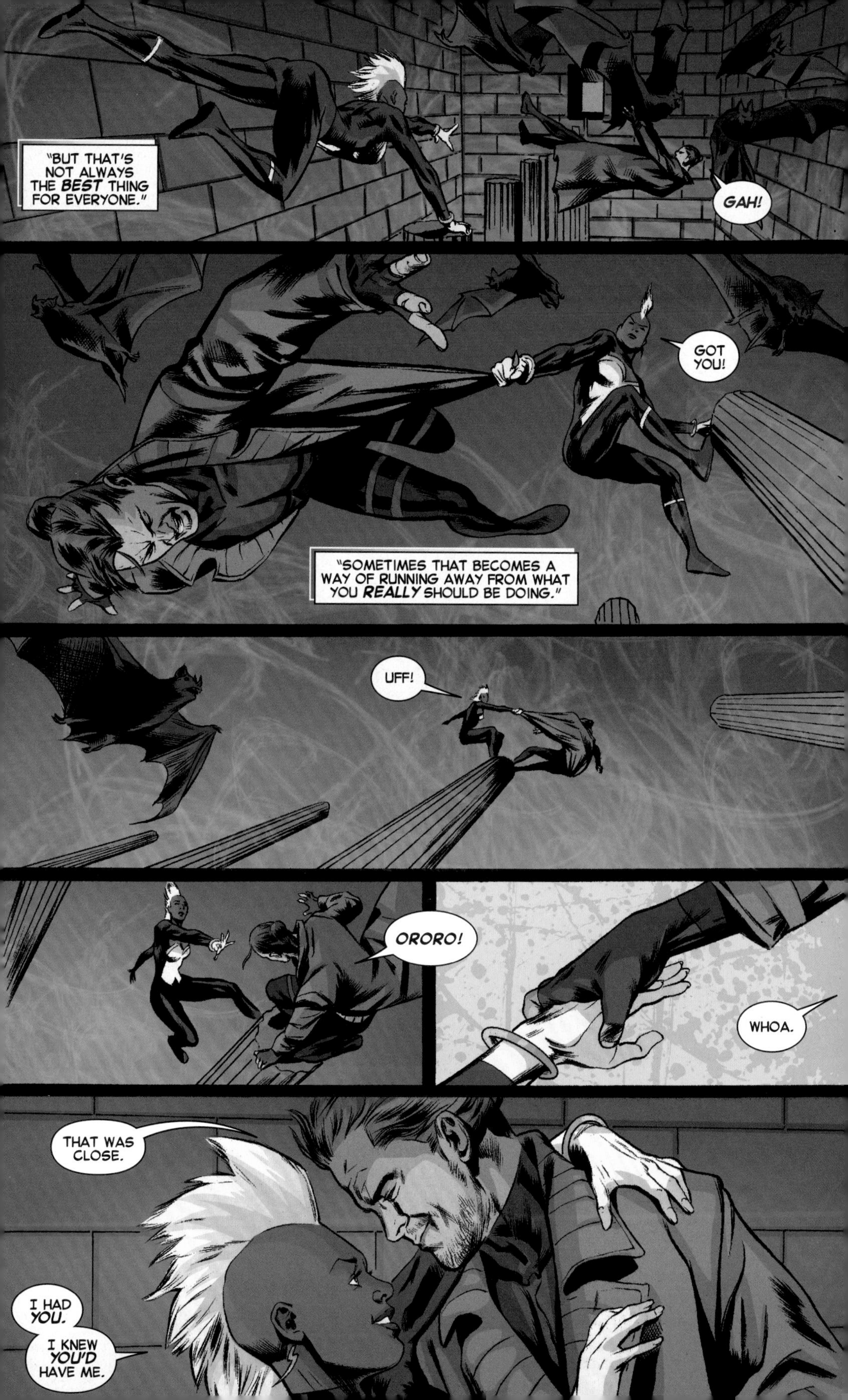
"BUT THAT'S NOT ALWAYS THE BEST THING FOR EVERYONE."
GAH!
GOT YOU!
"SOMETIMES THAT BECOMES A WAY OF RUNNING AWAY FROM WHAT YOU REALLY SHOULD BE DOING."
UFF!
ORORO!
WHOA.
THAT WAS CLOSE.
I HAD YOU.
I KNEW YOU'D HAVE ME.

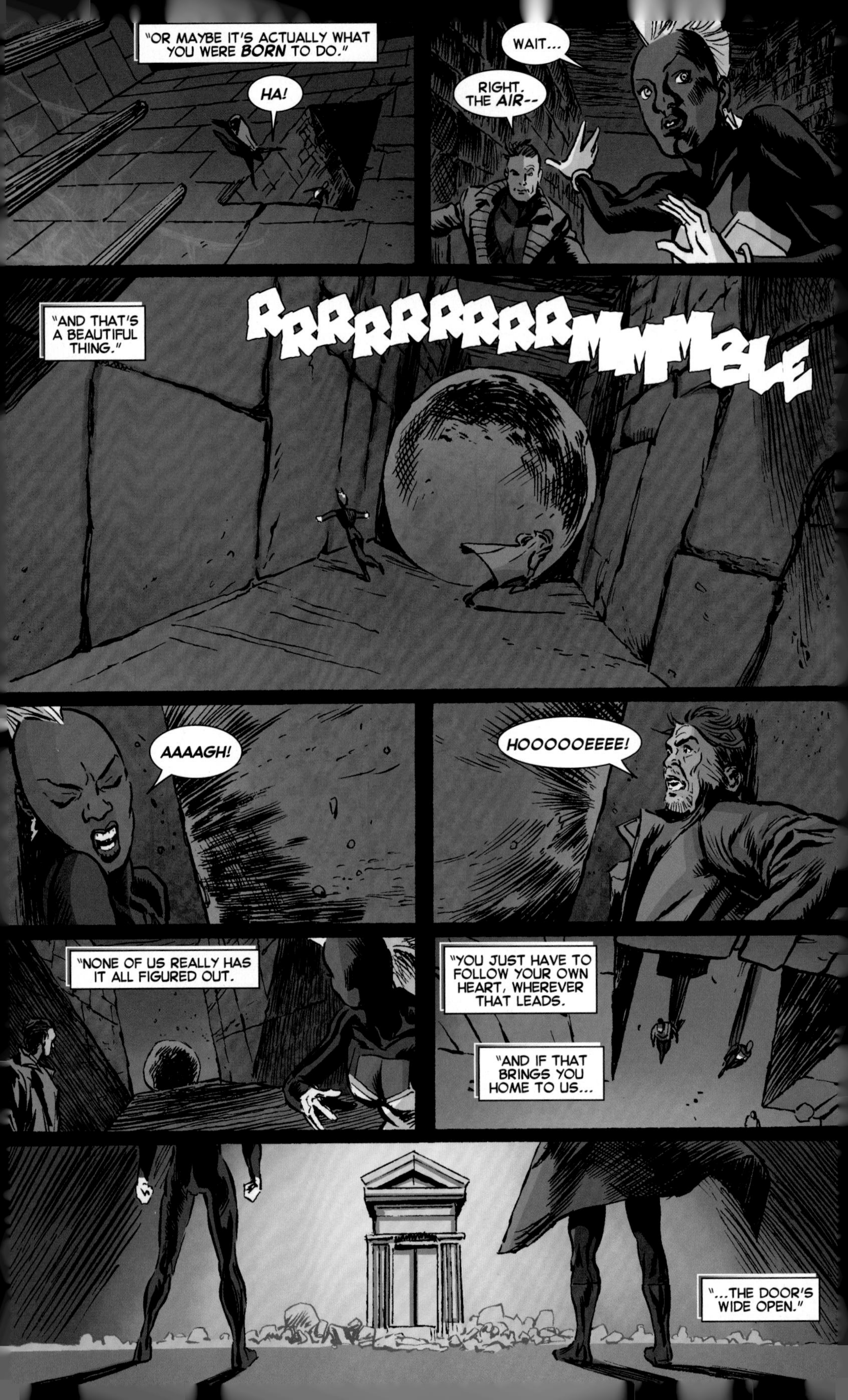

"OR MAYBE IT'S ACTUALLY WHAT YOU WERE **BORN** TO DO."
HA!
WAIT...
RIGHT. THE **AIR**--
"AND THAT'S A BEAUTIFUL THING."
RRRRRRRRRRMMMMBLE
AAAAGH!
HOOOOOEEEE!
"NONE OF US REALLY HAS IT ALL FIGURED OUT.
"YOU JUST HAVE TO FOLLOW YOUR OWN HEART, WHEREVER THAT LEADS.
"AND IF THAT BRINGS YOU HOME TO US...
"...THE DOOR'S WIDE OPEN."

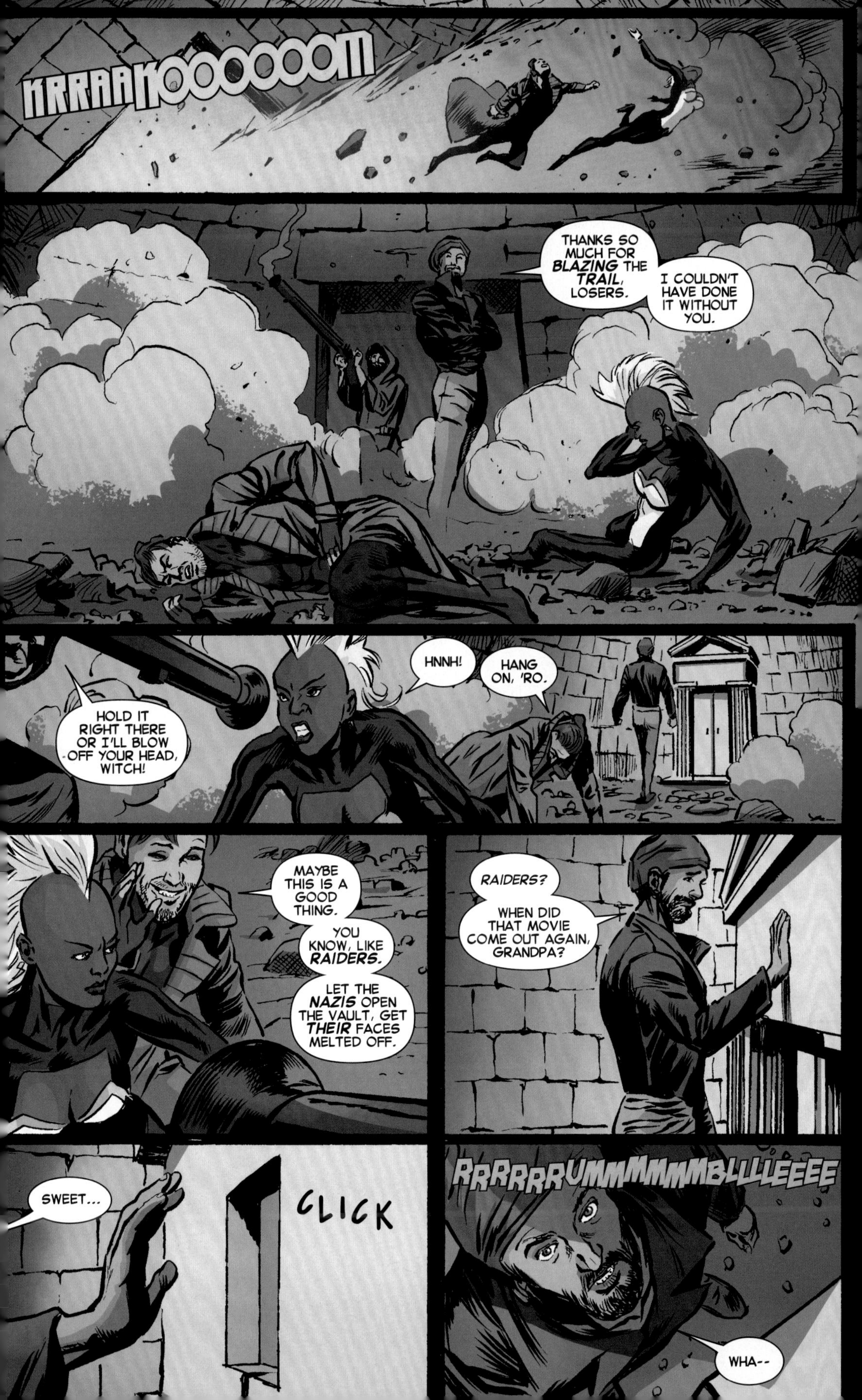
KRRAAKOOOOOOM
THANKS SO MUCH FOR BLAZING THE TRAIL, LOSERS.
I COULDN'T HAVE DONE IT WITHOUT YOU.
HOLD IT RIGHT THERE OR I'LL BLOW OFF YOUR HEAD, WITCH!
HNNH!
HANG ON, 'RO.
MAYBE THIS IS A GOOD THING.
YOU KNOW, LIKE RAIDERS.
LET THE NAZIS OPEN THE VAULT, GET THEIR FACES MELTED OFF.
RAIDERS?
WHEN DID THAT MOVIE COME OUT AGAIN, GRANDPA?
SWEET...
CLICK
RRRRRRUMMMMMMBLLLLEEEE
WHA--

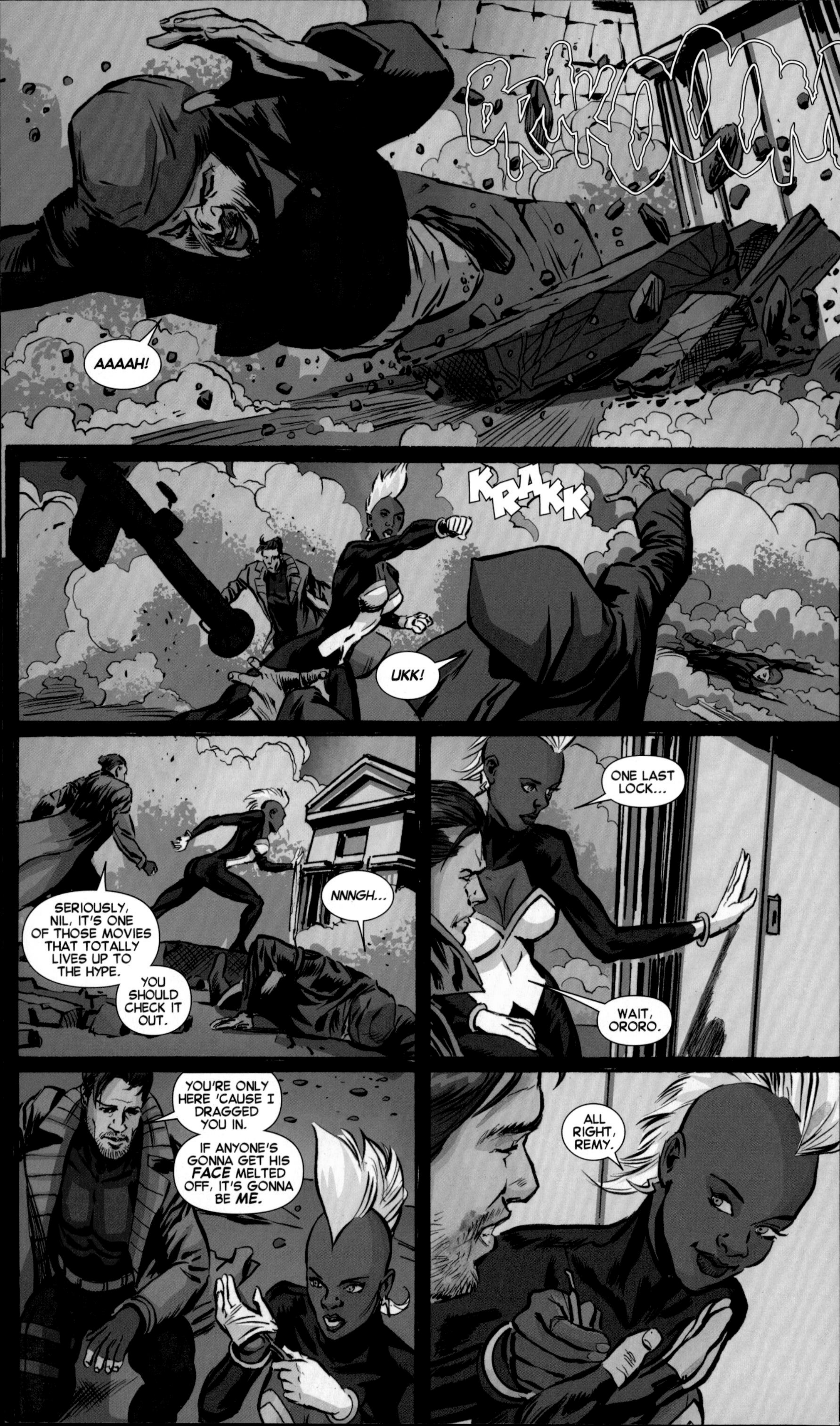
BRAKOOM
AAAAH!
KRAKK
UKK!
SERIOUSLY, NIL, IT'S ONE OF THOSE MOVIES THAT TOTALLY LIVES UP TO THE HYPE.
YOU SHOULD CHECK IT OUT.
NNNGH...
ONE LAST LOCK...
WAIT, ORORO.
YOU'RE ONLY HERE 'CAUSE I DRAGGED YOU IN.
IF ANYONE'S GONNA GET HIS FACE MELTED OFF, IT'S GONNA BE ME.
ALL RIGHT, REMY.

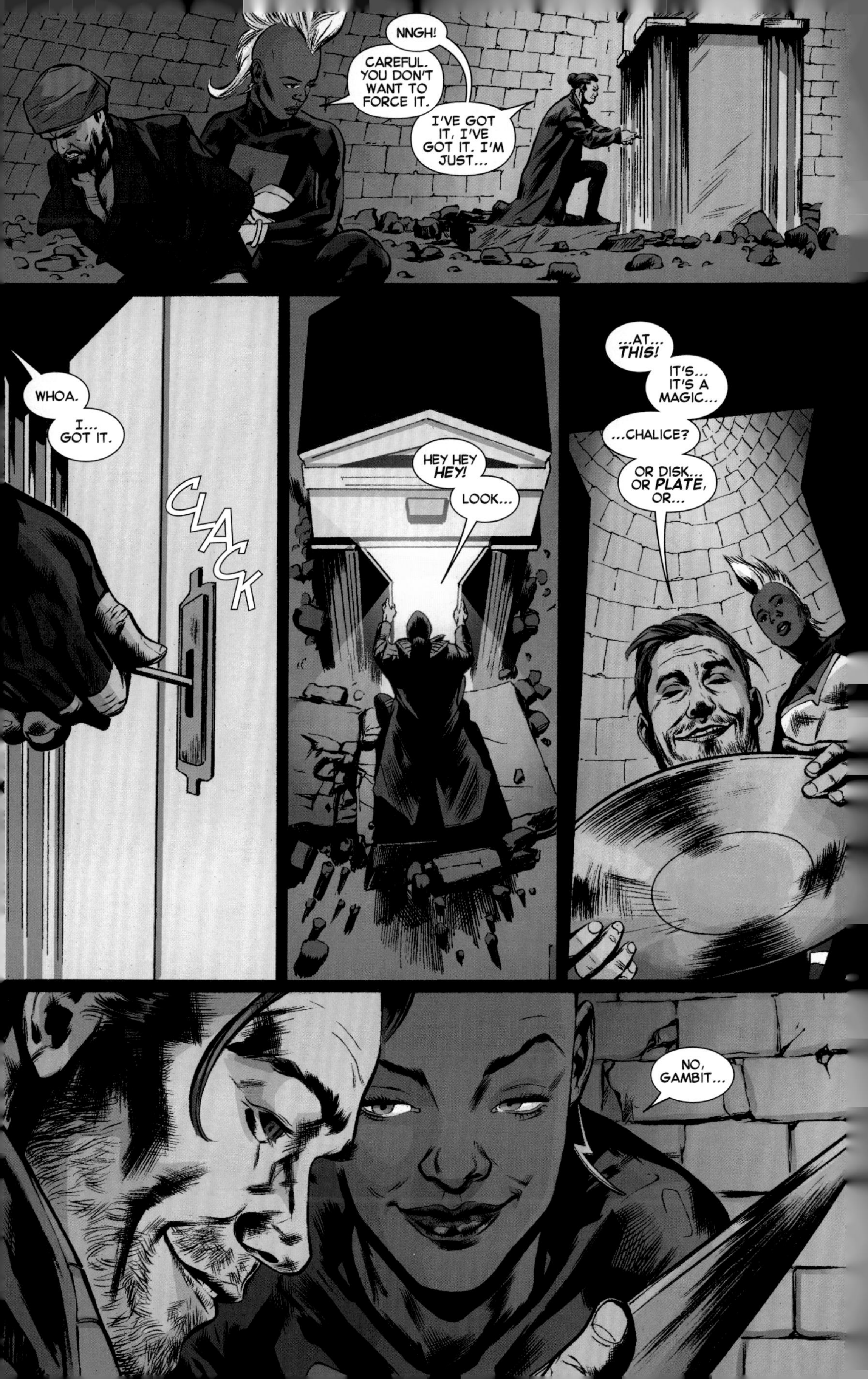
NNGH!
CAREFUL. YOU DON'T WANT TO FORCE IT.
I'VE GOT IT, I'VE GOT IT. I'M JUST...
WHOA.
I... GOT IT.
CLACK
HEY HEY HEY!
LOOK...
...AT... THIS!
IT'S... IT'S A MAGIC...
...CHALICE?
OR DISK... OR PLATE, OR...
NO, GAMBIT...

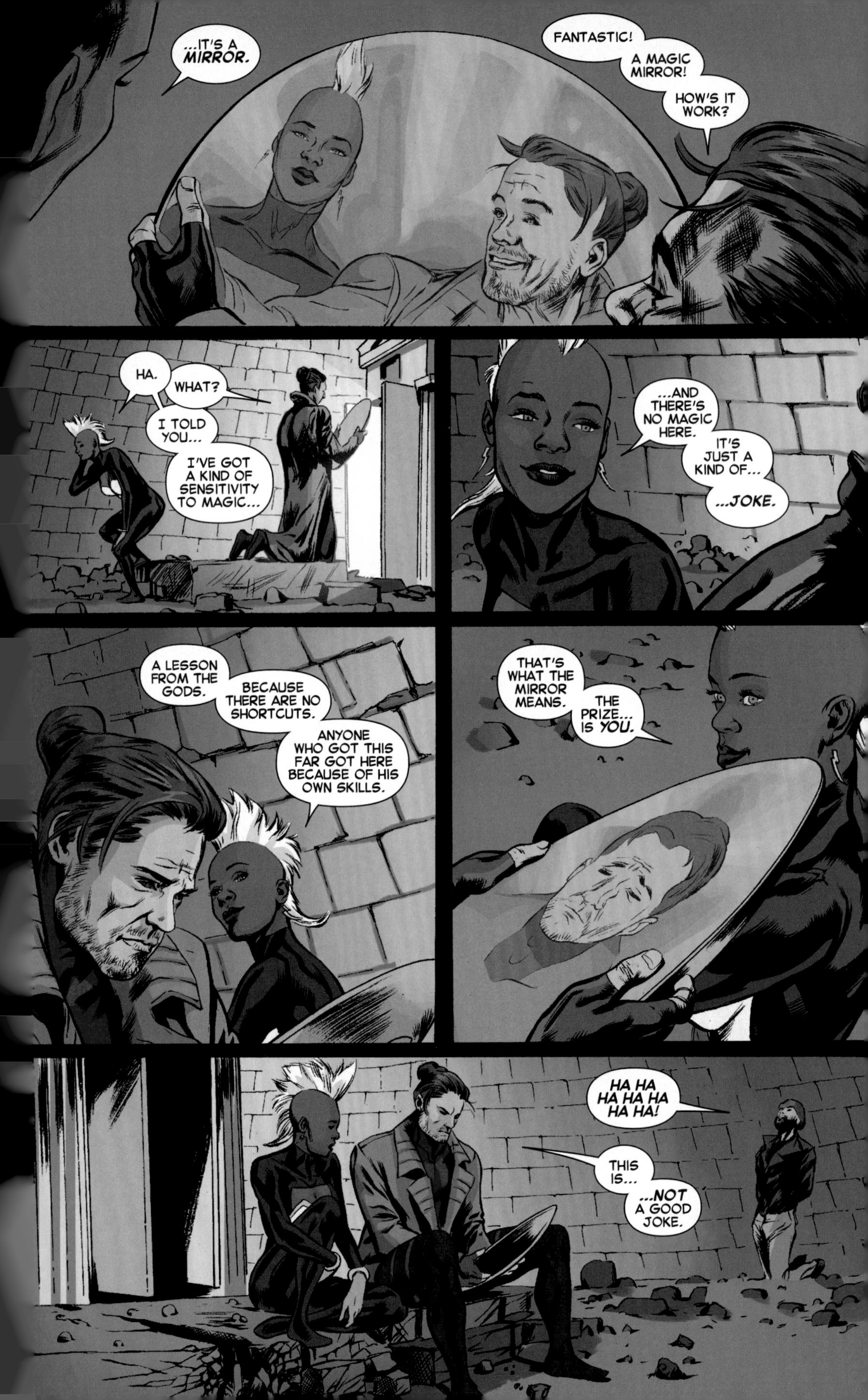
...IT'S A MIRROR.
FANTASTIC!
A MAGIC MIRROR!
HOW'S IT WORK?
HA.
WHAT?
I TOLD YOU...
I'VE GOT A KIND OF SENSITIVITY TO MAGIC...
...AND THERE'S NO MAGIC HERE.
IT'S JUST A KIND OF...
...JOKE.
A LESSON FROM THE GODS.
BECAUSE THERE ARE NO SHORTCUTS.
ANYONE WHO GOT THIS FAR GOT HERE BECAUSE OF HIS OWN SKILLS.
THAT'S WHAT THE MIRROR MEANS.
THE PRIZE... IS YOU.
HA HA HA HA HA HA HA!
THIS IS...
...NOT A GOOD JOKE.

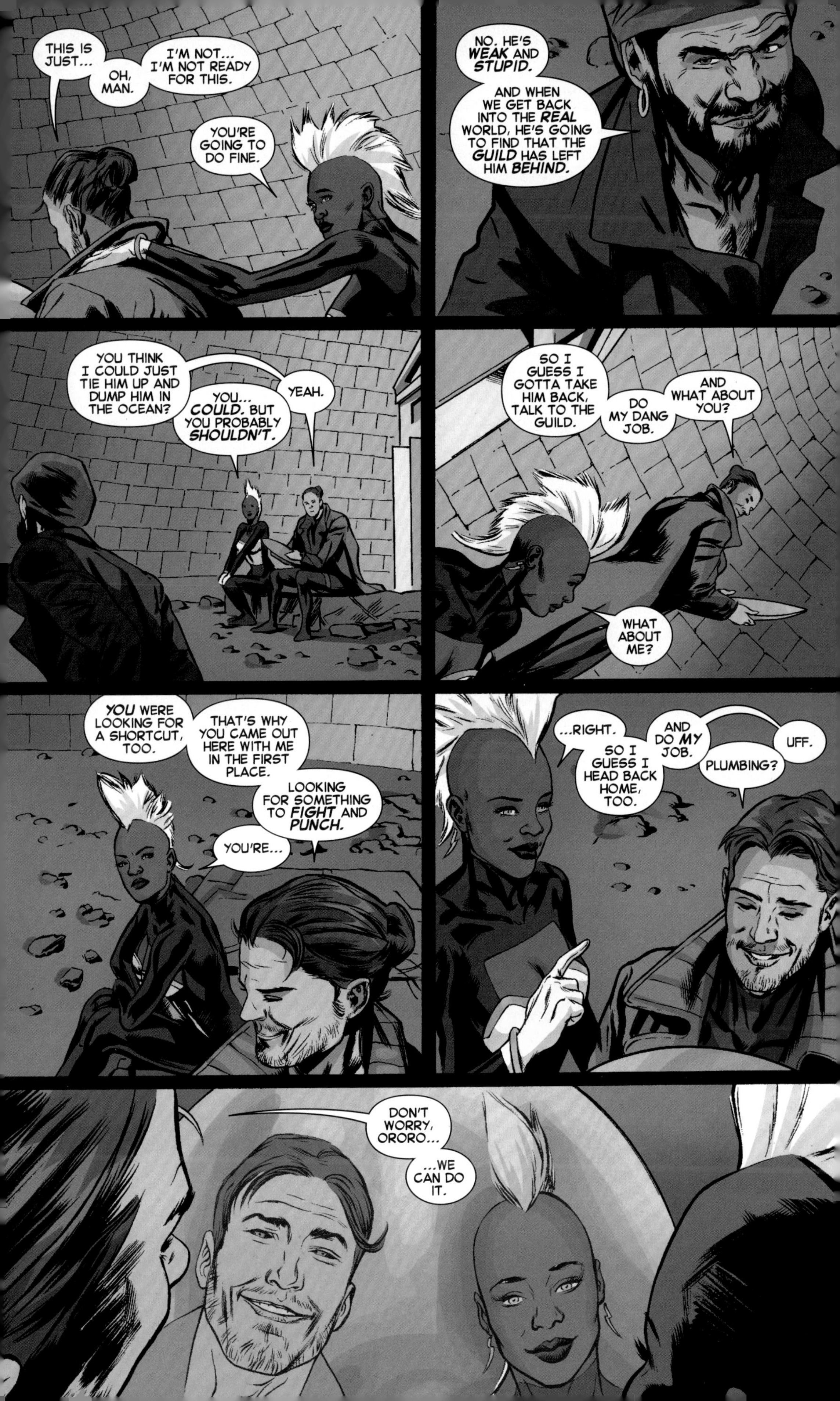
THIS IS JUST...
OH, MAN.
I'M NOT... I'M NOT READY FOR THIS.
YOU'RE GOING TO DO FINE.
NO. HE'S WEAK AND STUPID.
AND WHEN WE GET BACK INTO THE REAL WORLD, HE'S GOING TO FIND THAT THE GUILD HAS LEFT HIM BEHIND.
YOU THINK I COULD JUST TIE HIM UP AND DUMP HIM IN THE OCEAN?
YEAH.
YOU... COULD. BUT YOU PROBABLY SHOULDN'T.
SO I GUESS I GOTTA TAKE HIM BACK, TALK TO THE GUILD.
DO MY DANG JOB.
AND WHAT ABOUT YOU?
WHAT ABOUT ME?
YOU WERE LOOKING FOR A SHORTCUT, TOO.
THAT'S WHY YOU CAME OUT HERE WITH ME IN THE FIRST PLACE.
LOOKING FOR SOMETHING TO FIGHT AND PUNCH.
YOU'RE...
...RIGHT.
SO I GUESS I HEAD BACK HOME, TOO.
AND DO MY JOB.
UFF.
PLUMBING?
DON'T WORRY, ORORO...
...WE CAN DO IT.

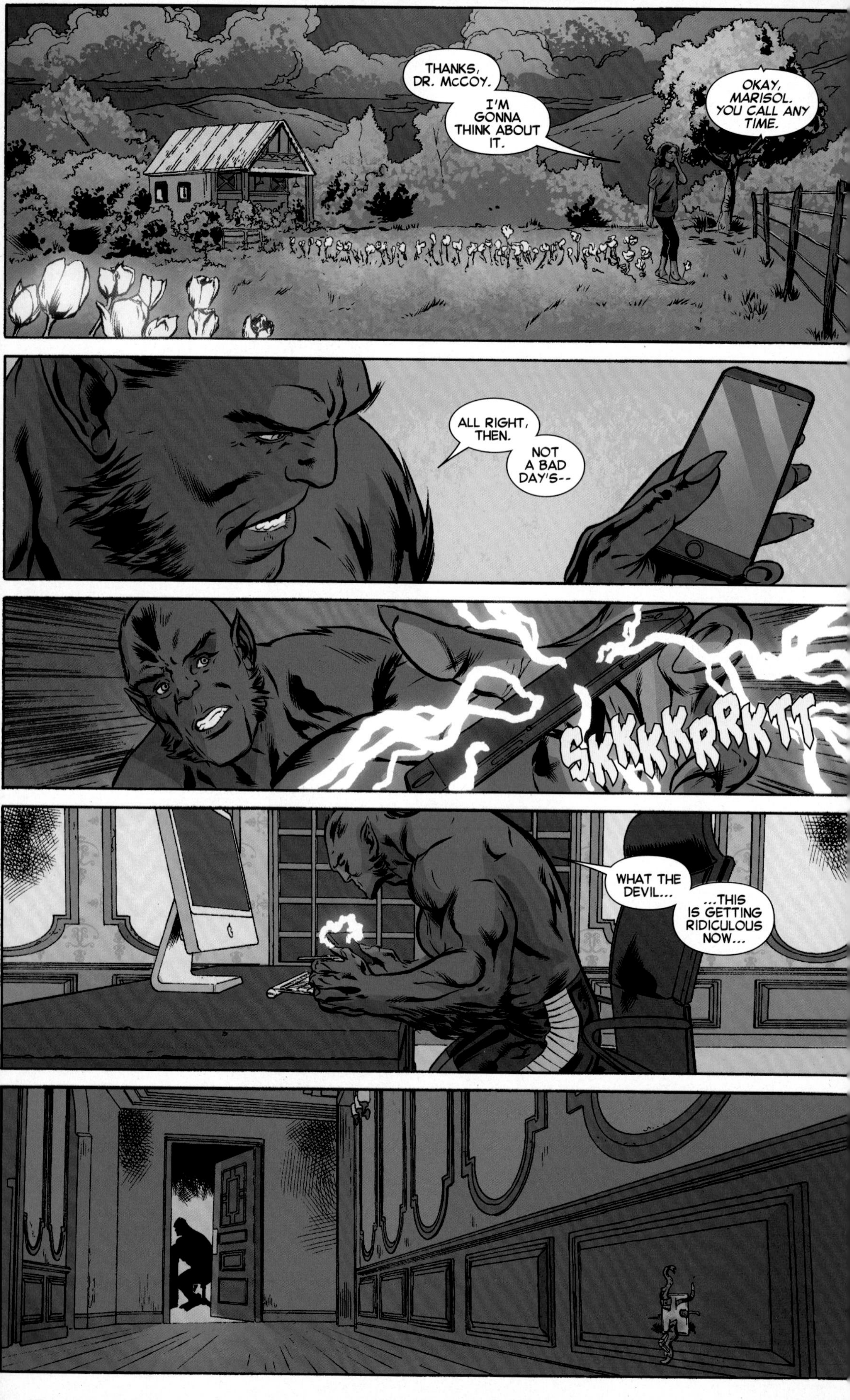
THANKS, DR. McCOY.
I'M GONNA THINK ABOUT IT.
OKAY, MARISOL. YOU CALL ANY TIME.
ALL RIGHT, THEN.
NOT A BAD DAY'S--
SKKKRRKTT
WHAT THE DEVIL...
...THIS IS GETTING RIDICULOUS NOW...

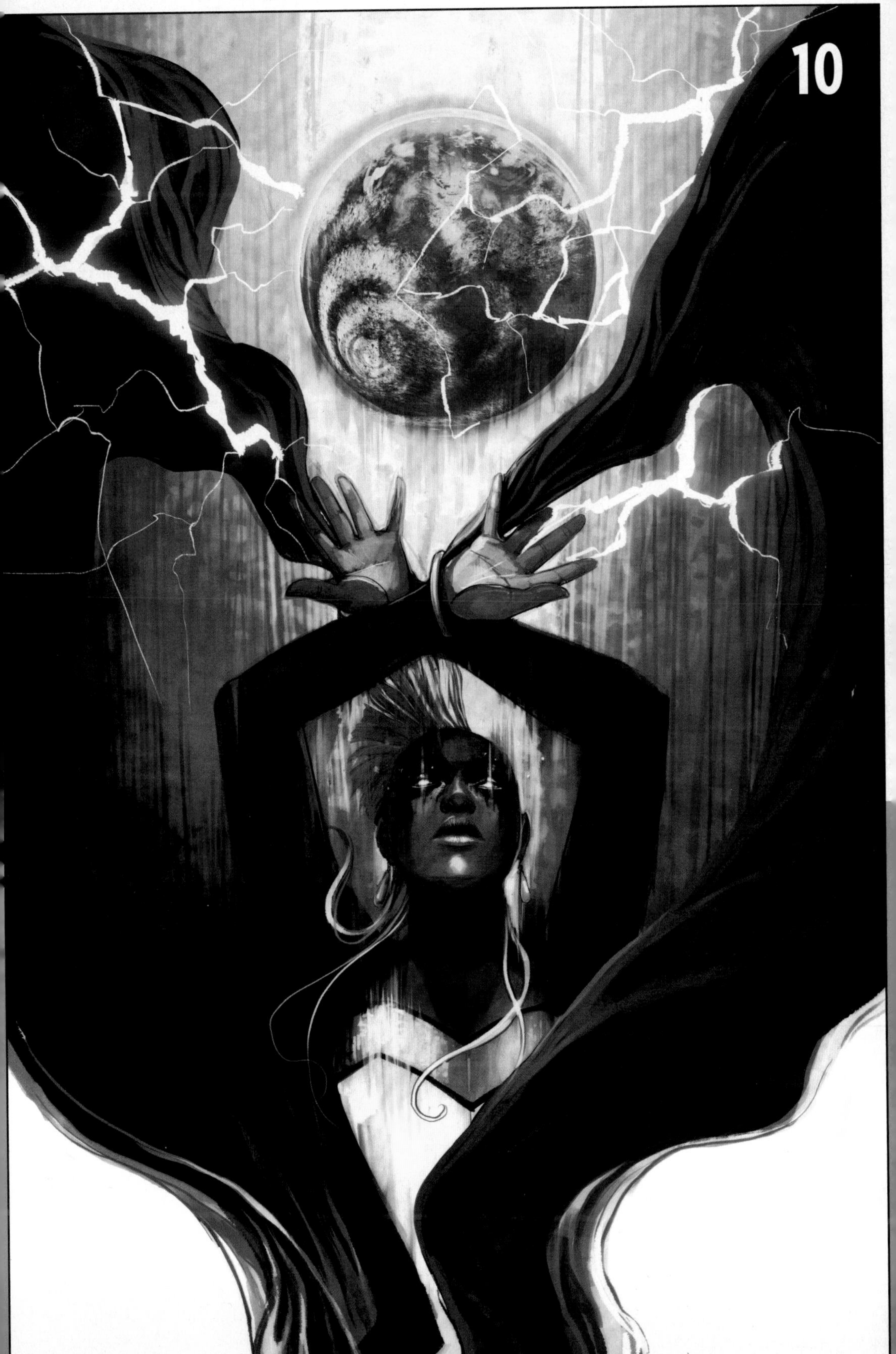
10

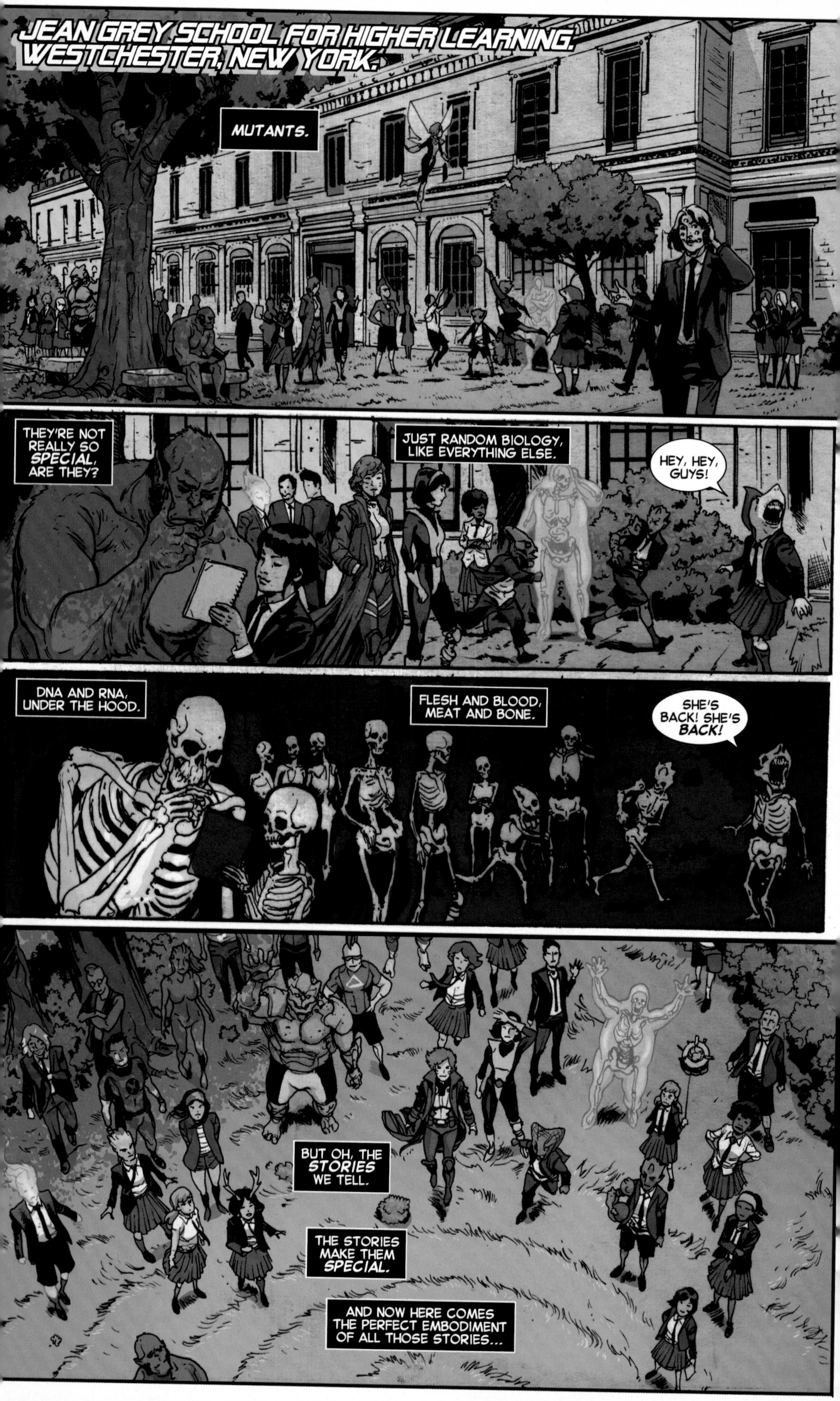
JEAN GREY SCHOOL FOR HIGHER LEARNING. WESTCHESTER, NEW YORK.
MUTANTS.
THEY'RE NOT REALLY SO SPECIAL, ARE THEY?
JUST RANDOM BIOLOGY, LIKE EVERYTHING ELSE.
HEY, HEY, GUYS!
DNA AND RNA, UNDER THE HOOD.
FLESH AND BLOOD, MEAT AND BONE.
SHE'S BACK! SHE'S BACK!
BUT OH, THE STORIES WE TELL.
THE STORIES MAKE THEM SPECIAL.
AND NOW HERE COMES THE PERFECT EMBODIMENT OF ALL THOSE STORIES...

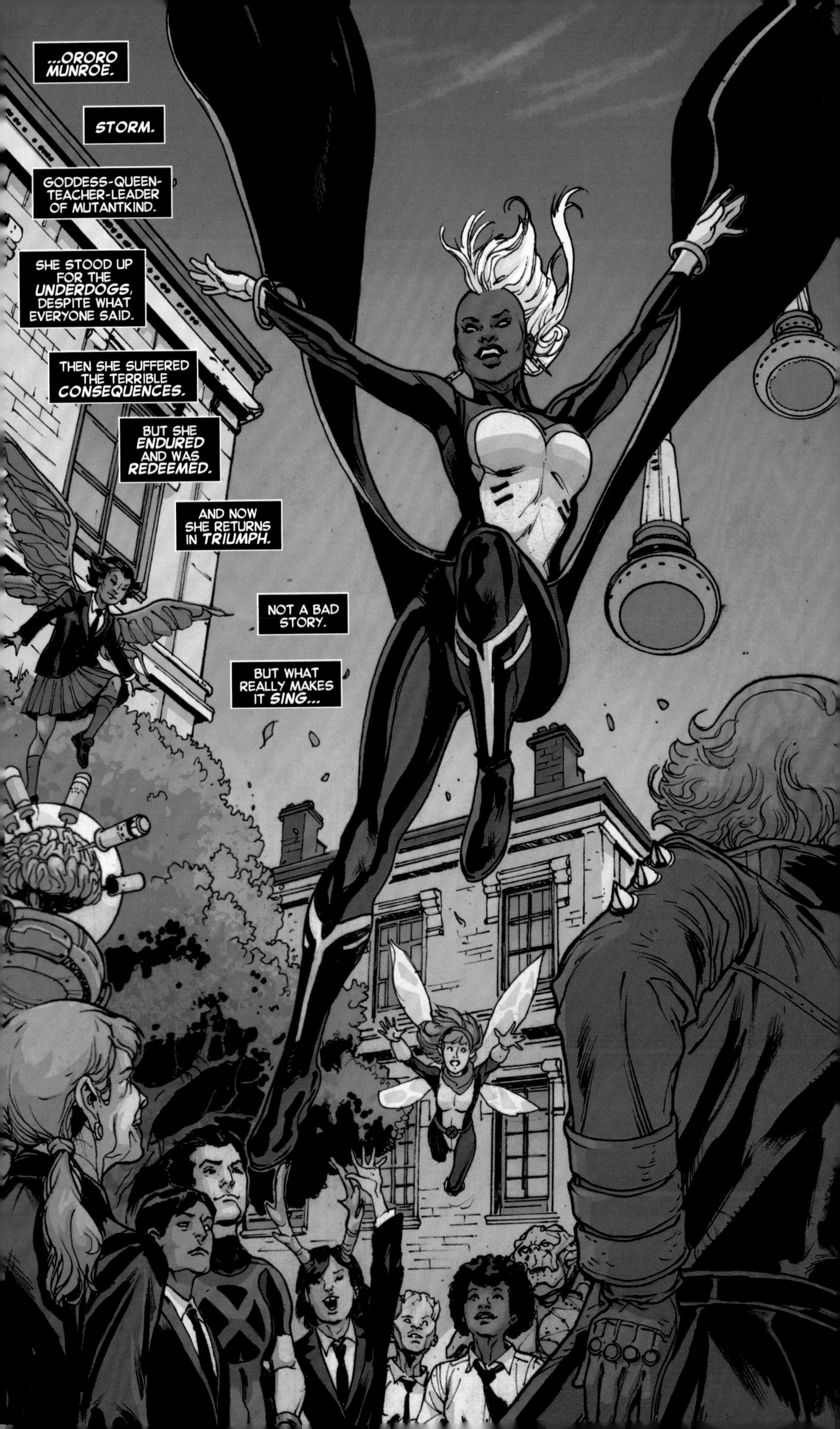
...ORORO MUNROE.
STORM.
GODDESS-QUEEN-TEACHER-LEADER OF MUTANTKIND.
SHE STOOD UP FOR THE UNDERDOGS, DESPITE WHAT EVERYONE SAID.
THEN SHE SUFFERED THE TERRIBLE CONSEQUENCES.
BUT SHE ENDURED AND WAS REDEEMED.
AND NOW SHE RETURNS IN TRIUMPH.
NOT A BAD STORY.
BUT WHAT REALLY MAKES IT SING...

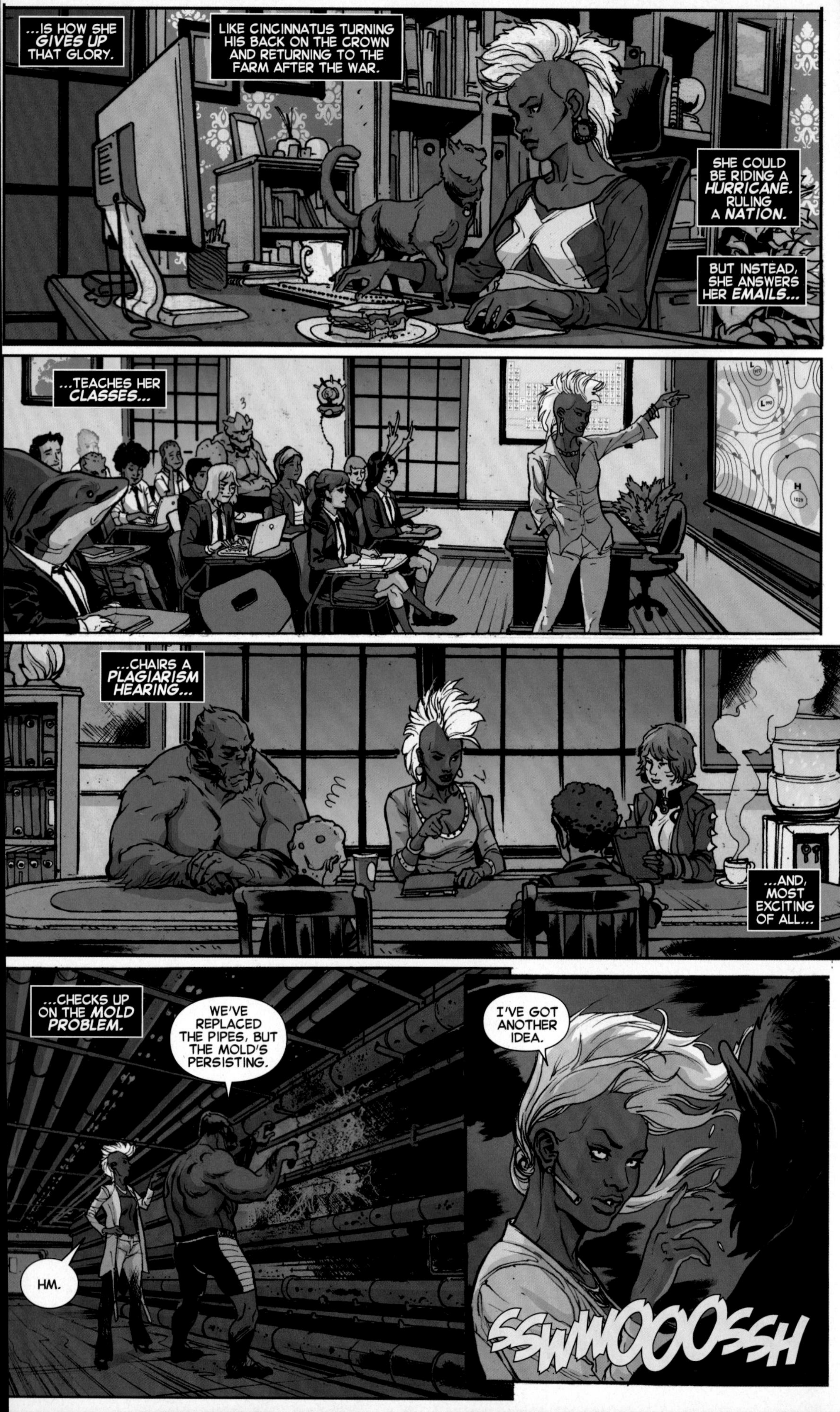
...IS HOW SHE GIVES UP THAT GLORY.
LIKE CINCINNATUS TURNING HIS BACK ON THE CROWN AND RETURNING TO THE FARM AFTER THE WAR.
SHE COULD BE RIDING A HURRICANE. RULING A NATION.
BUT INSTEAD, SHE ANSWERS HER EMAILS...
...TEACHES HER CLASSES...
...CHAIRS A PLAGIARISM HEARING...
...AND, MOST EXCITING OF ALL...
...CHECKS UP ON THE MOLD PROBLEM.
WE'VE REPLACED THE PIPES, BUT THE MOLD'S PERSISTING.
HM.
I'VE GOT ANOTHER IDEA.
SSWMOOOSSH

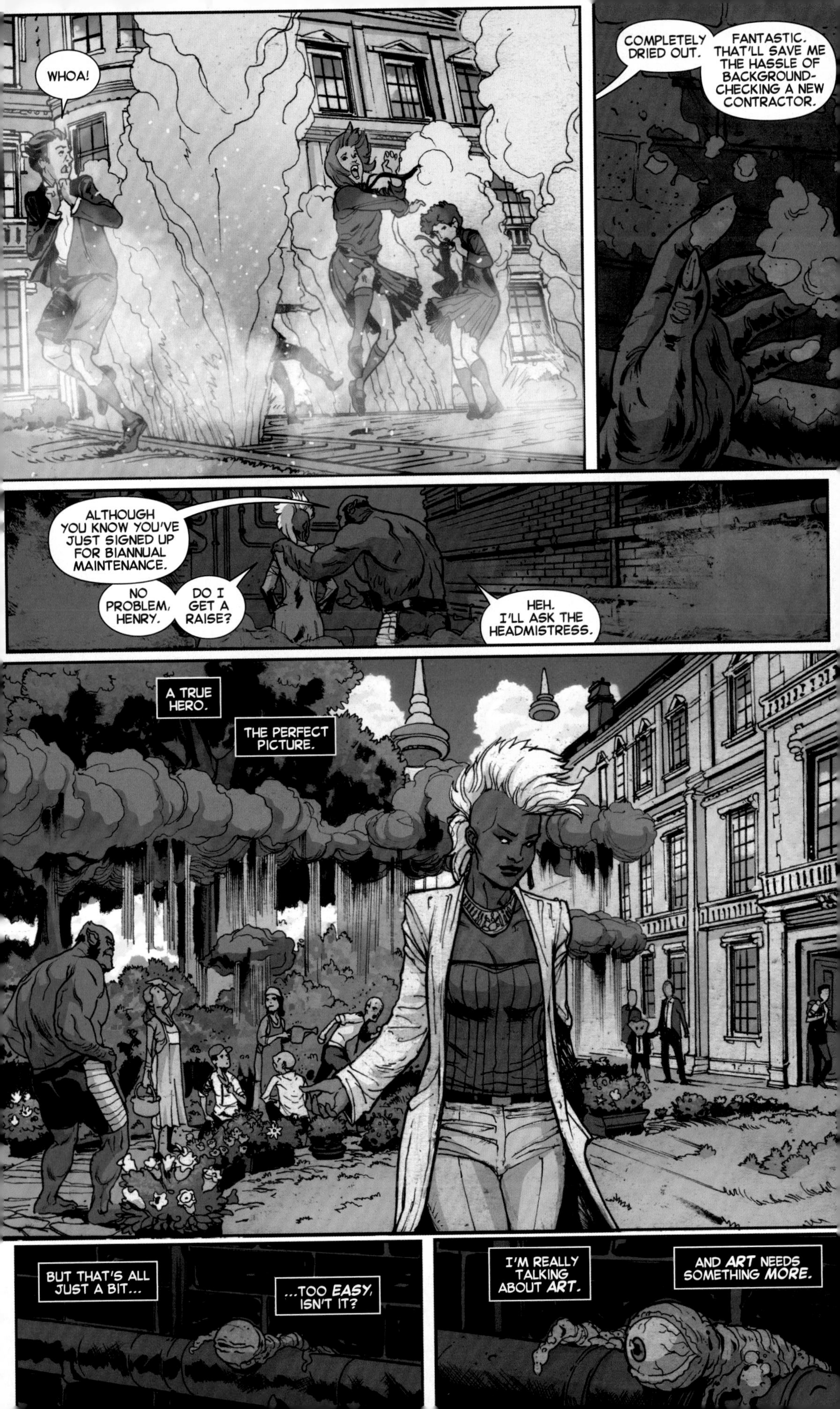
WHOA!
COMPLETELY DRIED OUT.
FANTASTIC. THAT'LL SAVE ME THE HASSLE OF BACKGROUND-CHECKING A NEW CONTRACTOR.
ALTHOUGH YOU KNOW YOU'VE JUST SIGNED UP FOR BIANNUAL MAINTENANCE.
NO PROBLEM, HENRY.
DO I GET A RAISE?
HEH. I'LL ASK THE HEADMISTRESS.
A TRUE HERO.
THE PERFECT PICTURE.
BUT THAT'S ALL JUST A BIT...
...TOO EASY, ISN'T IT?
I'M REALLY TALKING ABOUT ART.
AND ART NEEDS SOMETHING MORE.

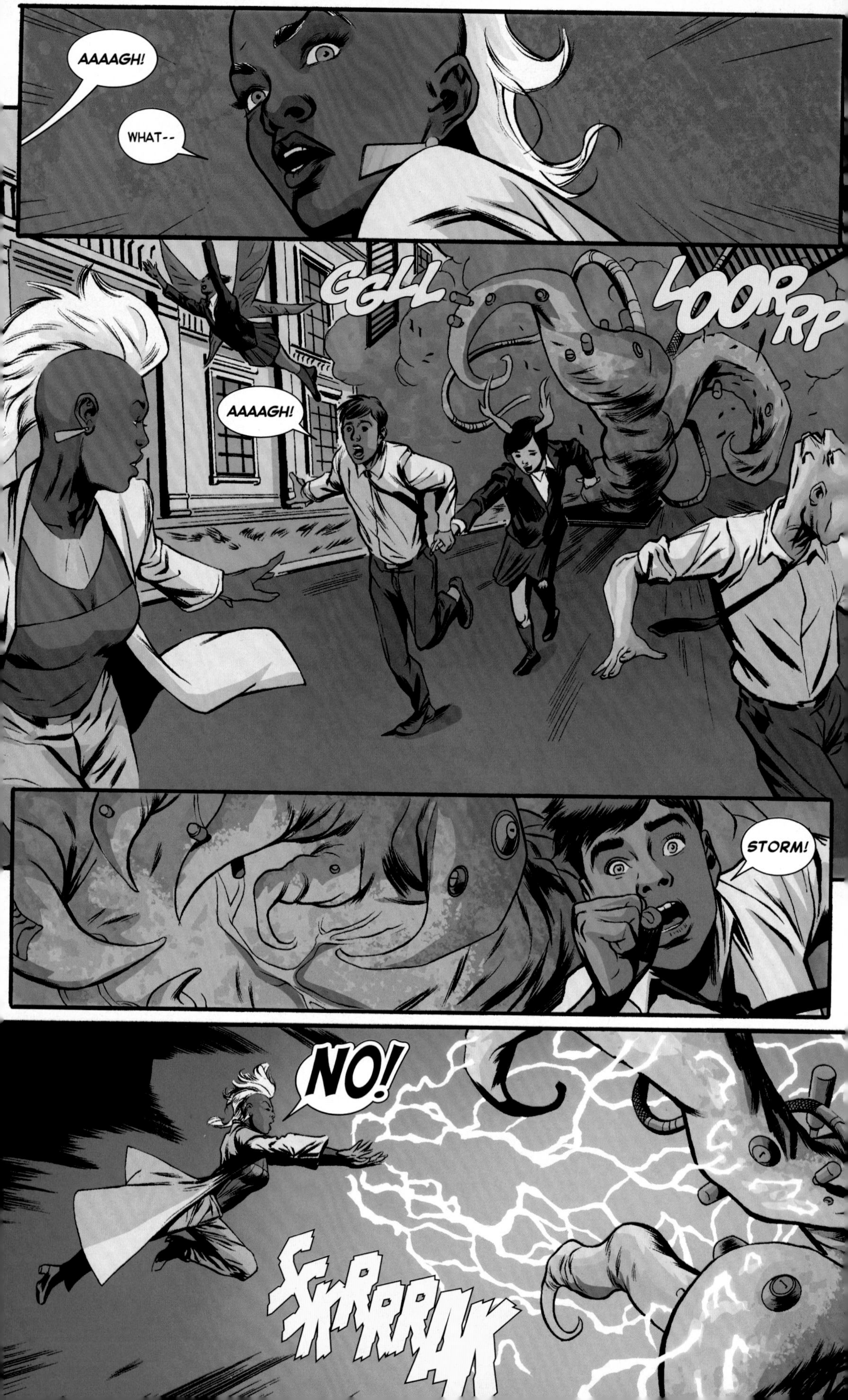
AAAAGH!
WHAT--
GGLL
LOORRP
AAAAGH!
STORM!
NO!
SKRRRAK

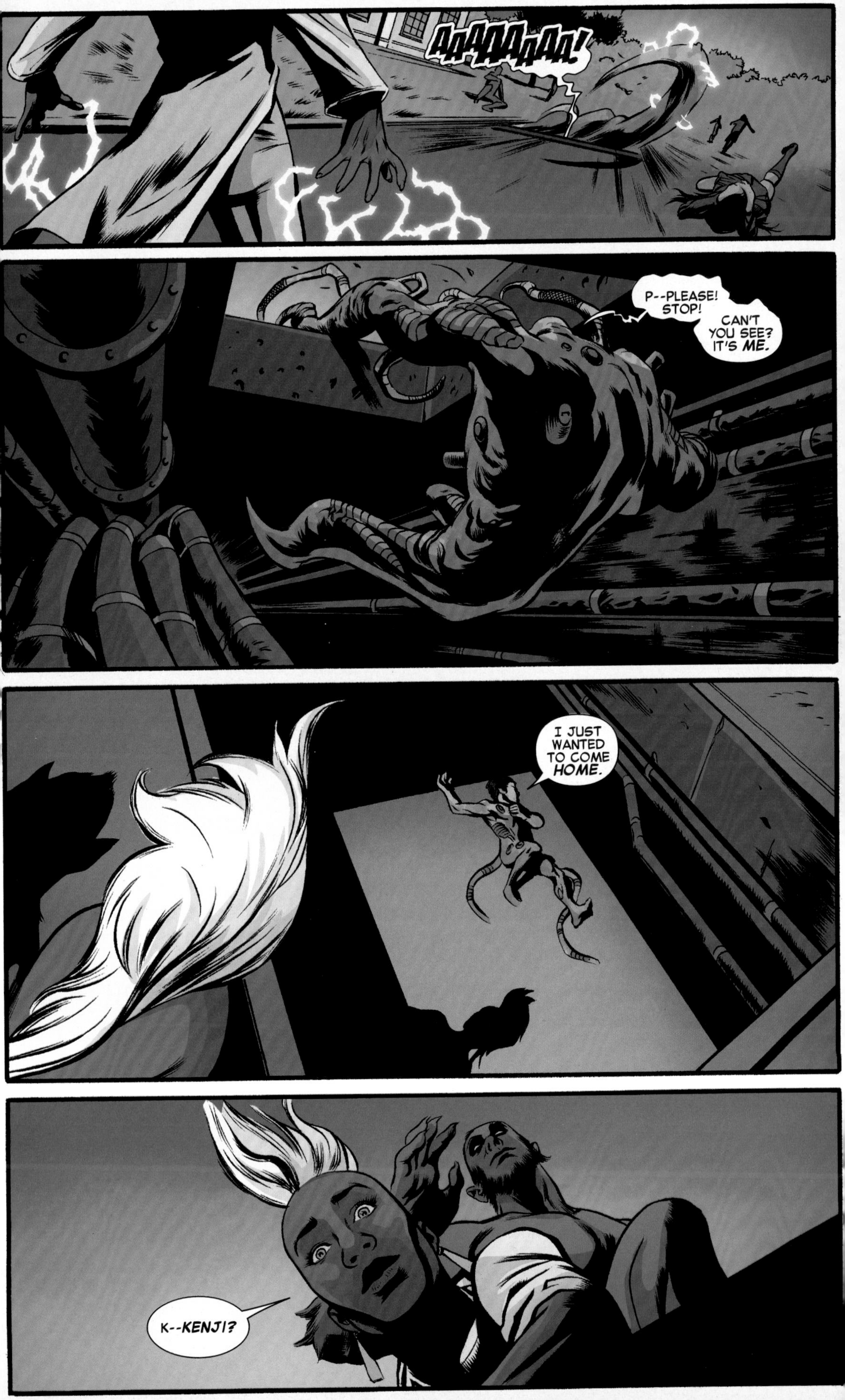
AAAAAAAA!
P--PLEASE! STOP!
CAN'T YOU SEE? IT'S ME.
I JUST WANTED TO COME HOME.
K--KENJI?

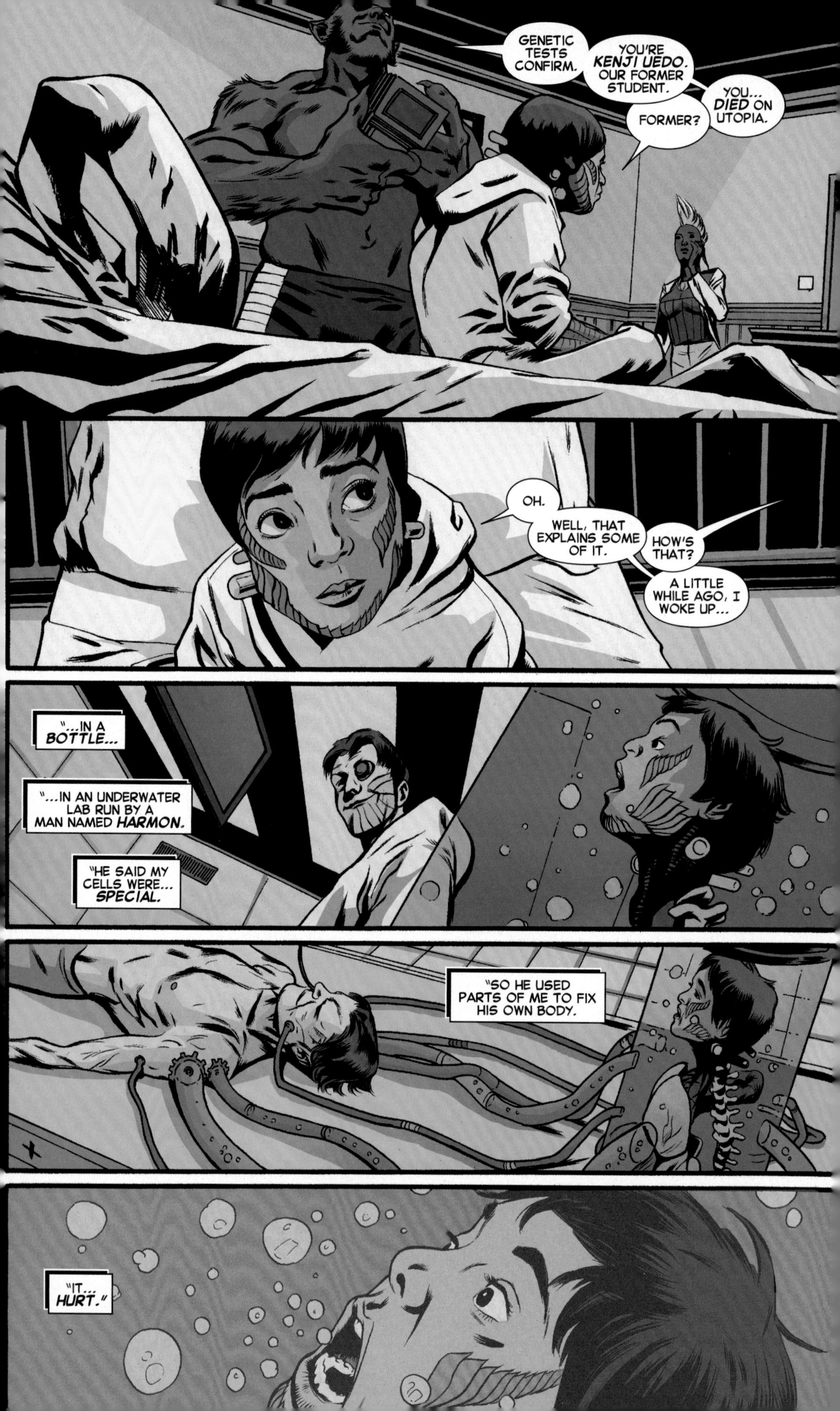

GENETIC TESTS CONFIRM.
YOU'RE KENJI UEDO. OUR FORMER STUDENT.
YOU... DIED ON UTOPIA.
FORMER?
OH.
WELL, THAT EXPLAINS SOME OF IT.
HOW'S THAT?
A LITTLE WHILE AGO, I WOKE UP...
"...IN A BOTTLE...
"...IN AN UNDERWATER LAB RUN BY A MAN NAMED HARMON.
"HE SAID MY CELLS WERE... SPECIAL.
"SO HE USED PARTS OF ME TO FIX HIS OWN BODY.
"IT... HURT."

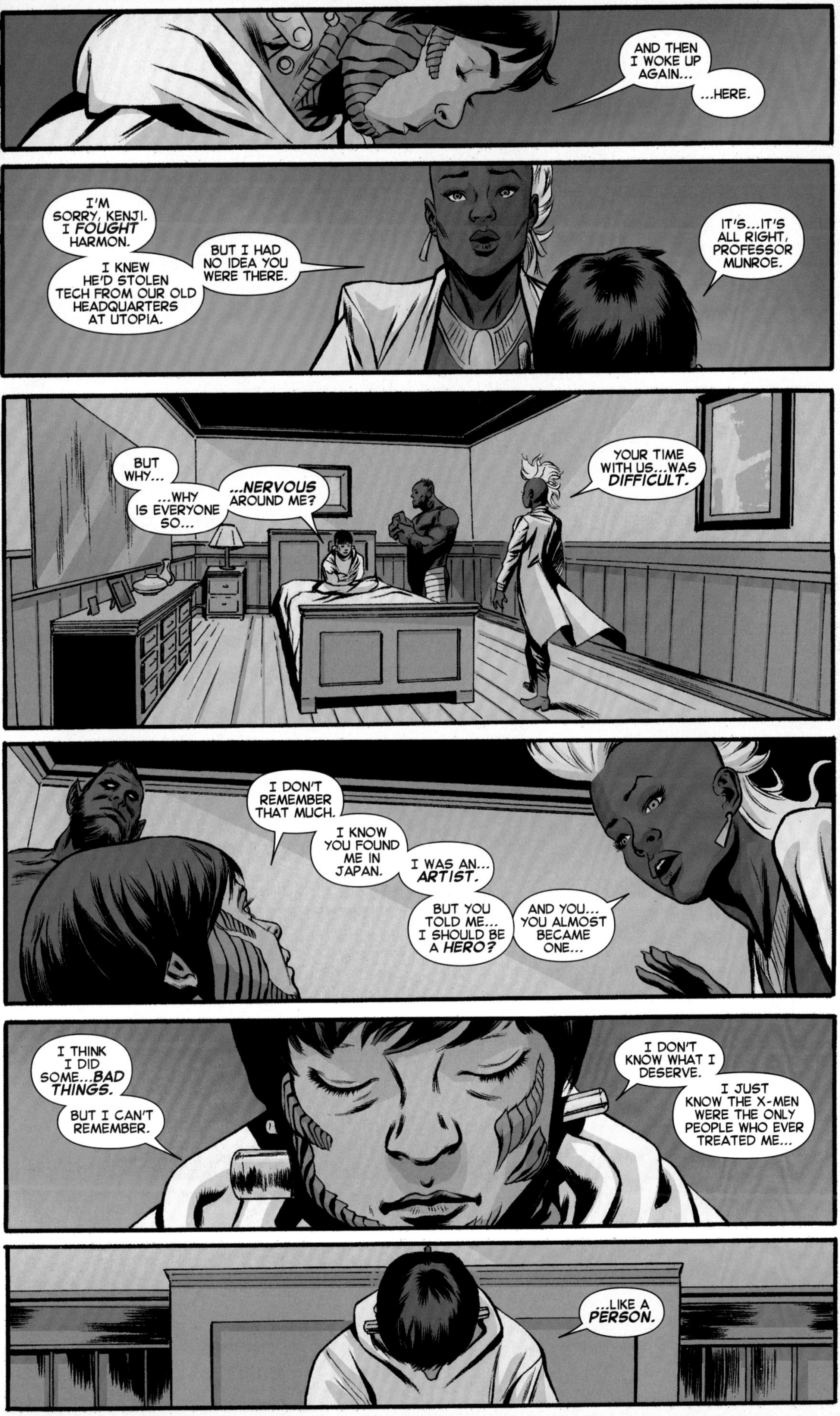
AND THEN I WOKE UP AGAIN...
...HERE.
I'M SORRY, KENJI. I FOUGHT HARMON.
I KNEW HE'D STOLEN TECH FROM OUR OLD HEADQUARTERS AT UTOPIA.
BUT I HAD NO IDEA YOU WERE THERE.
IT'S...IT'S ALL RIGHT, PROFESSOR MUNROE.
BUT WHY...
...WHY IS EVERYONE SO...
...NERVOUS AROUND ME?
YOUR TIME WITH US...WAS DIFFICULT.
I DON'T REMEMBER THAT MUCH.
I KNOW YOU FOUND ME IN JAPAN.
I WAS AN... ARTIST.
BUT YOU TOLD ME... I SHOULD BE A HERO?
AND YOU... YOU ALMOST BECAME ONE...
I THINK I DID SOME...BAD THINGS.
BUT I CAN'T REMEMBER.
I DON'T KNOW WHAT I DESERVE.
I JUST KNOW THE X-MEN WERE THE ONLY PEOPLE WHO EVER TREATED ME...
...LIKE A PERSON.

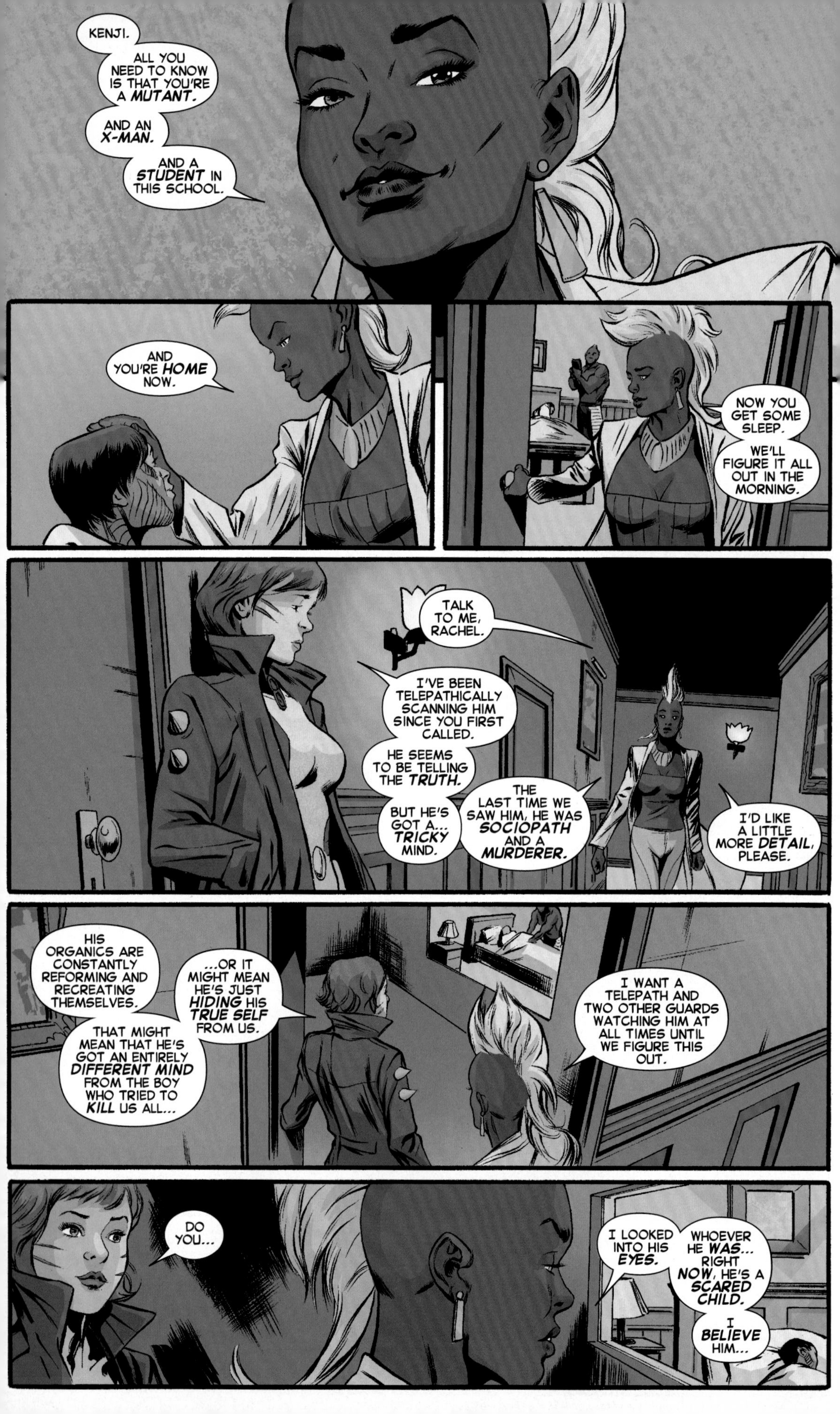

KENJI.
ALL YOU NEED TO KNOW IS THAT YOU'RE A MUTANT.
AND AN X-MAN.
AND A STUDENT IN THIS SCHOOL.
AND YOU'RE HOME NOW.
NOW YOU GET SOME SLEEP.
WE'LL FIGURE IT ALL OUT IN THE MORNING.
TALK TO ME, RACHEL.
I'VE BEEN TELEPATHICALLY SCANNING HIM SINCE YOU FIRST CALLED.
HE SEEMS TO BE TELLING THE TRUTH.
BUT HE'S GOT A... TRICKY MIND.
THE LAST TIME WE SAW HIM, HE WAS SOCIOPATH AND A MURDERER.
I'D LIKE A LITTLE MORE DETAIL, PLEASE.
HIS ORGANICS ARE CONSTANTLY REFORMING AND RECREATING THEMSELVES.
THAT MIGHT MEAN THAT HE'S GOT AN ENTIRELY DIFFERENT MIND FROM THE BOY WHO TRIED TO KILL US ALL...
...OR IT MIGHT MEAN HE'S JUST HIDING HIS TRUE SELF FROM US.
I WANT A TELEPATH AND TWO OTHER GUARDS WATCHING HIM AT ALL TIMES UNTIL WE FIGURE THIS OUT.
DO YOU...
I LOOKED INTO HIS EYES.
WHOEVER HE WAS... RIGHT NOW, HE'S A SCARED CHILD.
I BELIEVE HIM...

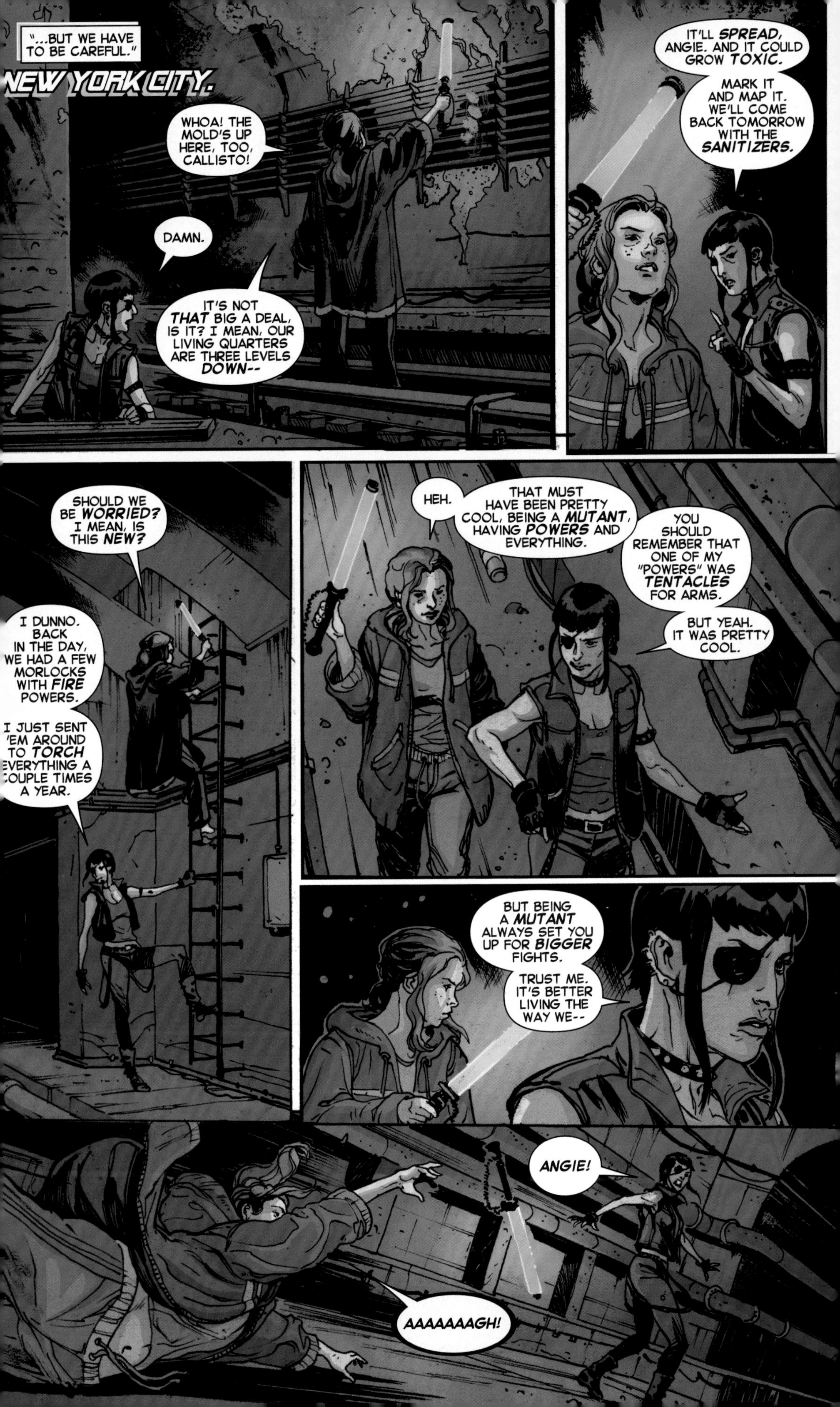

"...BUT WE HAVE TO BE CAREFUL."
NEW YORK CITY.
WHOA! THE MOLD'S UP HERE, TOO, CALLISTO!
DAMN.
IT'S NOT THAT BIG A DEAL, IS IT? I MEAN, OUR LIVING QUARTERS ARE THREE LEVELS DOWN--
IT'LL SPREAD, ANGIE. AND IT COULD GROW TOXIC.
MARK IT AND MAP IT. WE'LL COME BACK TOMORROW WITH THE SANITIZERS.
SHOULD WE BE WORRIED? I MEAN, IS THIS NEW?
I DUNNO. BACK IN THE DAY, WE HAD A FEW MORLOCKS WITH FIRE POWERS.
I JUST SENT 'EM AROUND TO TORCH EVERYTHING A COUPLE TIMES A YEAR.
HEH.
THAT MUST HAVE BEEN PRETTY COOL, BEING A MUTANT, HAVING POWERS AND EVERYTHING.
YOU SHOULD REMEMBER THAT ONE OF MY "POWERS" WAS TENTACLES FOR ARMS.
BUT YEAH. IT WAS PRETTY COOL.
BUT BEING A MUTANT ALWAYS SET YOU UP FOR BIGGER FIGHTS.
TRUST ME. IT'S BETTER LIVING THE WAY WE--
ANGIE!
AAAAAAAGH!

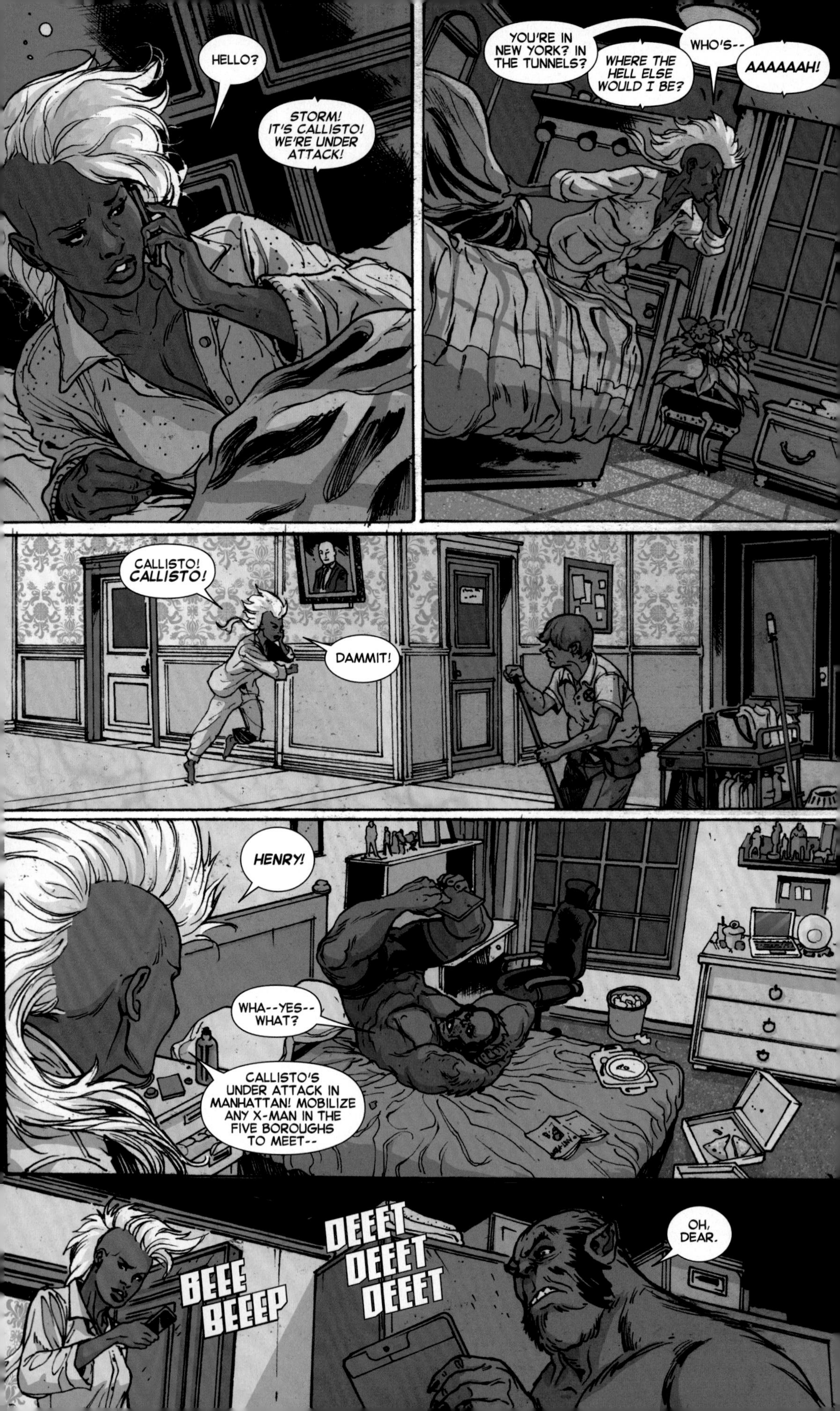
HELLO?
STORM! IT'S CALLISTO! WE'RE UNDER ATTACK!
YOU'RE IN NEW YORK? IN THE TUNNELS?
WHERE THE HELL ELSE WOULD I BE?
WHO'S--
AAAAAAH!
CALLISTO! CALLISTO!
DAMMIT!
HENRY!
WHA--YES-- WHAT?
CALLISTO'S UNDER ATTACK IN MANHATTAN! MOBILIZE ANY X-MAN IN THE FIVE BOROUGHS TO MEET--
BEEE BEEEP
DEEET DEEET DEEET
OH, DEAR.

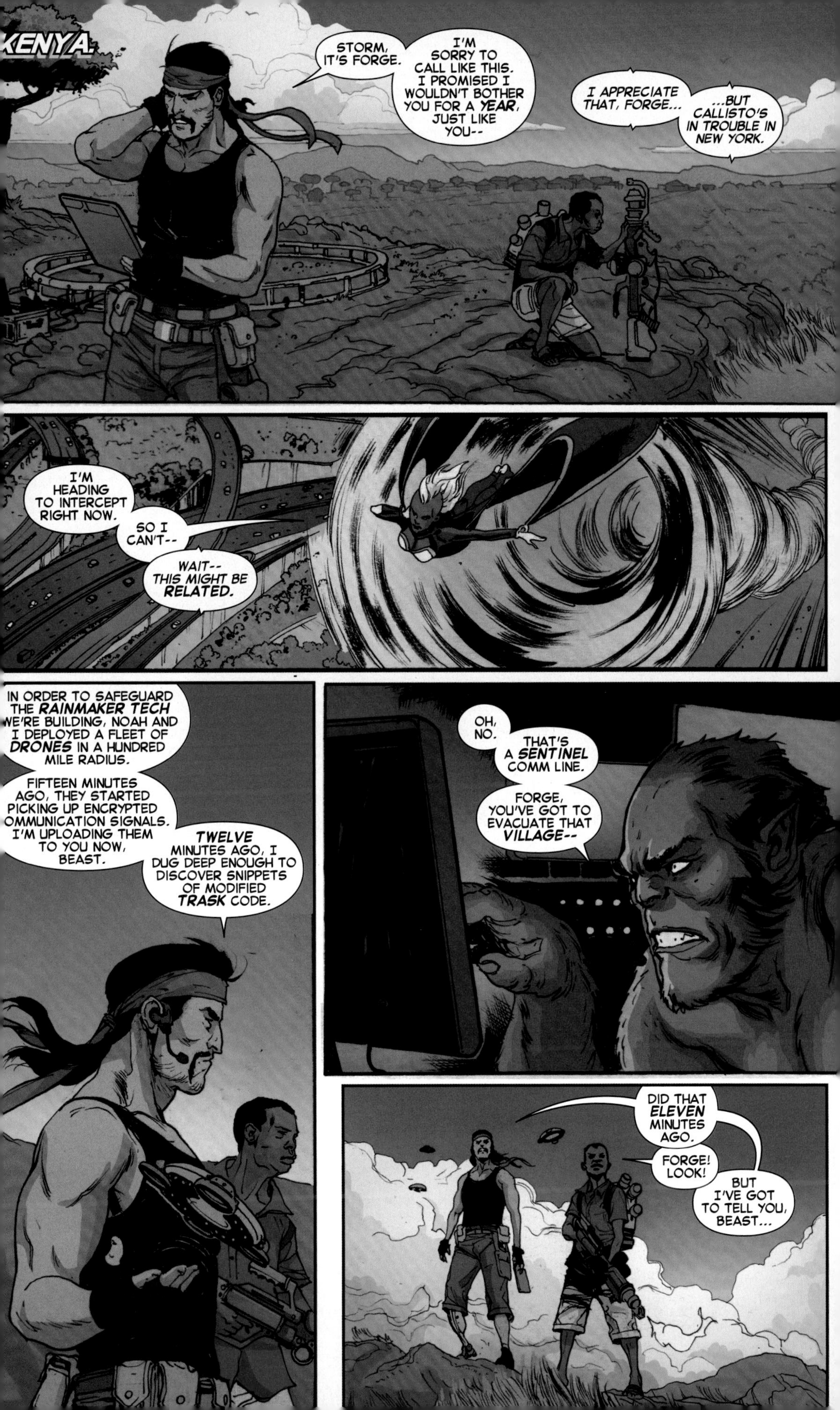
KENYA.
STORM, IT'S FORGE.
I'M SORRY TO CALL LIKE THIS. I PROMISED I WOULDN'T BOTHER YOU FOR A YEAR, JUST LIKE YOU--
I APPRECIATE THAT, FORGE...
...BUT CALLISTO'S IN TROUBLE IN NEW YORK.
I'M HEADING TO INTERCEPT RIGHT NOW.
SO I CAN'T--
WAIT-- THIS MIGHT BE RELATED.
IN ORDER TO SAFEGUARD THE RAINMAKER TECH WE'RE BUILDING, NOAH AND I DEPLOYED A FLEET OF DRONES IN A HUNDRED MILE RADIUS.
FIFTEEN MINUTES AGO, THEY STARTED PICKING UP ENCRYPTED OMMUNICATION SIGNALS. I'M UPLOADING THEM TO YOU NOW, BEAST.
TWELVE MINUTES AGO, I DUG DEEP ENOUGH TO DISCOVER SNIPPETS OF MODIFIED TRASK CODE.
OH, NO.
THAT'S A SENTINEL COMM LINE.
FORGE, YOU'VE GOT TO EVACUATE THAT VILLAGE--
DID THAT ELEVEN MINUTES AGO.
FORGE! LOOK!
BUT I'VE GOT TO TELL YOU, BEAST...

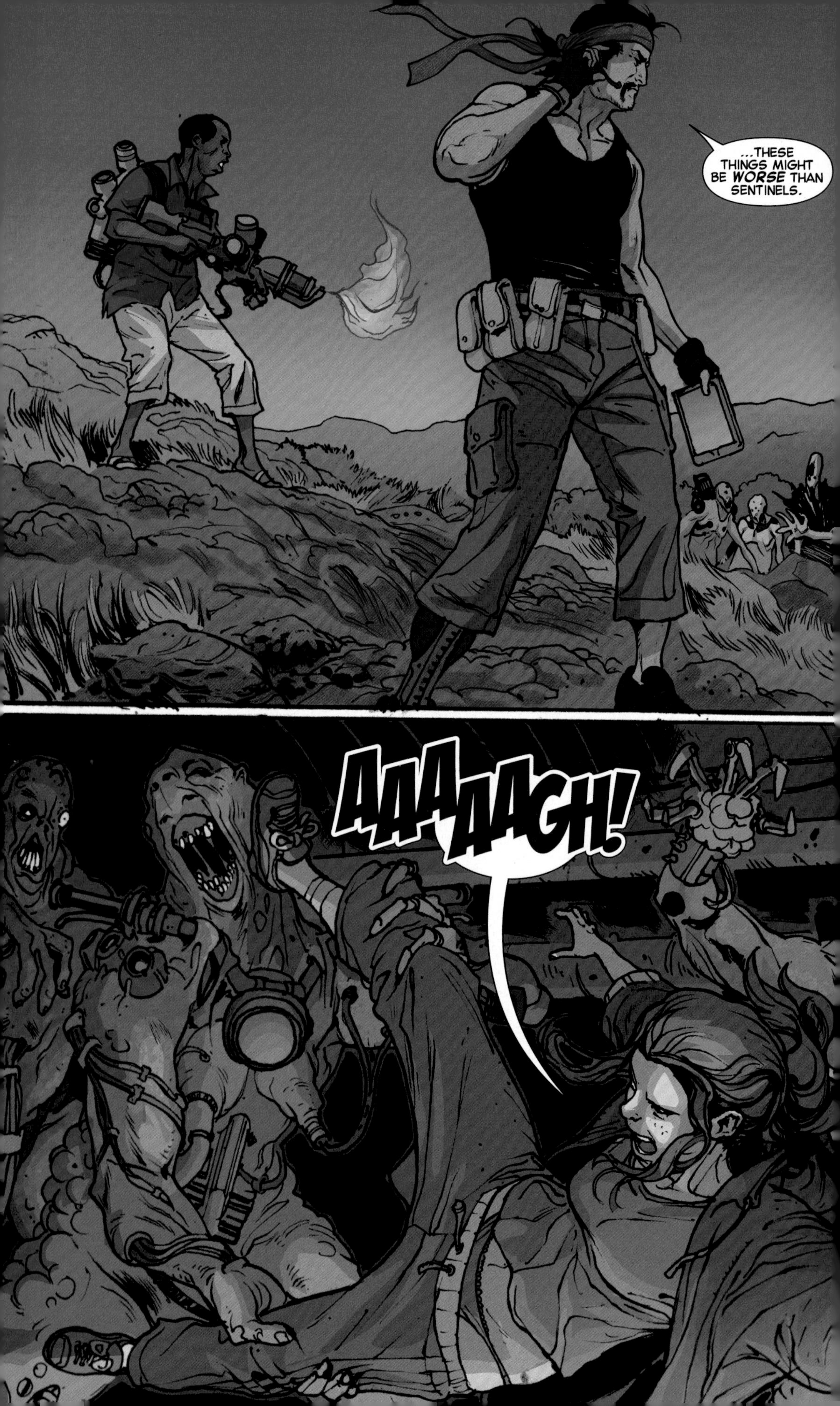
...THESE THINGS MIGHT BE WORSE THAN SENTINELS.
AAAAAAGH!

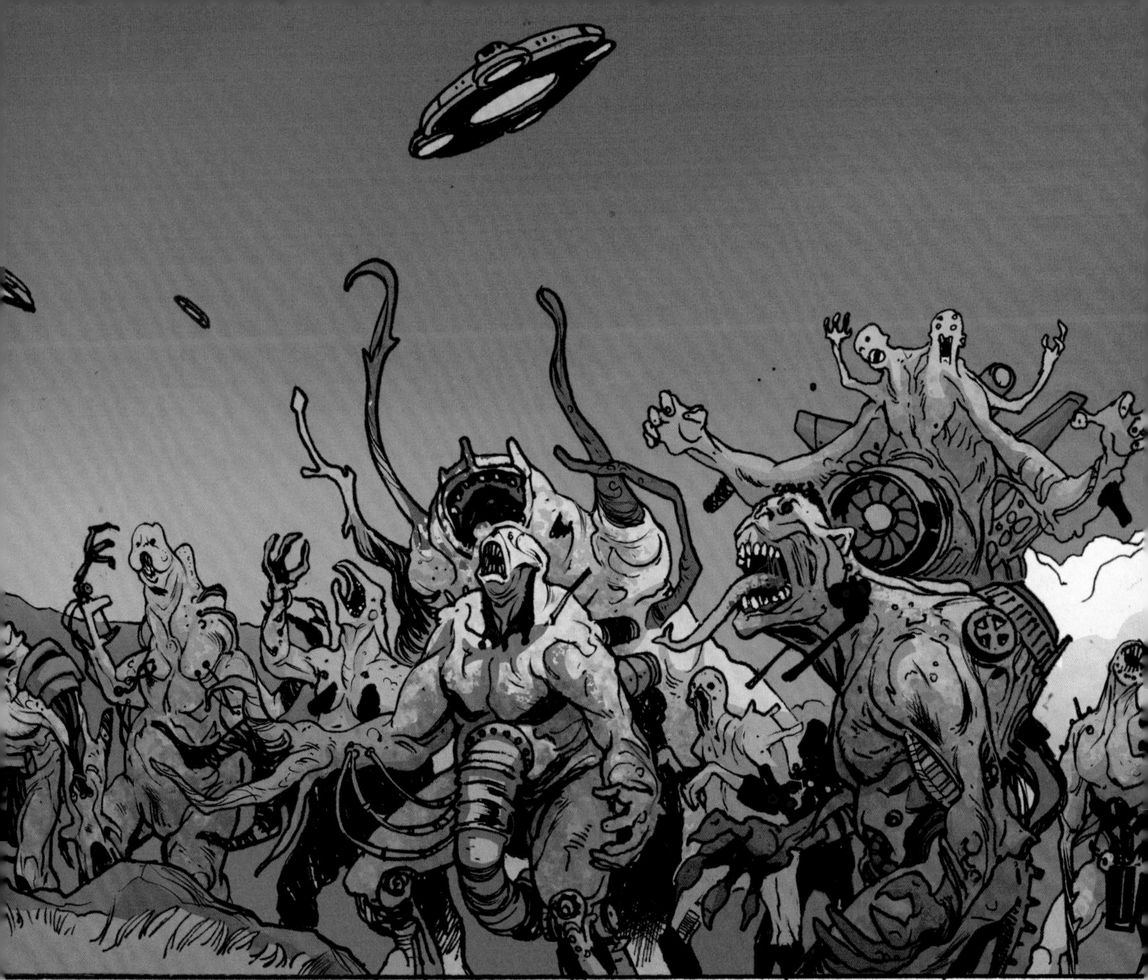
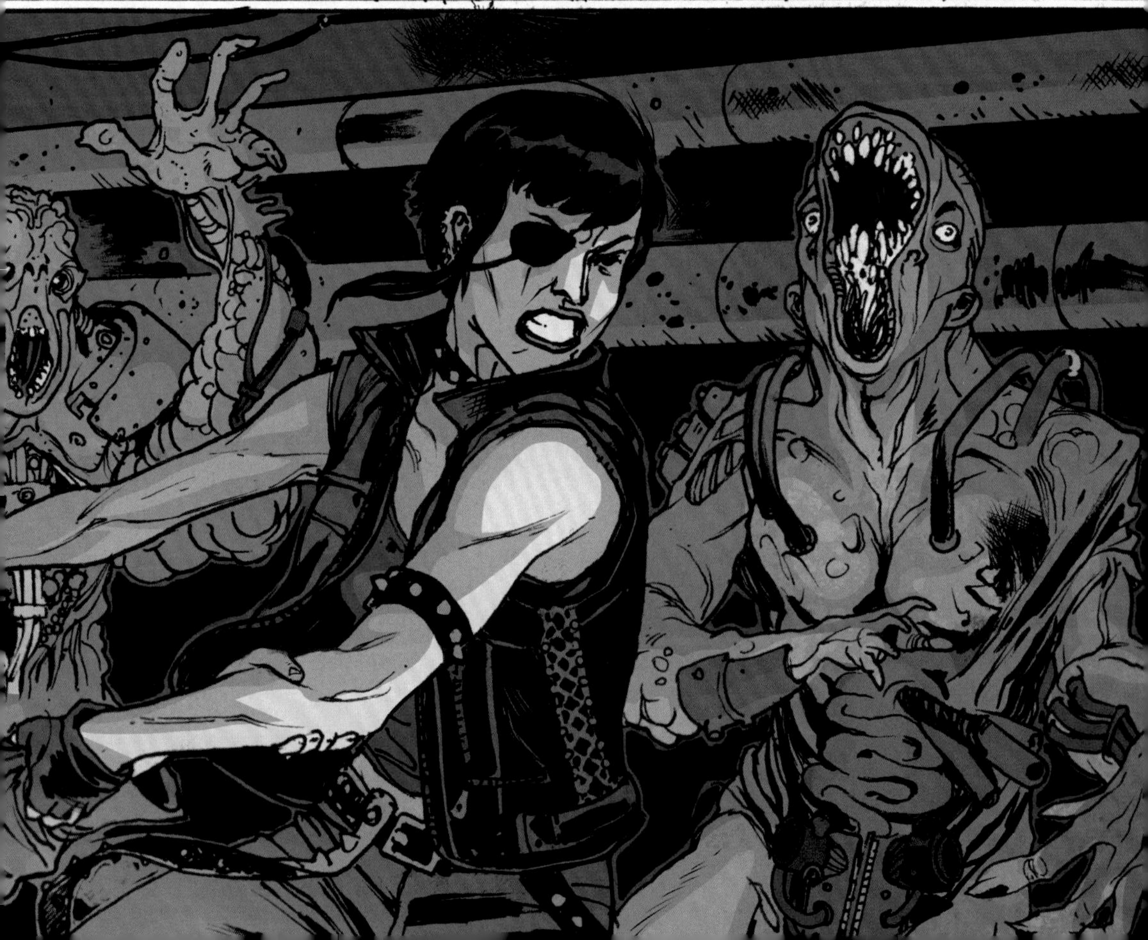

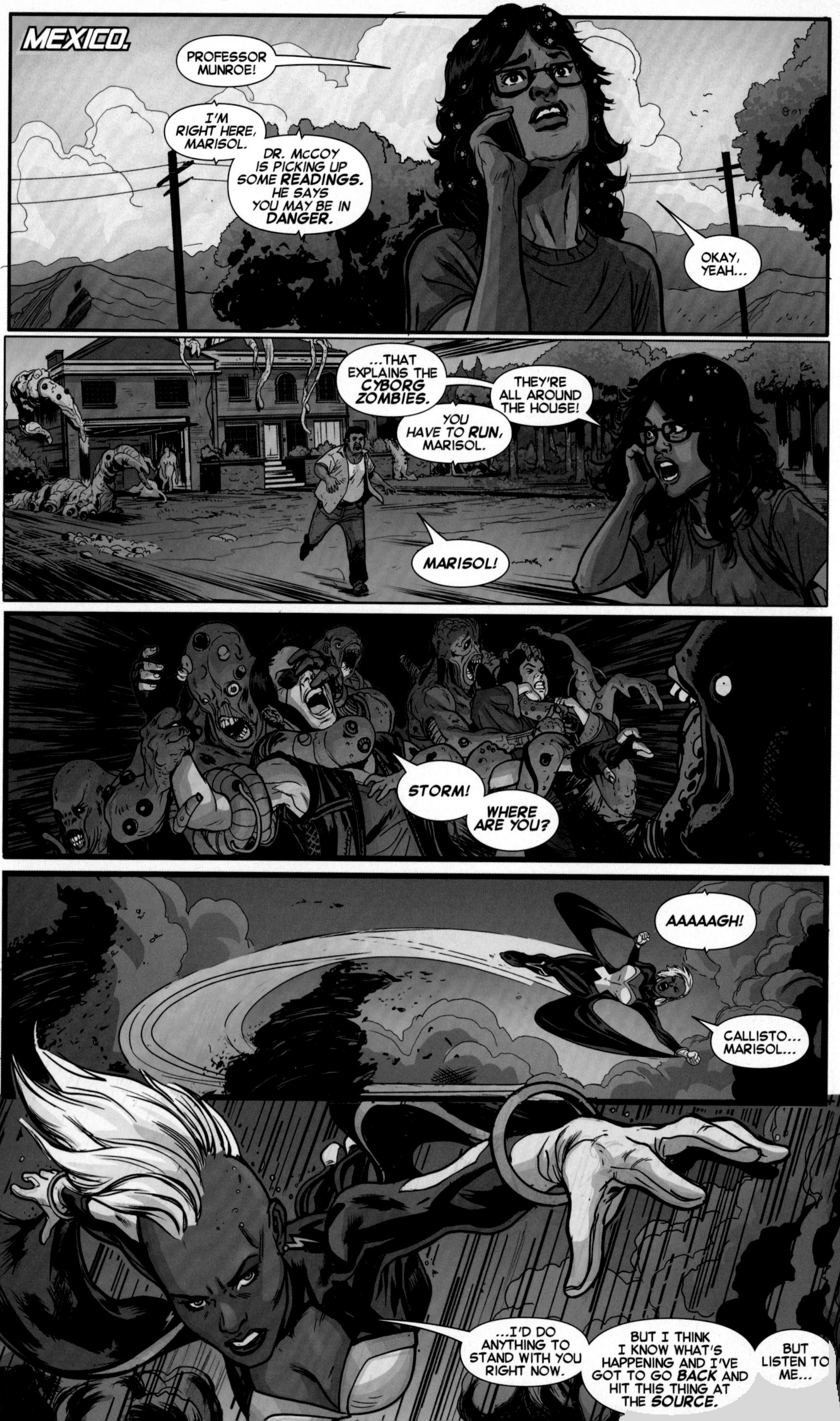
MEXICO.
PROFESSOR MUNROE!
I'M RIGHT HERE, MARISOL.
DR. McCOY IS PICKING UP SOME READINGS. HE SAYS YOU MAY BE IN DANGER.
OKAY, YEAH...
...THAT EXPLAINS THE CYBORG ZOMBIES.
THEY'RE ALL AROUND THE HOUSE!
YOU HAVE TO RUN, MARISOL.
MARISOL!
STORM!
WHERE ARE YOU?
AAAAAGH!
CALLISTO... MARISOL...
...I'D DO ANYTHING TO STAND WITH YOU RIGHT NOW.
BUT I THINK I KNOW WHAT'S HAPPENING AND I'VE GOT TO GO BACK AND HIT THIS THING AT THE SOURCE.
BUT LISTEN TO ME...

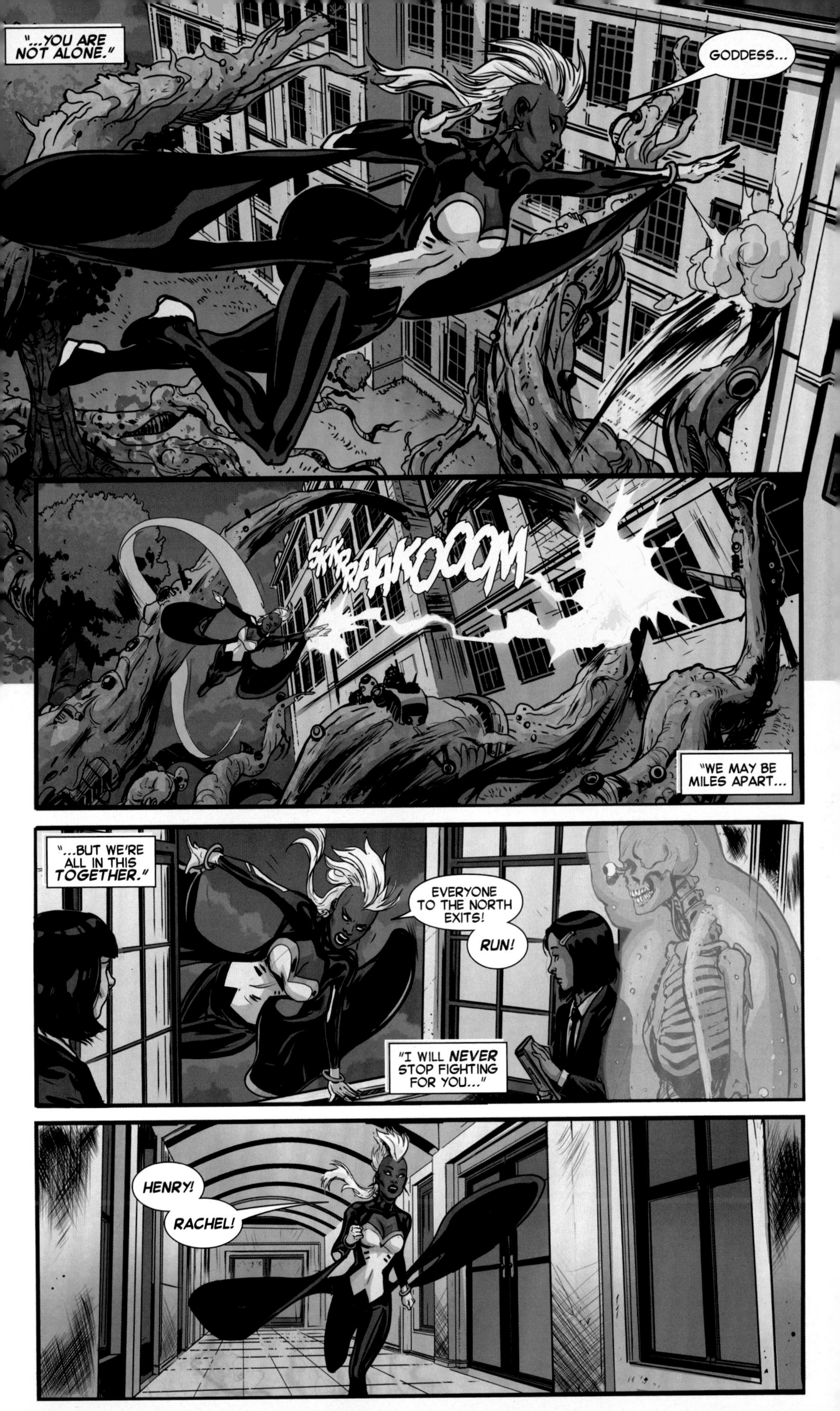
"...YOU ARE NOT ALONE."
GODDESS...
SKKRAAKOOOM
"WE MAY BE MILES APART...
"...BUT WE'RE ALL IN THIS TOGETHER."
EVERYONE TO THE NORTH EXITS!
RUN!
"I WILL NEVER STOP FIGHTING FOR YOU..."
HENRY!
RACHEL!

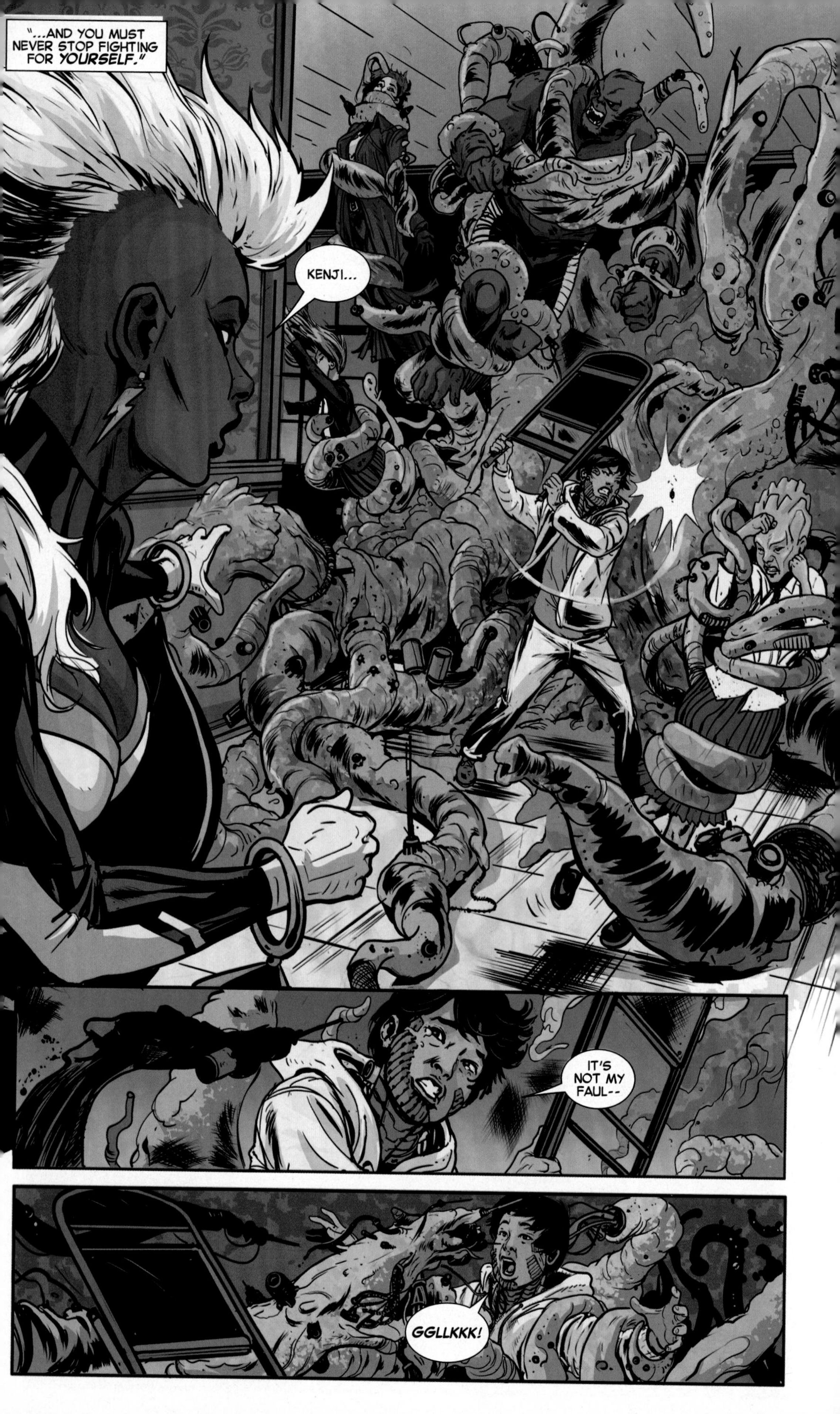
"...AND YOU MUST NEVER STOP FIGHTING FOR *YOURSELF.*"
KENJI...
IT'S NOT MY FAUL--
GGLLKKK!

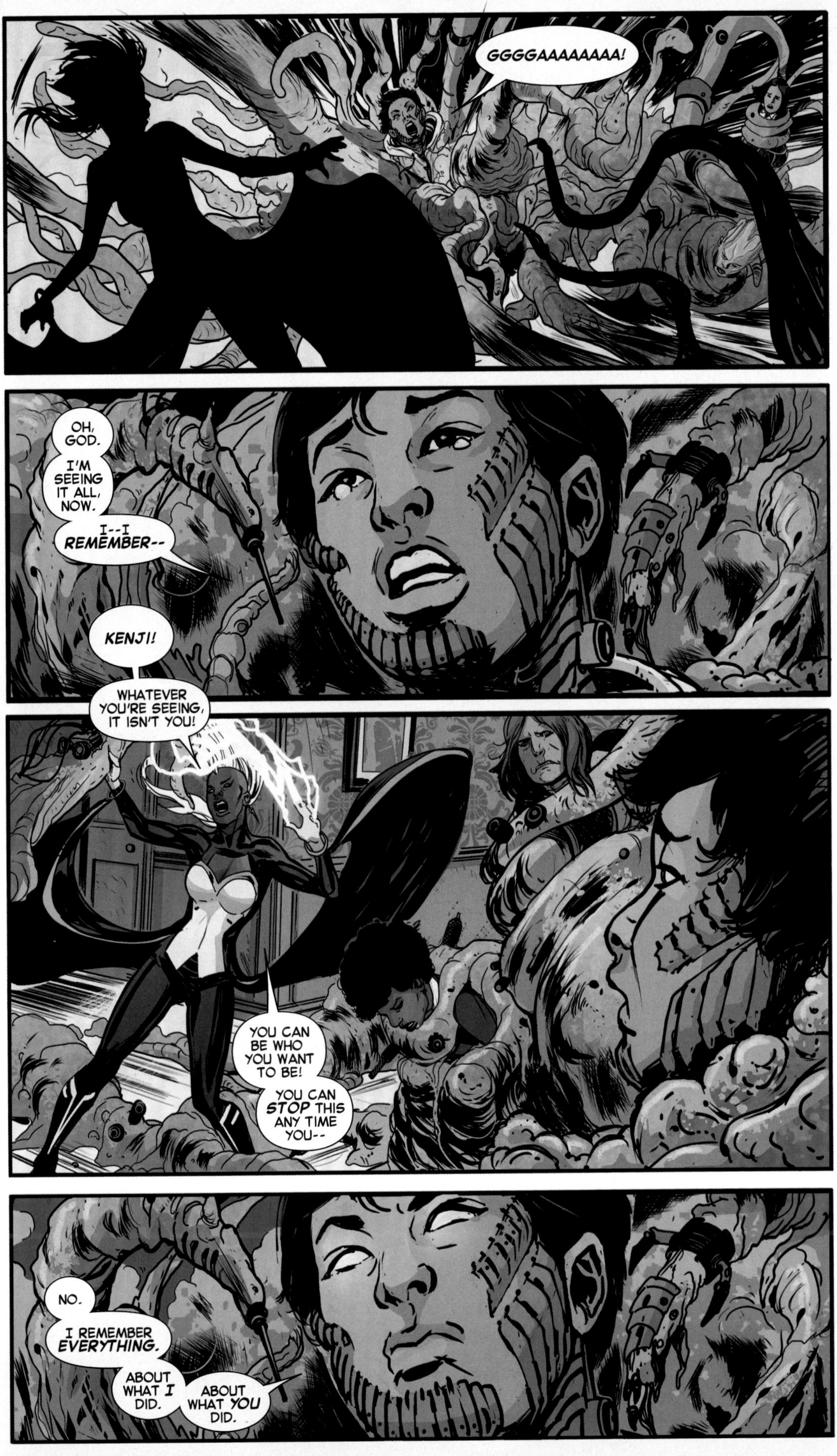
GGGGAAAAAAAA!
OH, GOD.
I'M SEEING IT ALL, NOW.
I--I REMEMBER--
KENJI!
WHATEVER YOU'RE SEEING, IT ISN'T YOU!
YOU CAN BE WHO YOU WANT TO BE!
YOU CAN STOP THIS ANY TIME YOU--
NO.
I REMEMBER EVERYTHING.
ABOUT WHAT I DID.
ABOUT WHAT YOU DID.

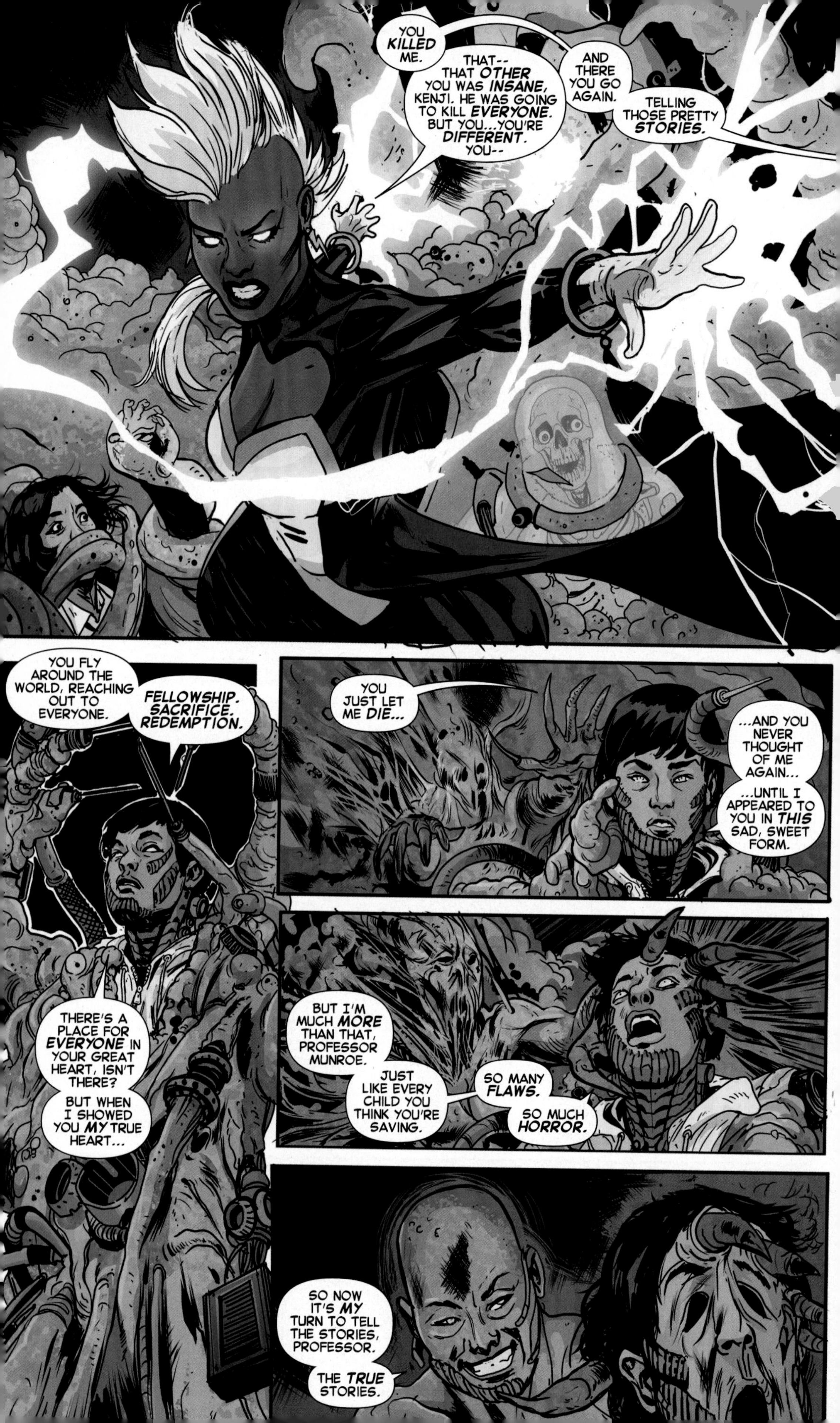

YOU KILLED ME.
THAT-- THAT OTHER YOU WAS INSANE, KENJI. HE WAS GOING TO KILL EVERYONE. BUT YOU...YOU'RE DIFFERENT. YOU--
AND THERE YOU GO AGAIN.
TELLING THOSE PRETTY STORIES.
YOU FLY AROUND THE WORLD, REACHING OUT TO EVERYONE.
FELLOWSHIP. SACRIFICE. REDEMPTION.
YOU JUST LET ME DIE...
...AND YOU NEVER THOUGHT OF ME AGAIN...
...UNTIL I APPEARED TO YOU IN THIS SAD, SWEET FORM.
THERE'S A PLACE FOR EVERYONE IN YOUR GREAT HEART, ISN'T THERE?
BUT WHEN I SHOWED YOU MY TRUE HEART...
BUT I'M MUCH MORE THAN THAT, PROFESSOR MUNROE.
JUST LIKE EVERY CHILD YOU THINK YOU'RE SAVING.
SO MANY FLAWS.
SO MUCH HORROR.
SO NOW IT'S MY TURN TO TELL THE STORIES, PROFESSOR.
THE TRUE STORIES.

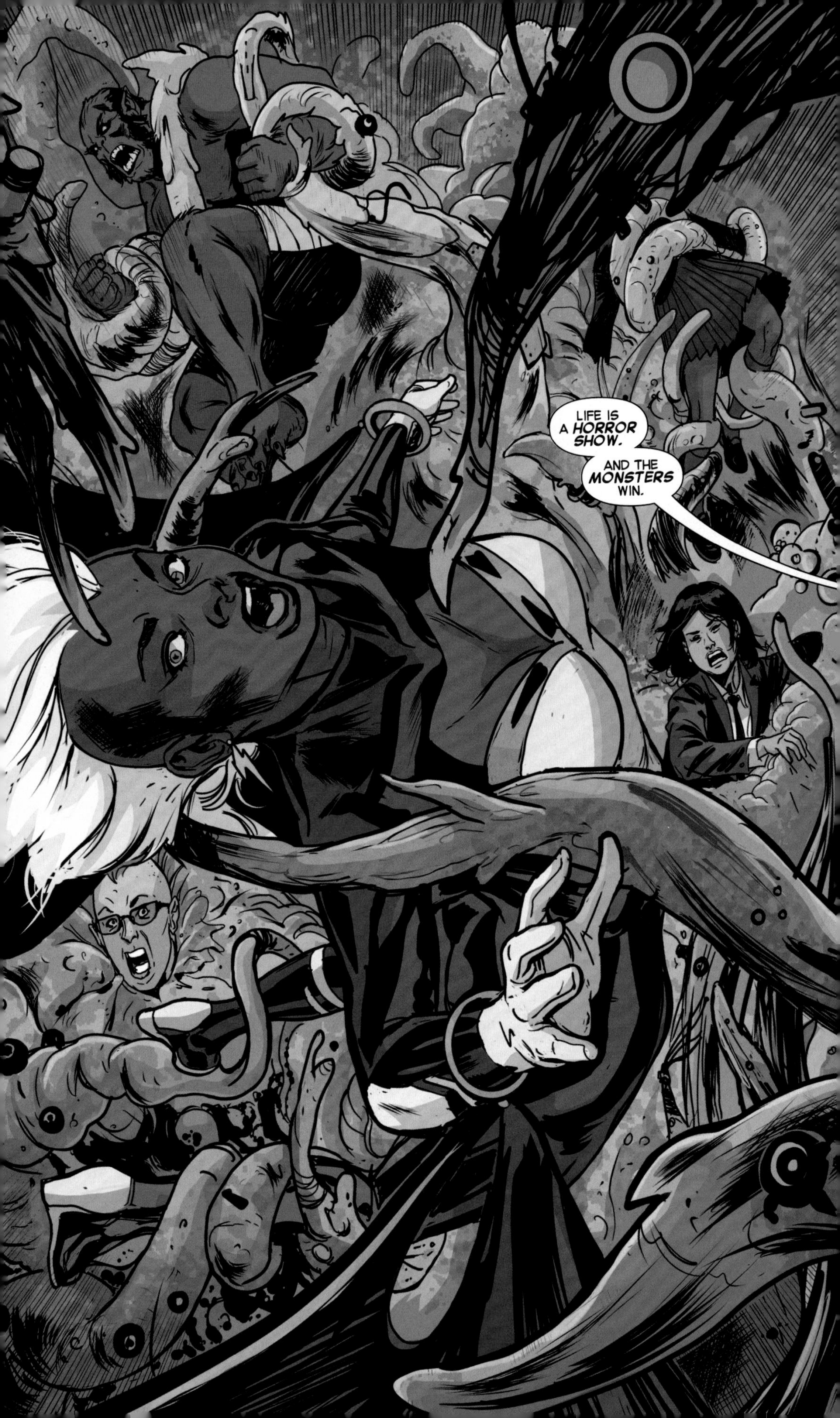
LIFE IS A HORROR SHOW.
AND THE MONSTERS WIN.

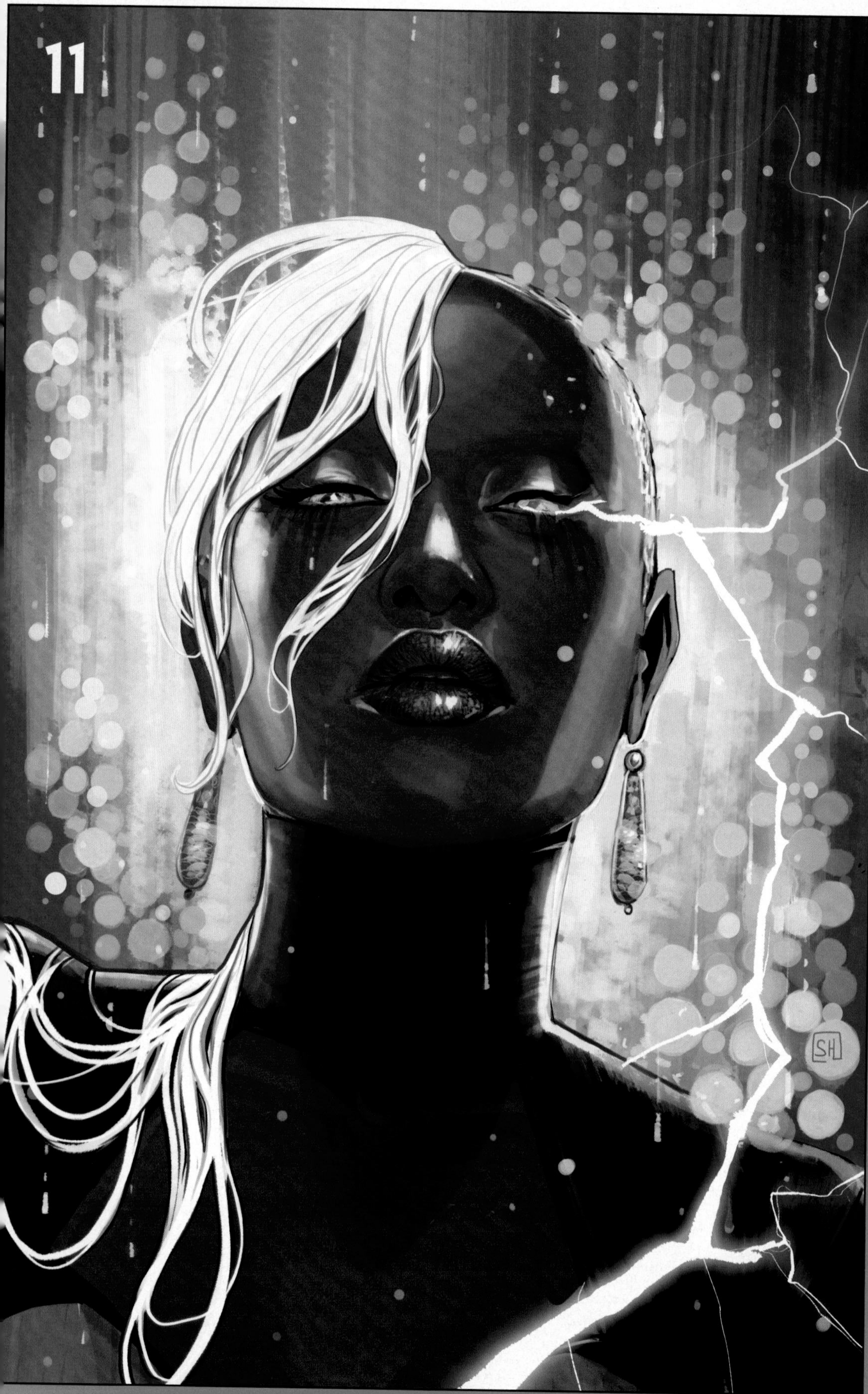
11
SH

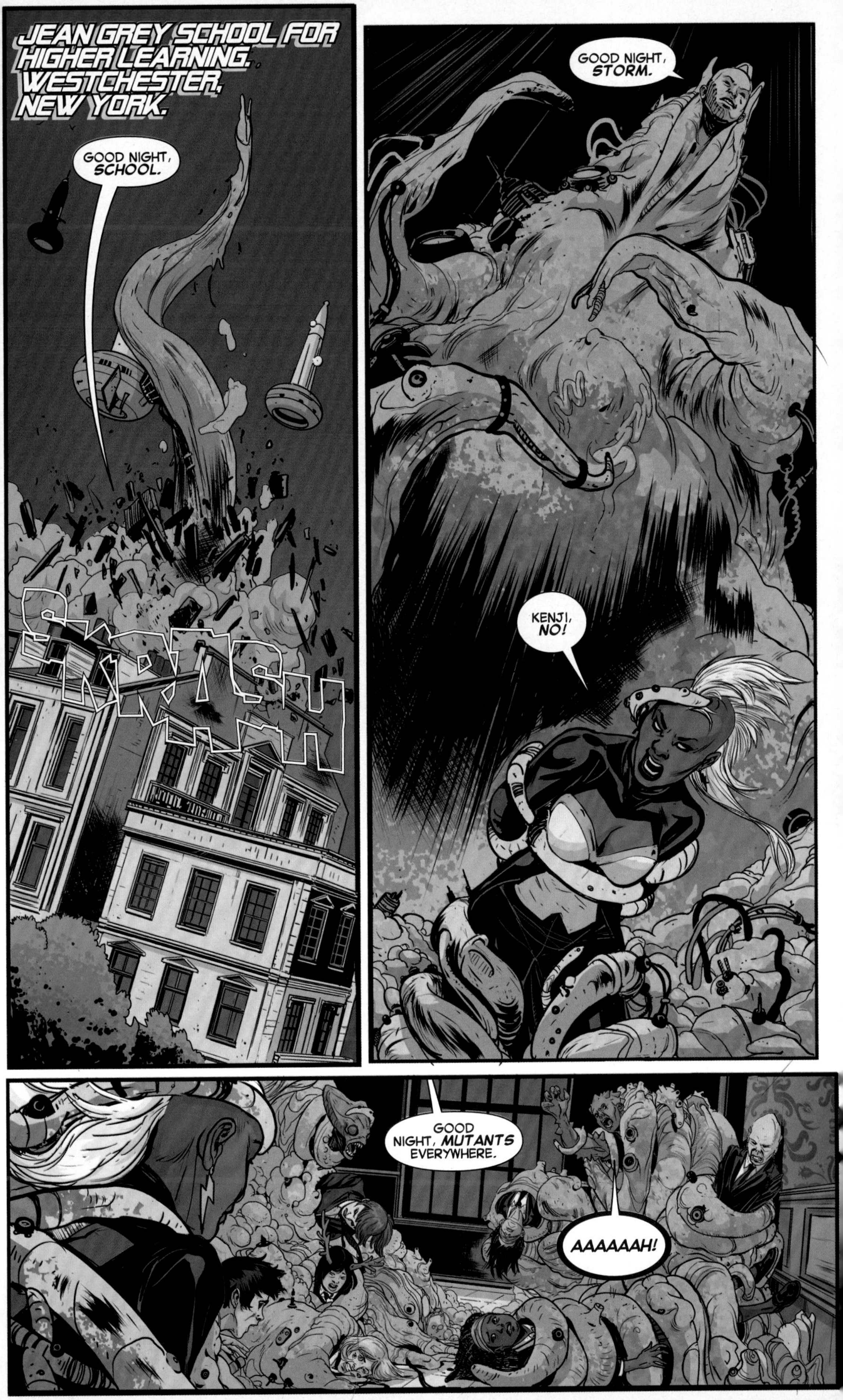
JEAN GREY SCHOOL FOR HIGHER LEARNING. WESTCHESTER, NEW YORK.
GOOD NIGHT, SCHOOL.
SMASH
GOOD NIGHT, STORM.
KENJI, NO!
GOOD NIGHT, MUTANTS EVERYWHERE.
AAAAAAH!

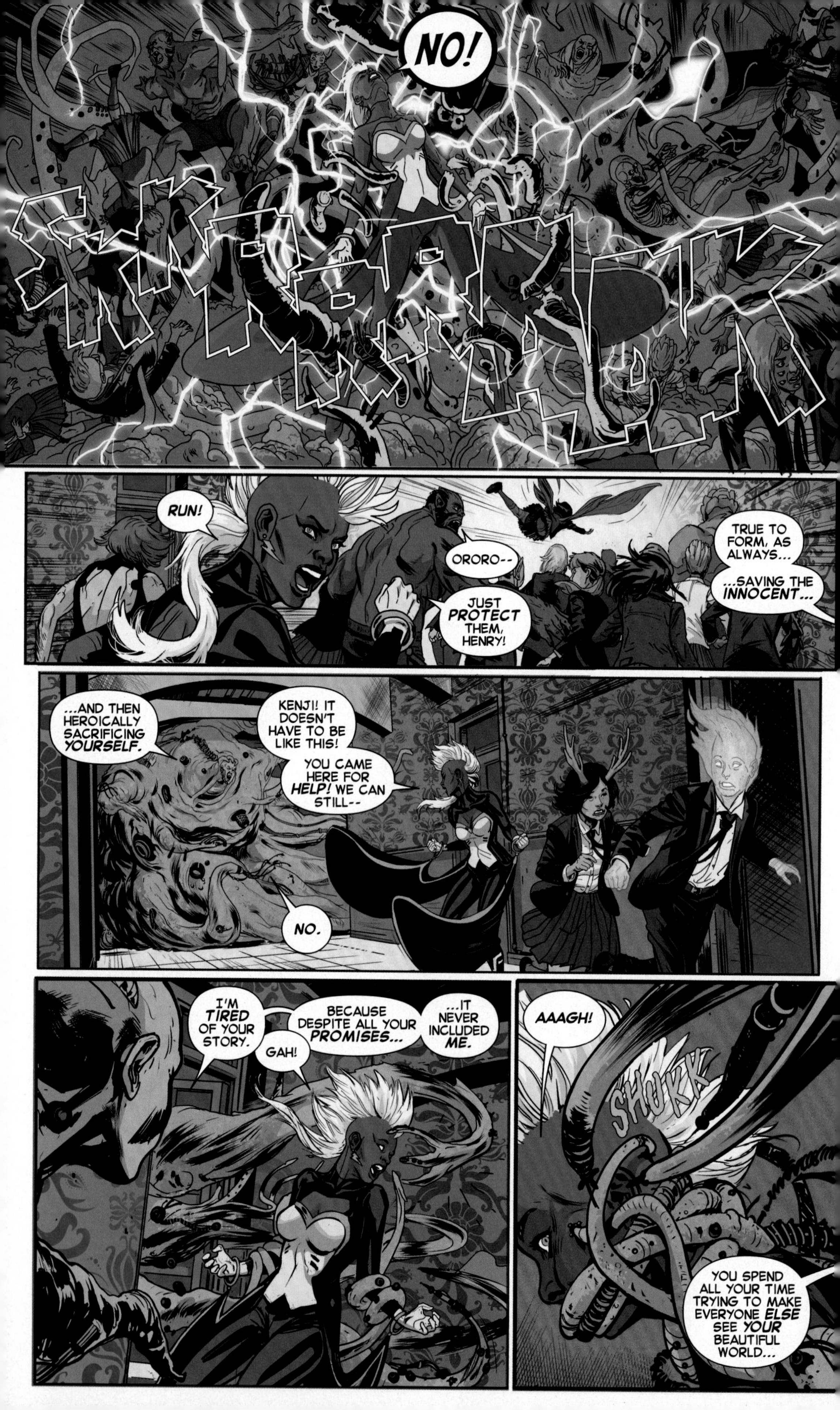
NO!
RUN!
ORORO--
JUST PROTECT THEM, HENRY!
TRUE TO FORM, AS ALWAYS...
...SAVING THE INNOCENT...
...AND THEN HEROICALLY SACRIFICING YOURSELF.
KENJI! IT DOESN'T HAVE TO BE LIKE THIS!
YOU CAME HERE FOR HELP! WE CAN STILL--
NO.
I'M TIRED OF YOUR STORY.
BECAUSE DESPITE ALL YOUR PROMISES...
...IT NEVER INCLUDED ME.
GAH!
AAAGH!
SHOKK
YOU SPEND ALL YOUR TIME TRYING TO MAKE EVERYONE ELSE SEE YOUR BEAUTIFUL WORLD...

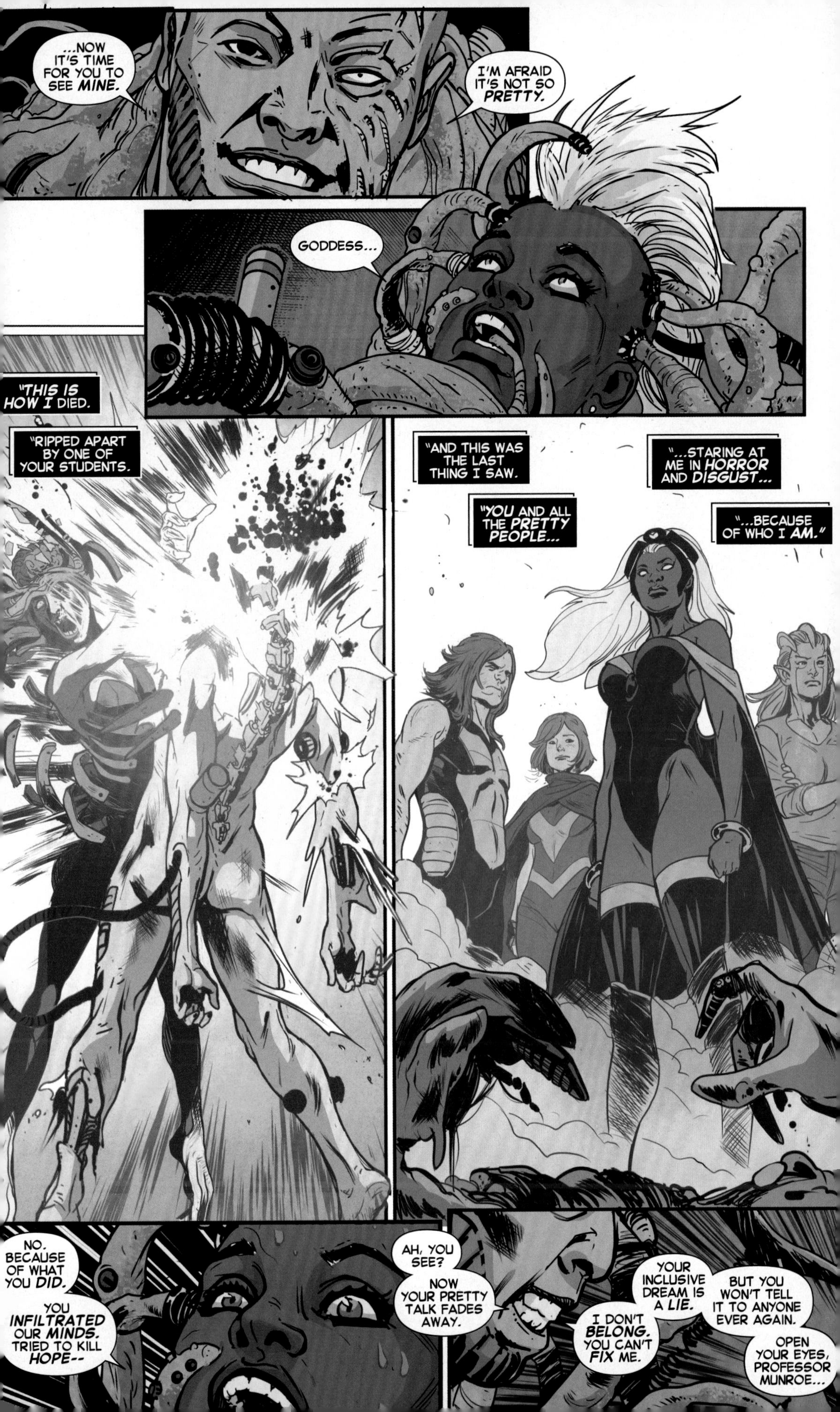

...NOW IT'S TIME FOR YOU TO SEE MINE.
I'M AFRAID IT'S NOT SO PRETTY.
GODDESS...
"THIS IS HOW I DIED.
"RIPPED APART BY ONE OF YOUR STUDENTS.
"AND THIS WAS THE LAST THING I SAW.
"YOU AND ALL THE PRETTY PEOPLE...
"...STARING AT ME IN HORROR AND DISGUST...
"...BECAUSE OF WHO I AM."
NO. BECAUSE OF WHAT YOU DID.
YOU INFILTRATED OUR MINDS. TRIED TO KILL HOPE--
AH, YOU SEE?
NOW YOUR PRETTY TALK FADES AWAY.
I DON'T BELONG. YOU CAN'T FIX ME.
YOUR INCLUSIVE DREAM IS A LIE.
BUT YOU WON'T TELL IT TO ANYONE EVER AGAIN.
OPEN YOUR EYES, PROFESSOR MUNROE...

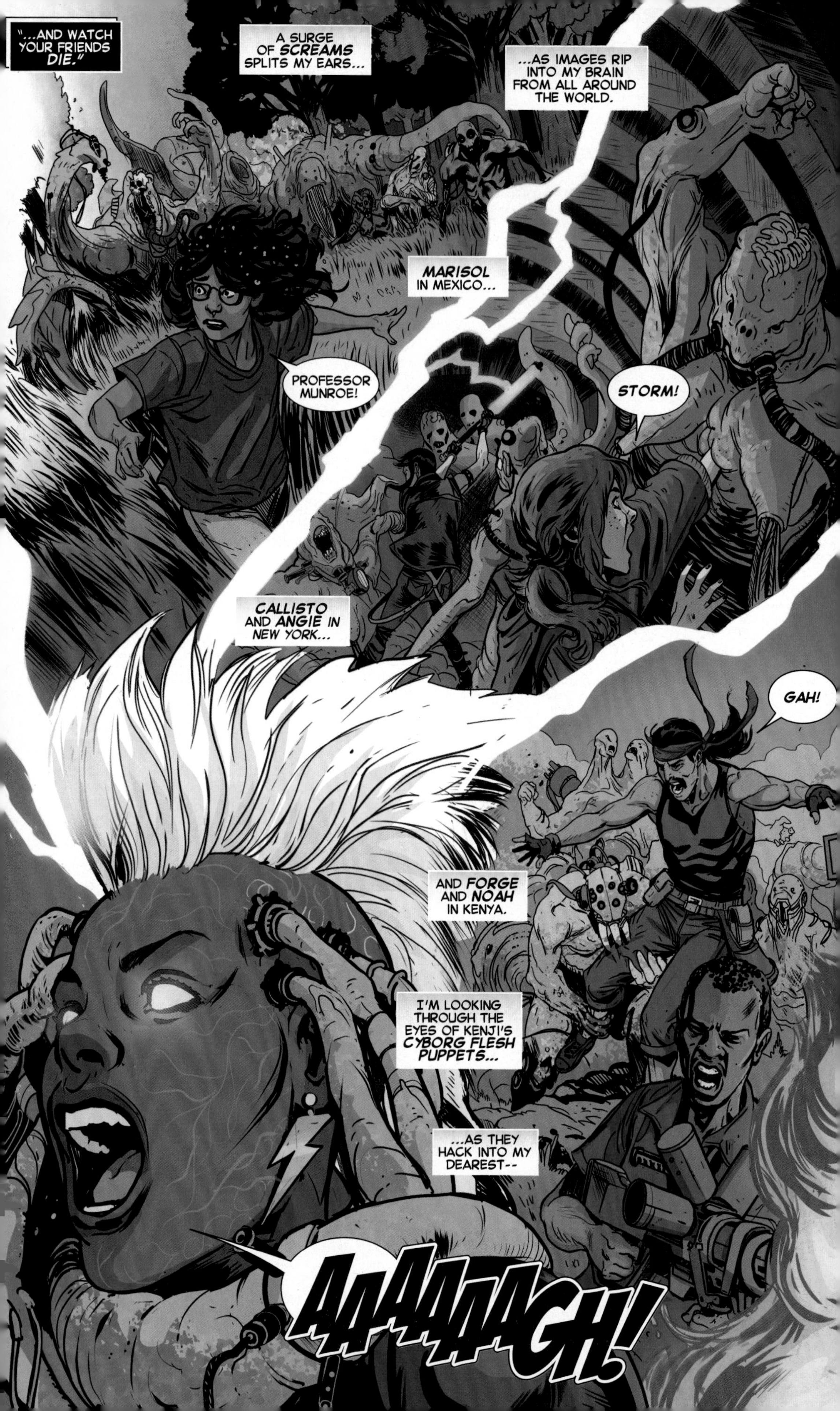
"...AND WATCH YOUR FRIENDS DIE."
A SURGE OF SCREAMS SPLITS MY EARS...
...AS IMAGES RIP INTO MY BRAIN FROM ALL AROUND THE WORLD.
MARISOL IN MEXICO...
PROFESSOR MUNROE!
STORM!
CALLISTO AND ANGIE IN NEW YORK...
GAH!
AND FORGE AND NOAH IN KENYA.
I'M LOOKING THROUGH THE EYES OF KENJI'S CYBORG FLESH PUPPETS...
...AS THEY HACK INTO MY DEAREST--
AAAAAAGH!

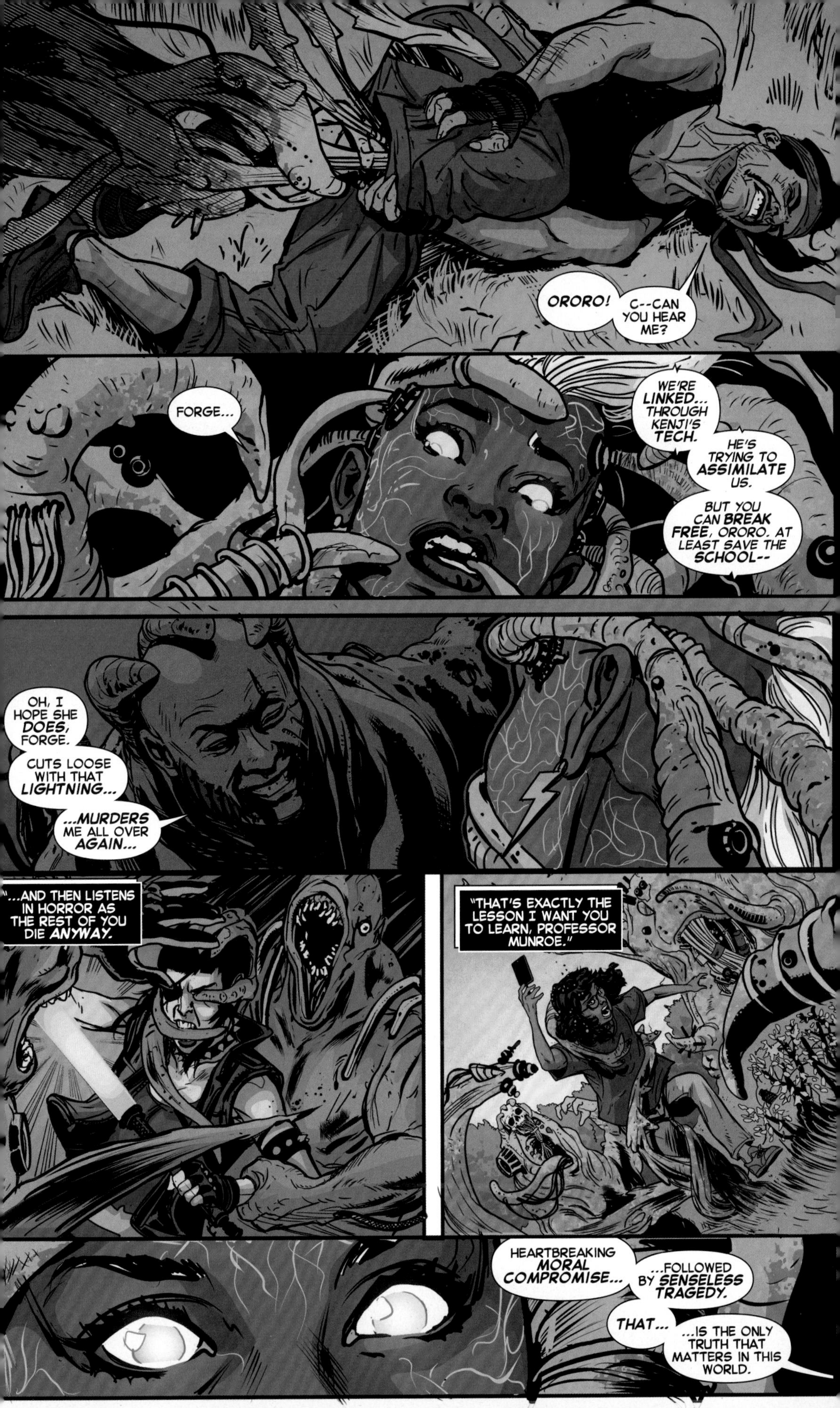
OROROR!
C--CAN YOU HEAR ME?
FORGE...
WE'RE LINKED... THROUGH KENJI'S TECH.
HE'S TRYING TO ASSIMILATE US.
BUT YOU CAN BREAK FREE, ORORO. AT LEAST SAVE THE SCHOOL--
OH, I HOPE SHE DOES, FORGE.
CUTS LOOSE WITH THAT LIGHTNING...
...MURDERS ME ALL OVER AGAIN...
"...AND THEN LISTENS IN HORROR AS THE REST OF YOU DIE ANYWAY.
"THAT'S EXACTLY THE LESSON I WANT YOU TO LEARN, PROFESSOR MUNROE."
HEARTBREAKING MORAL COMPROMISE...
...FOLLOWED BY SENSELESS TRAGEDY.
THAT...
...IS THE ONLY TRUTH THAT MATTERS IN THIS WORLD.

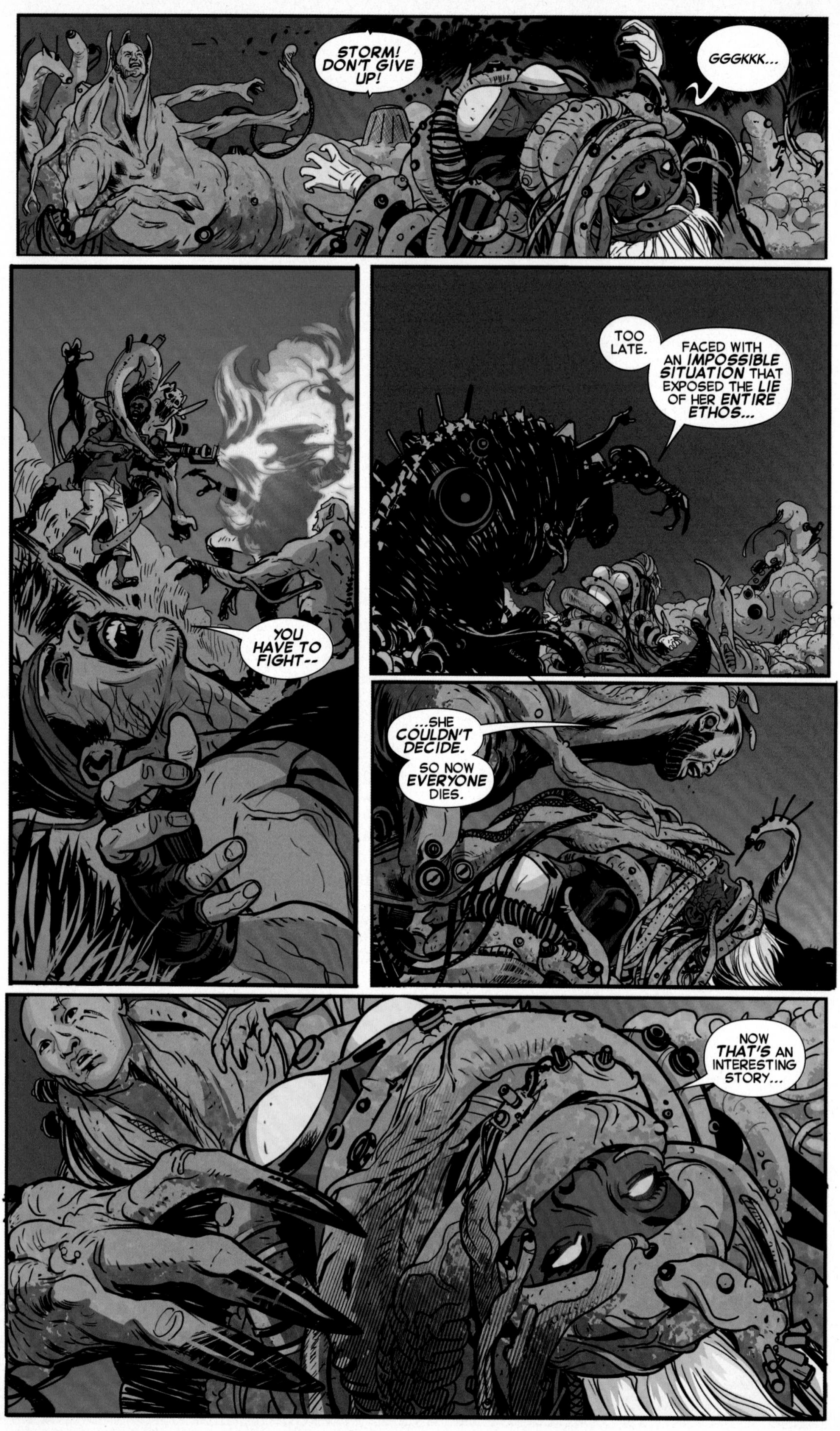
STORM! DON'T GIVE UP!
GGGKKK...
YOU HAVE TO FIGHT--
TOO LATE.
FACED WITH AN IMPOSSIBLE SITUATION THAT EXPOSED THE LIE OF HER ENTIRE ETHOS...
...SHE COULDN'T DECIDE.
SO NOW EVERYONE DIES.
NOW THAT'S AN INTERESTING STORY...

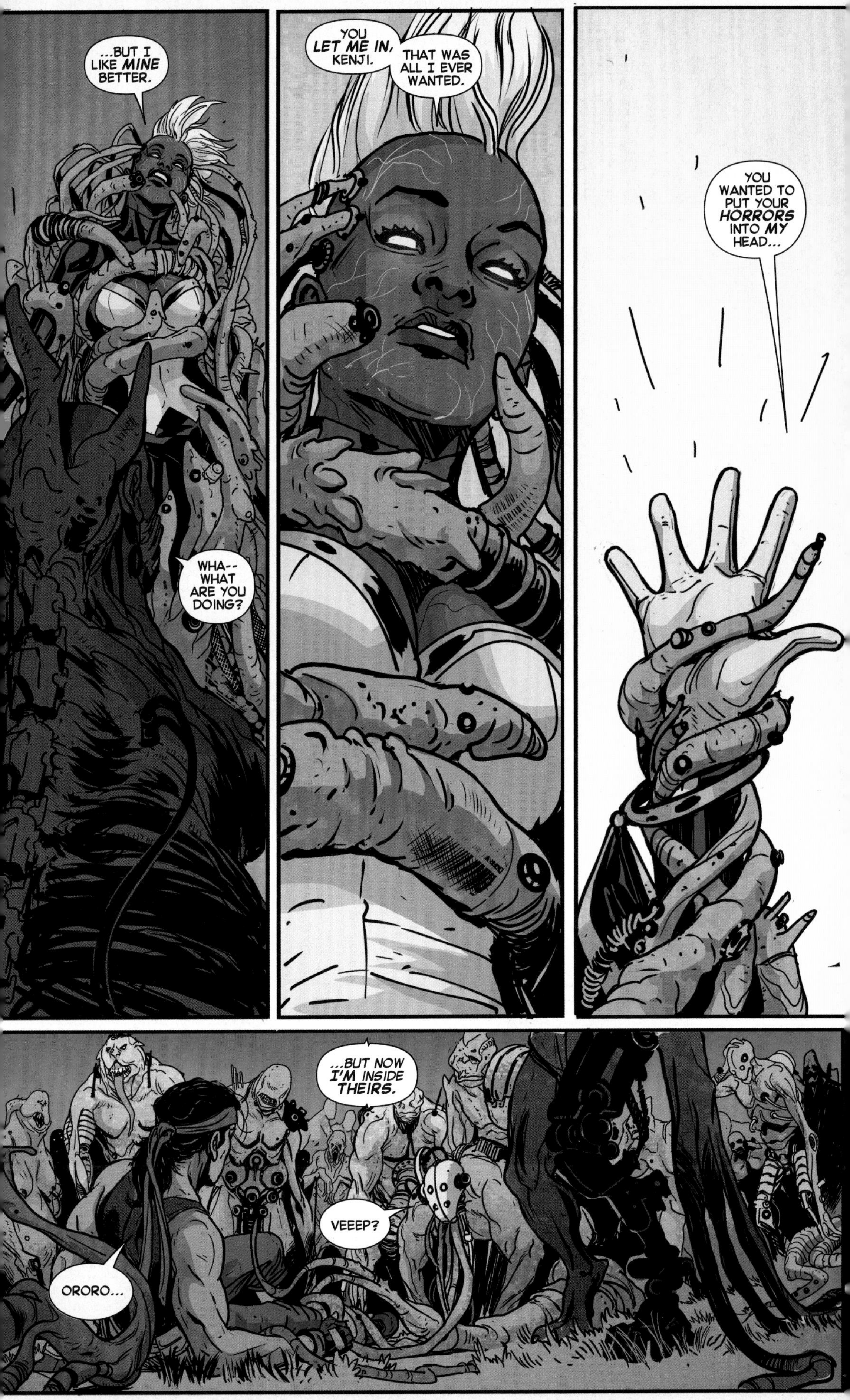
...BUT I LIKE MINE BETTER.
WHA--WHAT ARE YOU DOING?
YOU LET ME IN, KENJI.
THAT WAS ALL I EVER WANTED.
YOU WANTED TO PUT YOUR HORRORS INTO MY HEAD...
...BUT NOW I'M INSIDE THEIRS.
VEEEP?
ORORO...

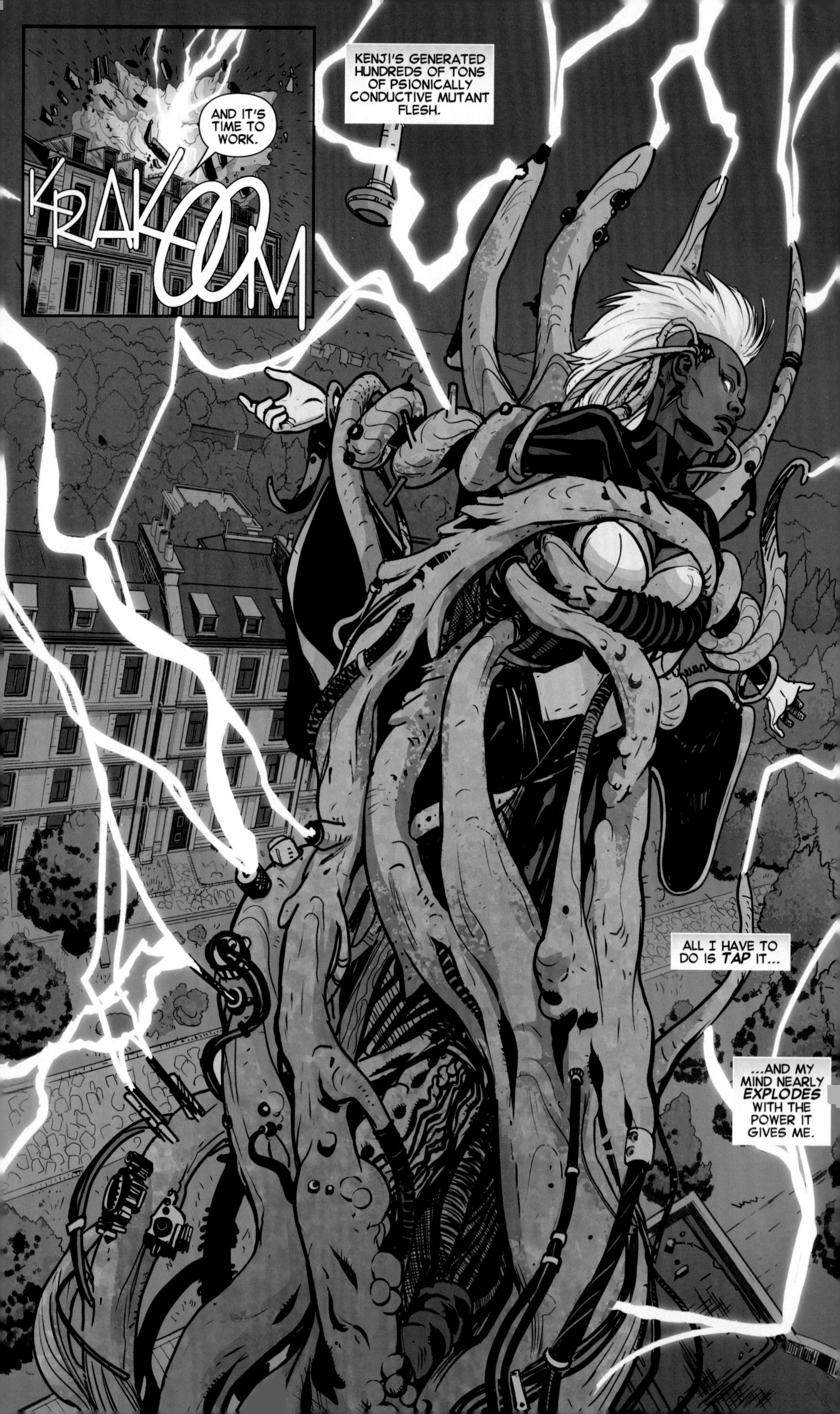
AND IT'S TIME TO WORK.
KRAKOOM
KENJI'S GENERATED HUNDREDS OF TONS OF PSIONICALLY CONDUCTIVE MUTANT FLESH.
ALL I HAVE TO DO IS *TAP* IT...
...AND MY MIND NEARLY *EXPLODES* WITH THE POWER IT GIVES ME.

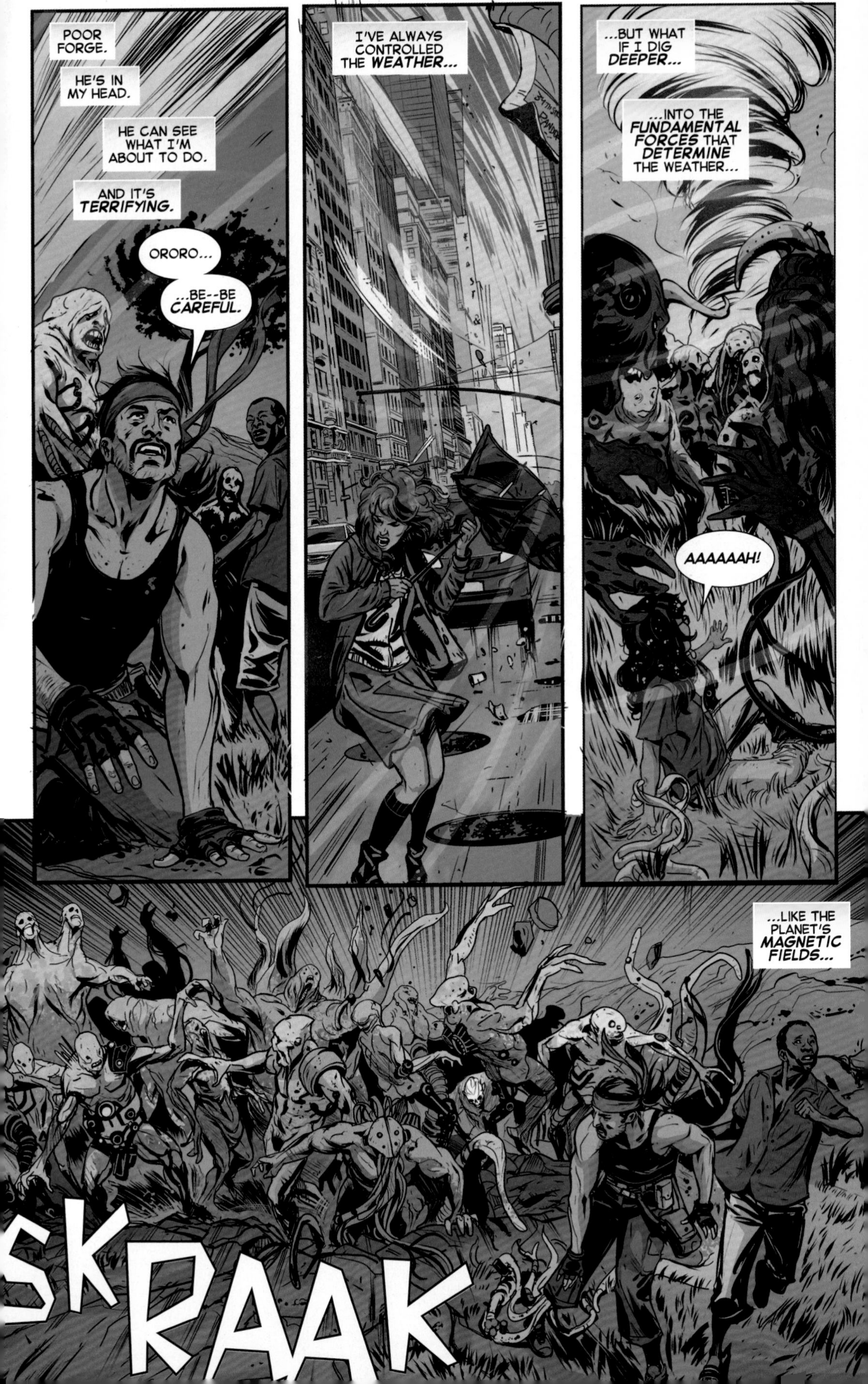
POOR FORGE.
HE'S IN MY HEAD.
HE CAN SEE WHAT I'M ABOUT TO DO.
AND IT'S TERRIFYING.
ORORO...
...BE--BE CAREFUL.
I'VE ALWAYS CONTROLLED THE WEATHER...
...BUT WHAT IF I DIG DEEPER...
...INTO THE FUNDAMENTAL FORCES THAT DETERMINE THE WEATHER...
AAAAAAH!
...LIKE THE PLANET'S MAGNETIC FIELDS...
SKRAAK

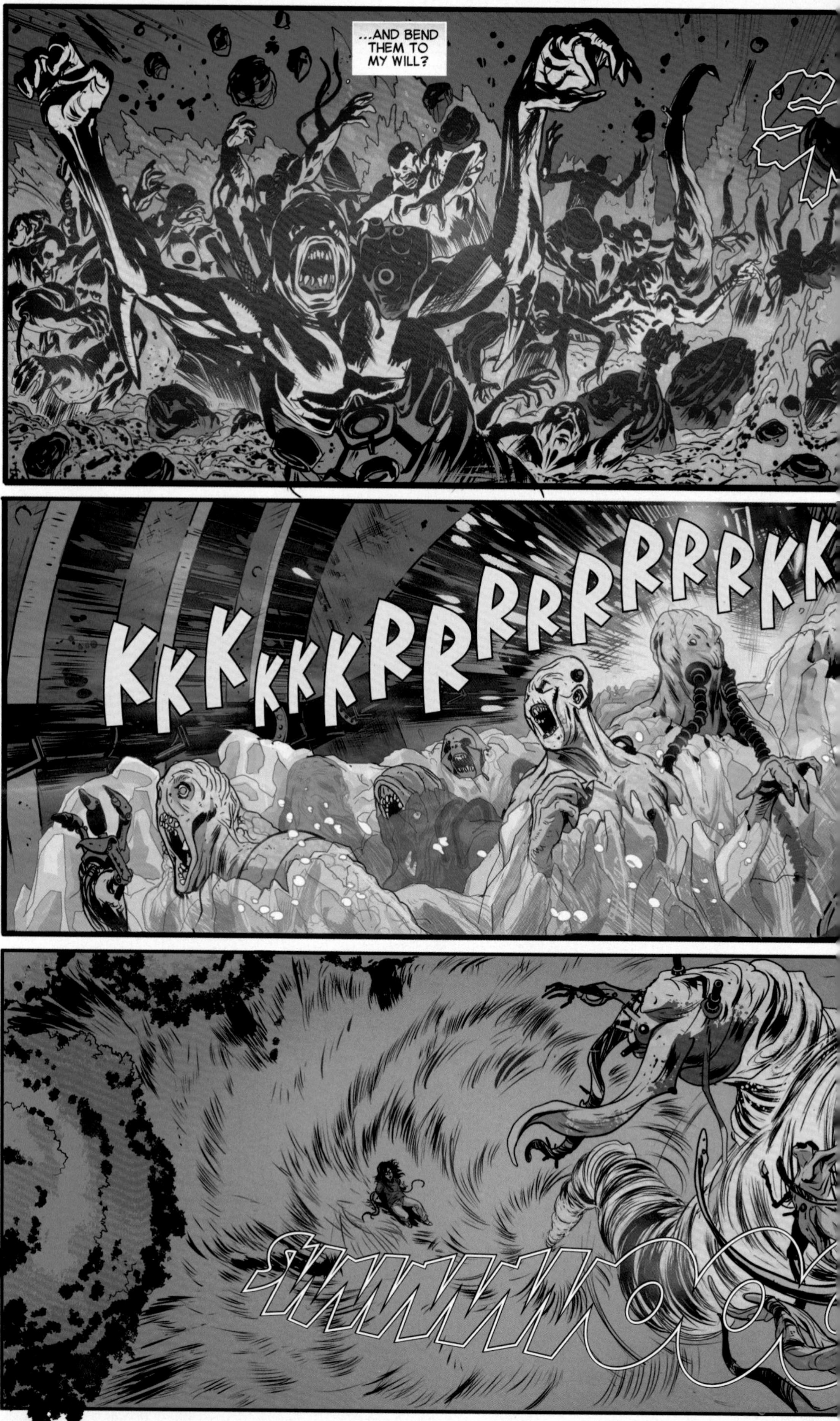
...AND BEND THEM TO MY WILL?
KKKKKKRRRRRRRRRRK

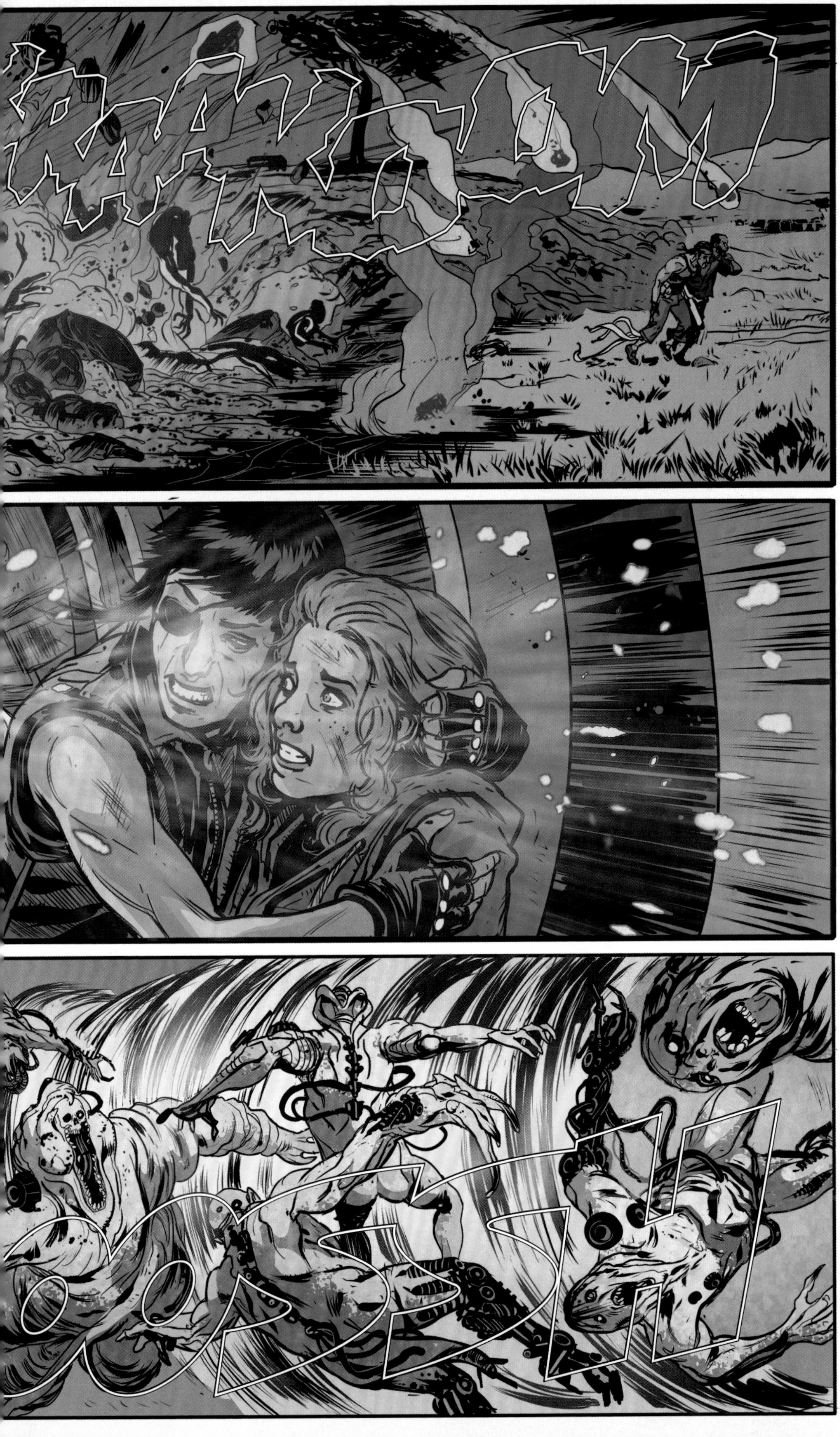
WOOSH

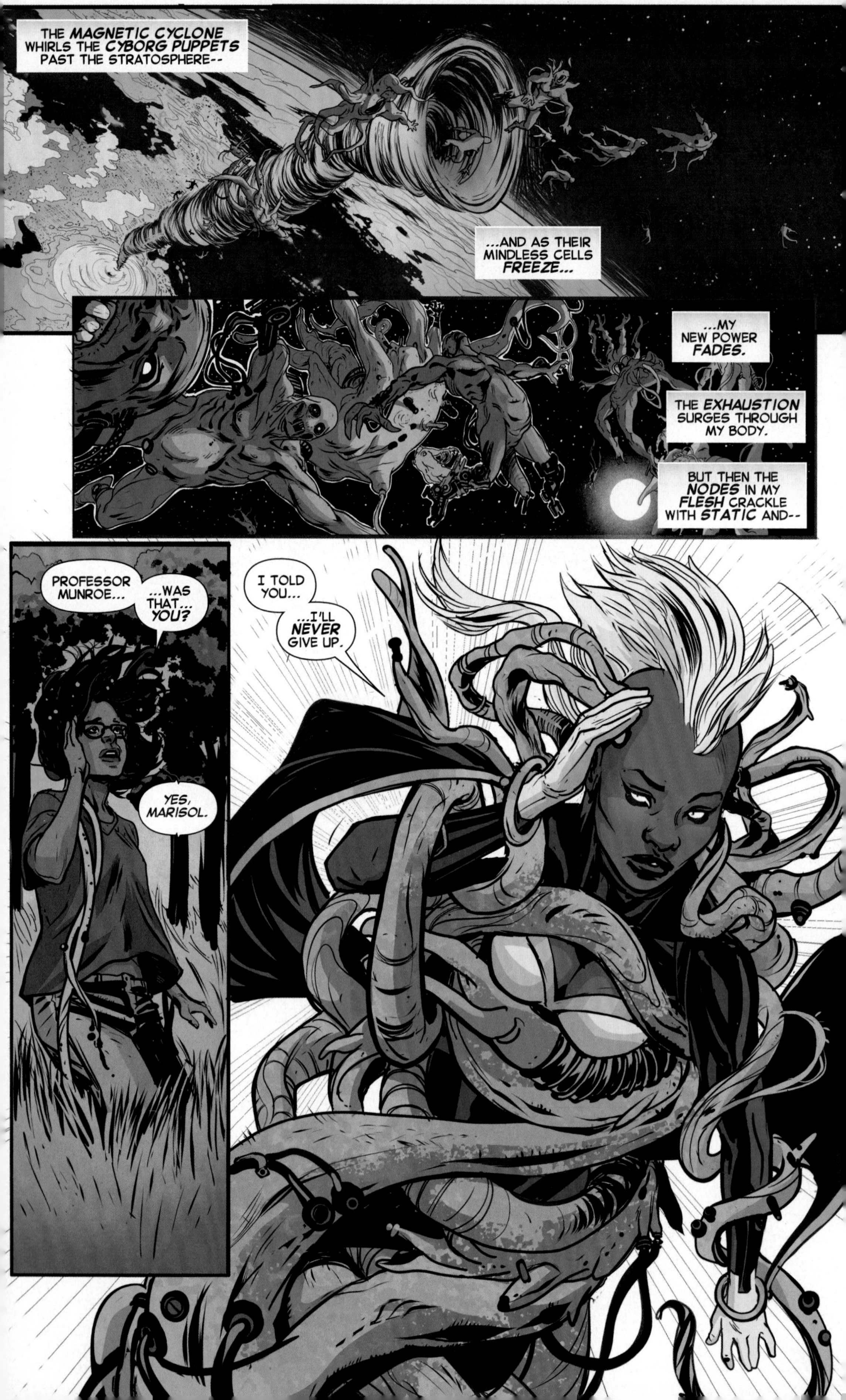

THE MAGNETIC CYCLONE WHIRLS THE CYBORG PUPPETS PAST THE STRATOSPHERE--
...AND AS THEIR MINDLESS CELLS FREEZE...
...MY NEW POWER FADES.
THE EXHAUSTION SURGES THROUGH MY BODY.
BUT THEN THE NODES IN MY FLESH CRACKLE WITH STATIC AND--
PROFESSOR MUNROE...
...WAS THAT... YOU?
YES, MARISOL.
I TOLD YOU...
...I'LL NEVER GIVE UP.

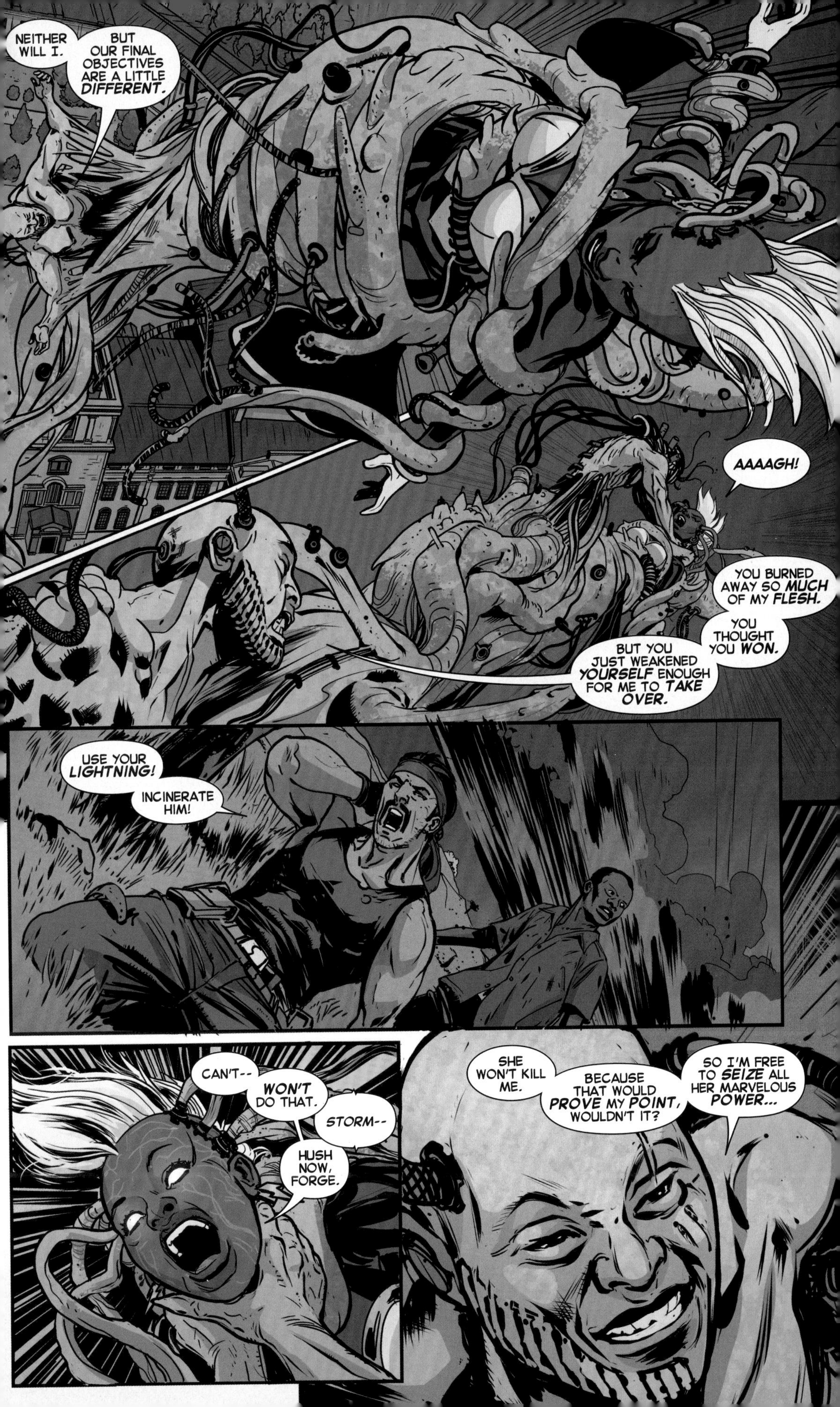

NEITHER WILL I.
BUT OUR FINAL OBJECTIVES ARE A LITTLE DIFFERENT.
AAAAGH!
YOU BURNED AWAY SO MUCH OF MY FLESH.
YOU THOUGHT YOU WON.
BUT YOU JUST WEAKENED YOURSELF ENOUGH FOR ME TO TAKE OVER.
USE YOUR LIGHTNING!
INCINERATE HIM!
CAN'T--
WON'T DO THAT.
STORM--
HUSH NOW, FORGE.
SHE WON'T KILL ME.
BECAUSE THAT WOULD PROVE MY POINT, WOULDN'T IT?
SO I'M FREE TO SEIZE ALL HER MARVELOUS POWER...

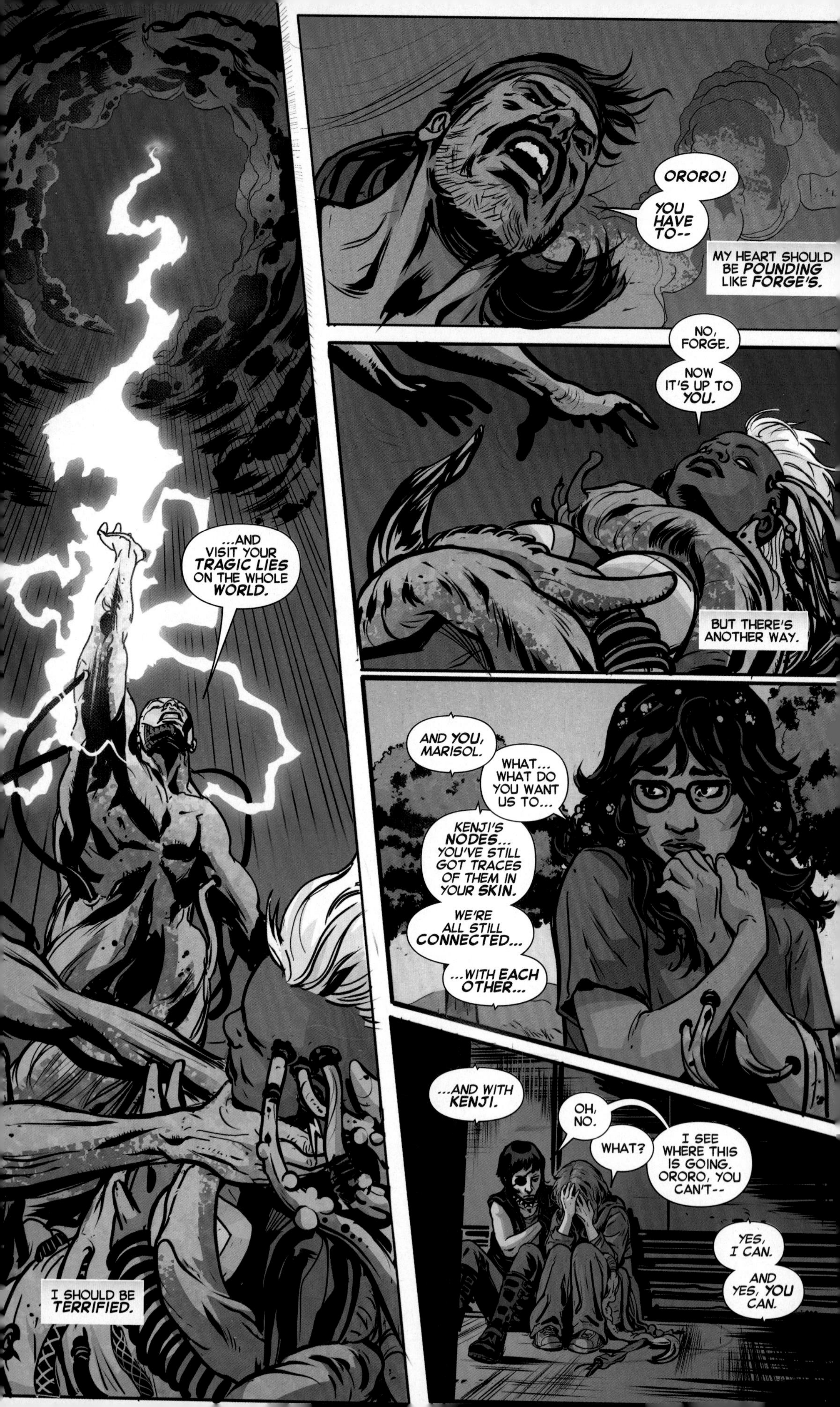

ORORO!
YOU HAVE TO--
MY HEART SHOULD BE POUNDING LIKE FORGE'S.
...AND VISIT YOUR TRAGIC LIES ON THE WHOLE WORLD.
NO, FORGE.
NOW IT'S UP TO YOU.
BUT THERE'S ANOTHER WAY.
AND YOU, MARISOL.
WHAT... WHAT DO YOU WANT US TO...
KENJI'S NODES... YOU'VE STILL GOT TRACES OF THEM IN YOUR SKIN.
WE'RE ALL STILL CONNECTED...
...WITH EACH OTHER...
I SHOULD BE TERRIFIED.
...AND WITH KENJI.
OH, NO.
WHAT?
I SEE WHERE THIS IS GOING. ORORO, YOU CAN'T--
YES, I CAN.
AND YES, YOU CAN.

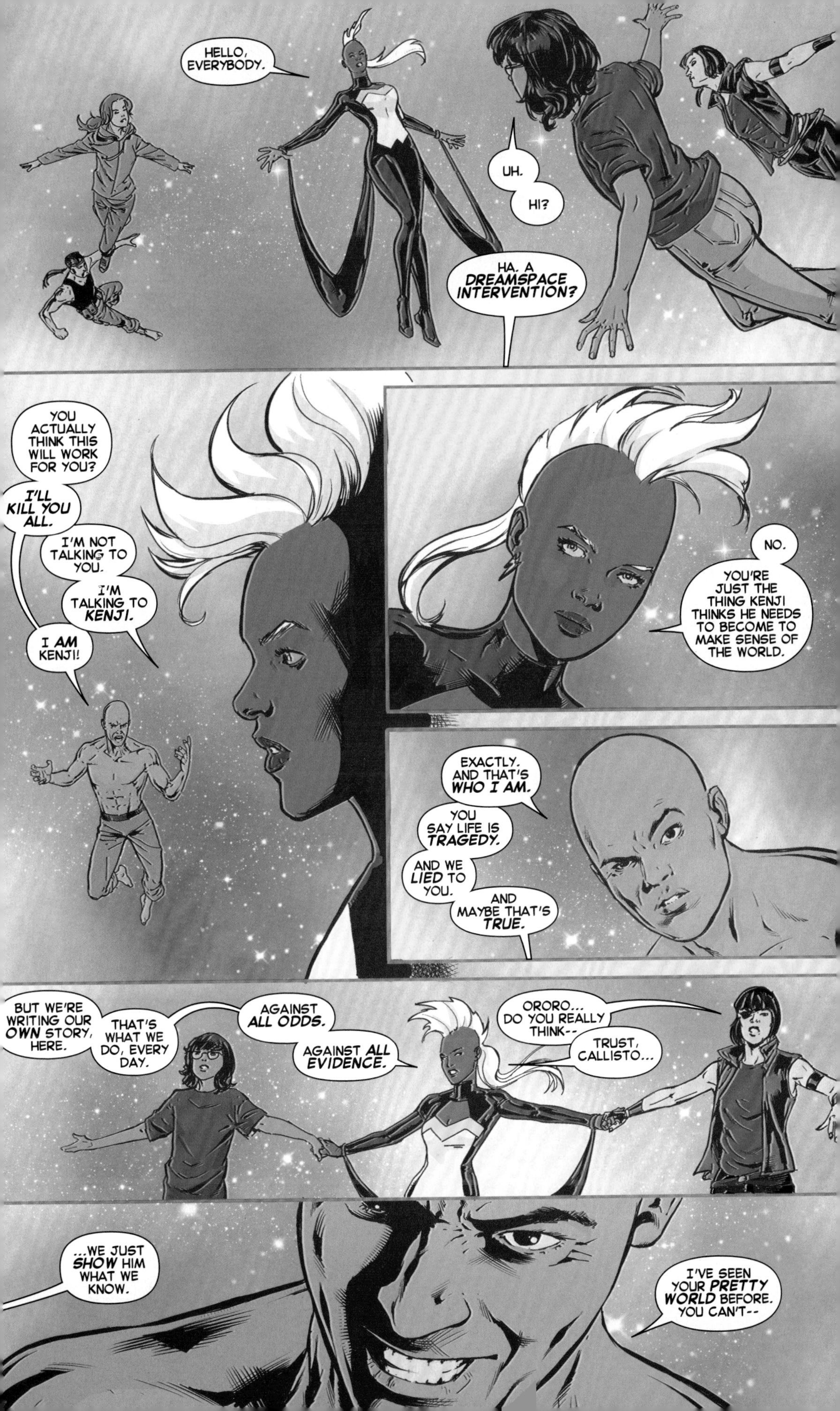
HELLO, EVERYBODY.
UH.
HI?
HA. A DREAMSPACE INTERVENTION?
YOU ACTUALLY THINK THIS WILL WORK FOR YOU?
I'LL KILL YOU ALL.
I'M NOT TALKING TO YOU.
I'M TALKING TO KENJI.
I AM KENJI!
NO.
YOU'RE JUST THE THING KENJI THINKS HE NEEDS TO BECOME TO MAKE SENSE OF THE WORLD.
EXACTLY. AND THAT'S WHO I AM.
YOU SAY LIFE IS TRAGEDY.
AND WE LIED TO YOU.
AND MAYBE THAT'S TRUE.
BUT WE'RE WRITING OUR OWN STORY, HERE.
THAT'S WHAT WE DO, EVERY DAY.
AGAINST ALL ODDS.
AGAINST ALL EVIDENCE.
ORORO... DO YOU REALLY THINK--
TRUST, CALLISTO...
...WE JUST SHOW HIM WHAT WE KNOW.
I'VE SEEN YOUR PRETTY WORLD BEFORE. YOU CAN'T--

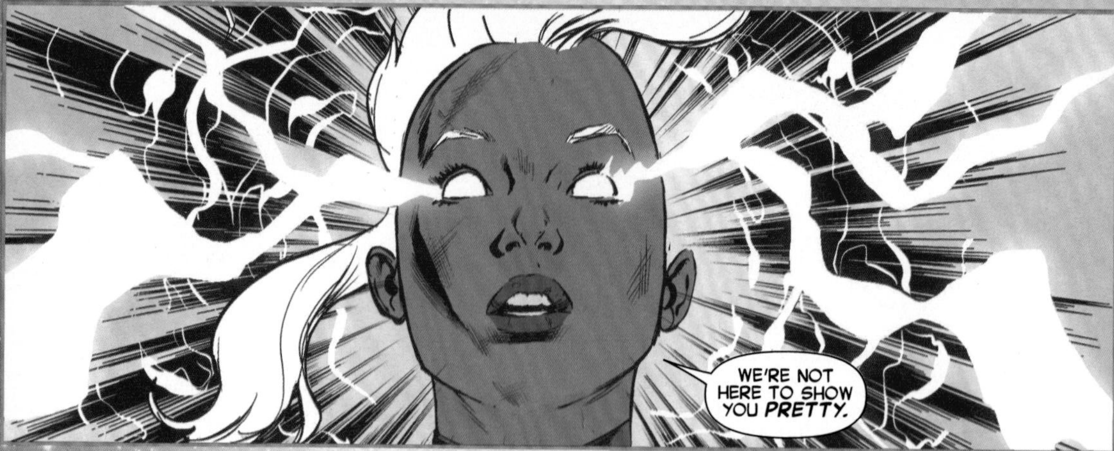
WE'RE NOT HERE TO SHOW YOU PRETTY.

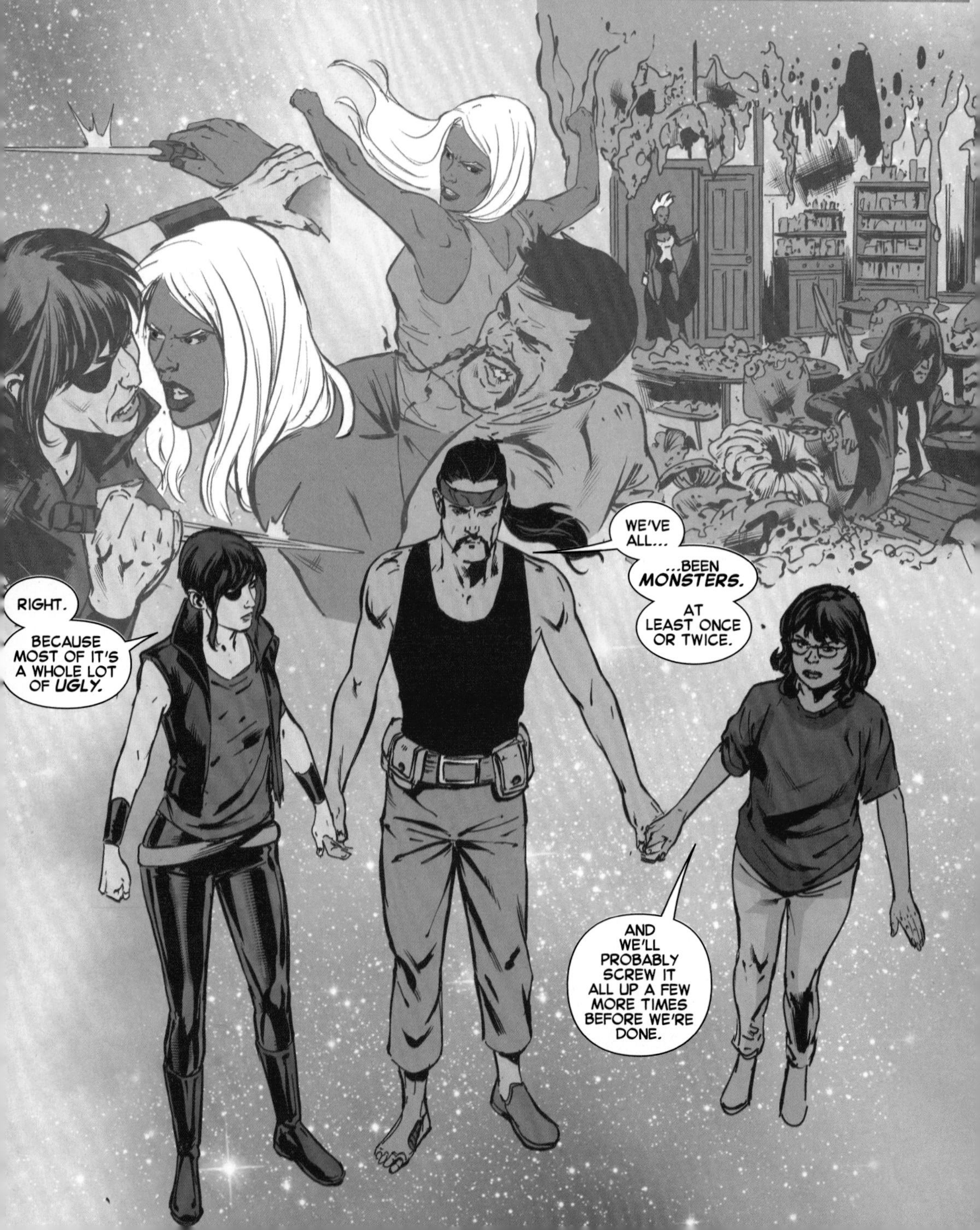
WE'VE ALL...
...BEEN MONSTERS.
AT LEAST ONCE OR TWICE.
RIGHT.
BECAUSE MOST OF IT'S A WHOLE LOT OF UGLY.
AND WE'LL PROBABLY SCREW IT ALL UP A FEW MORE TIMES BEFORE WE'RE DONE.

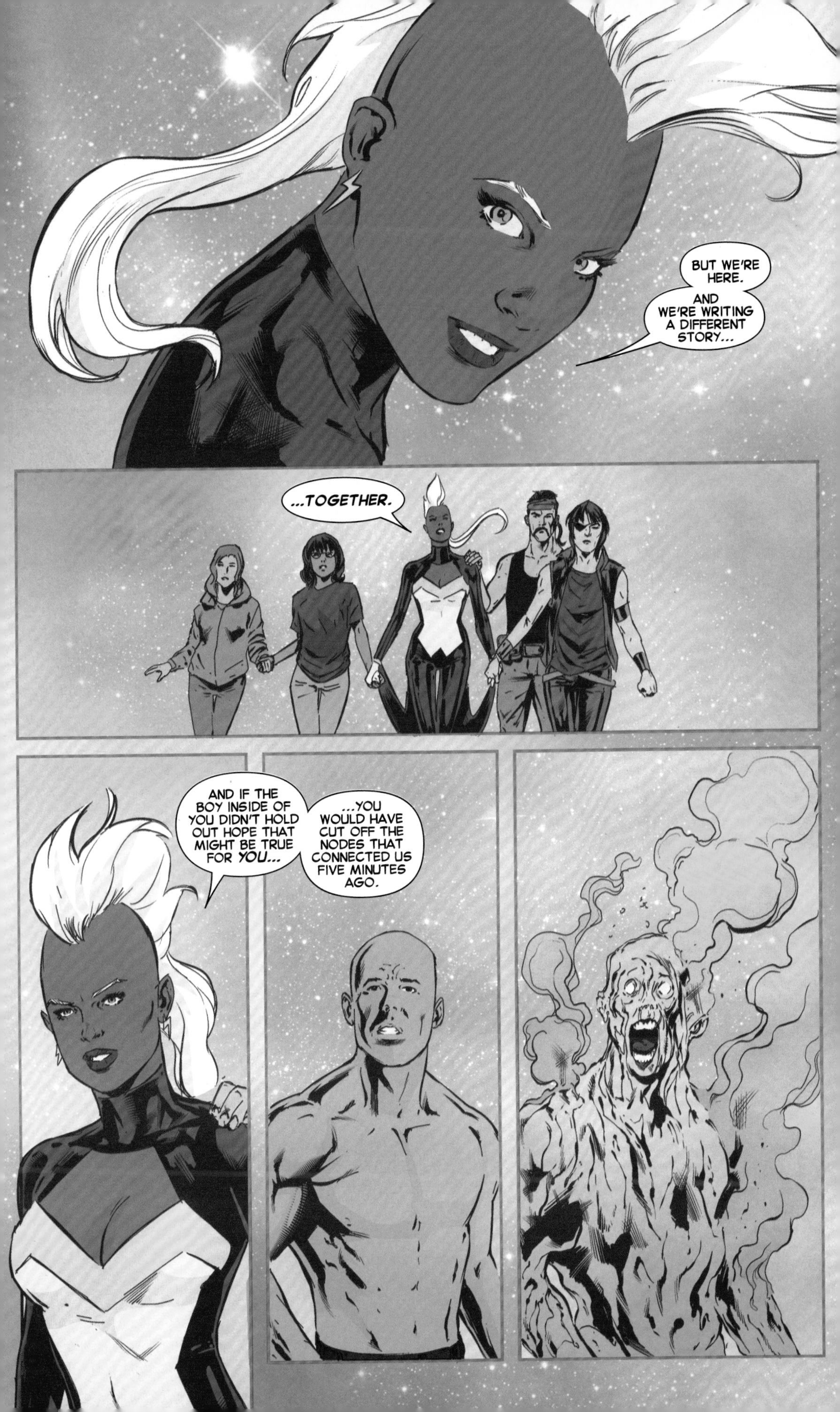
BUT WE'RE HERE.
AND WE'RE WRITING A DIFFERENT STORY...
...TOGETHER.
AND IF THE BOY INSIDE OF YOU DIDN'T HOLD OUT HOPE THAT MIGHT BE TRUE FOR YOU...
...YOU WOULD HAVE CUT OFF THE NODES THAT CONNECTED US FIVE MINUTES AGO.

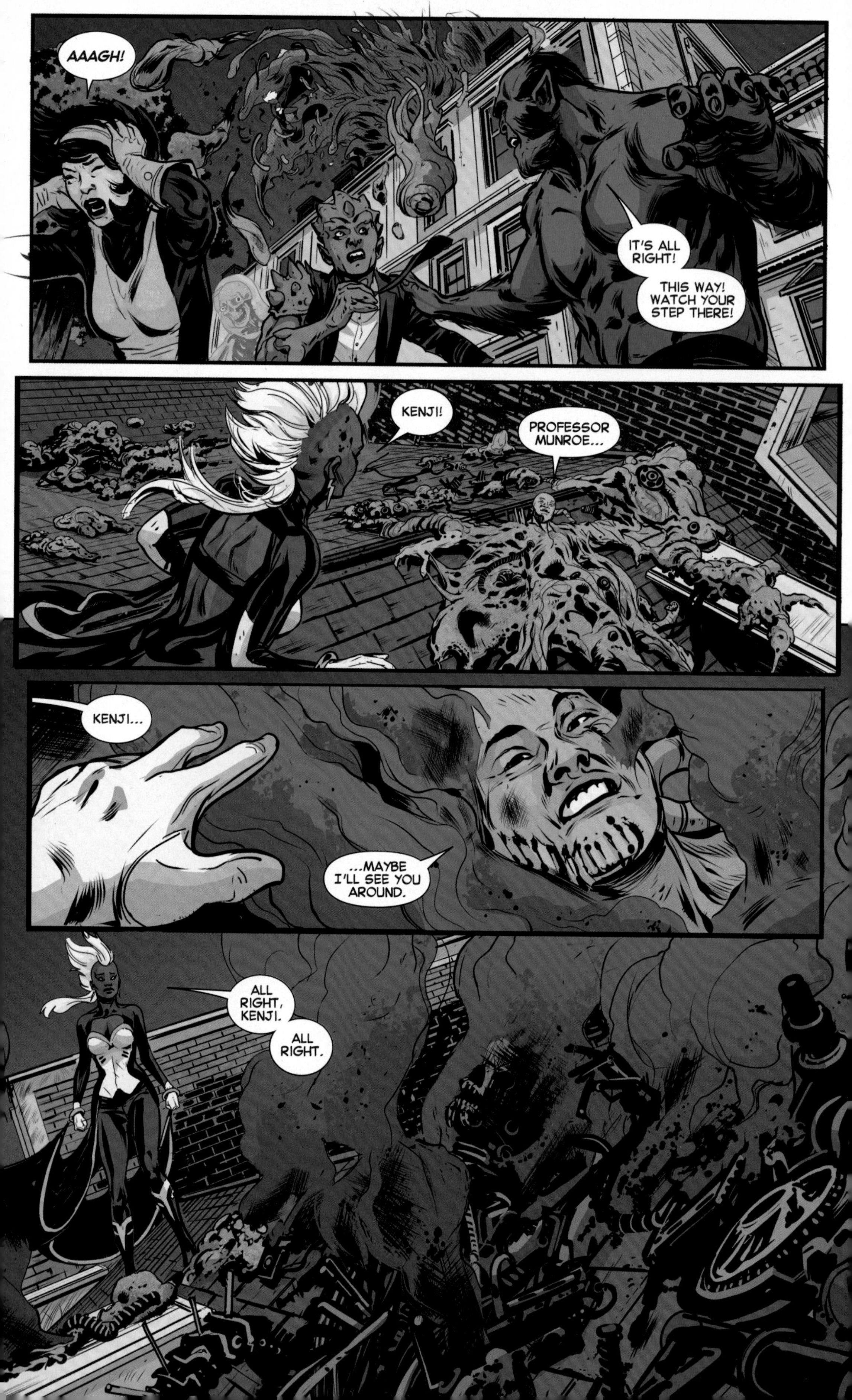
AAAGH!
IT'S ALL RIGHT!
THIS WAY! WATCH YOUR STEP THERE!
KENJI!
PROFESSOR MUNROE...
KENJI...
...MAYBE I'LL SEE YOU AROUND.
ALL RIGHT, KENJI.
ALL RIGHT.

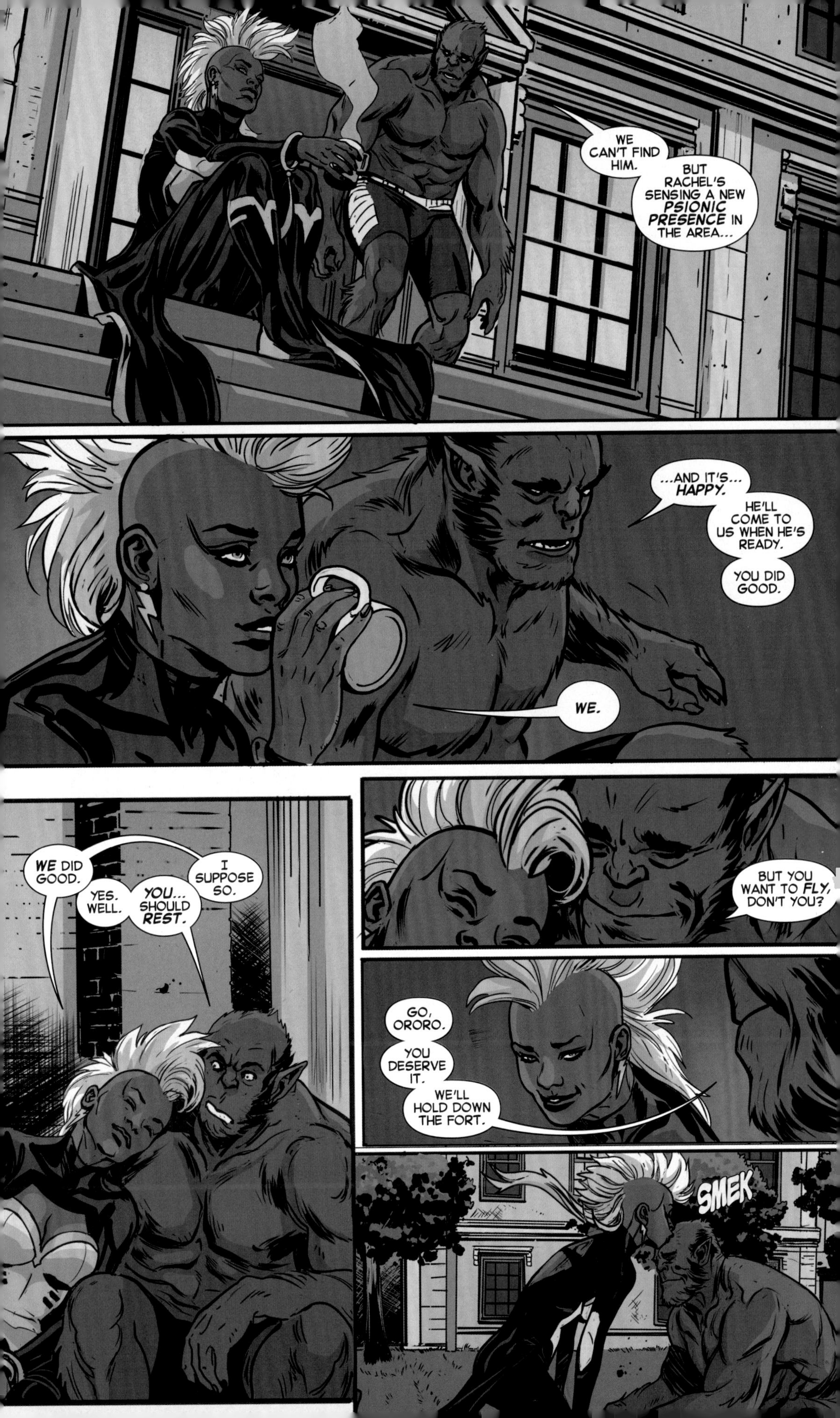
WE CAN'T FIND HIM.
BUT RACHEL'S SENSING A NEW PSIONIC PRESENCE IN THE AREA...
...AND IT'S... HAPPY.
HE'LL COME TO US WHEN HE'S READY.
YOU DID GOOD.
WE.
WE DID GOOD.
I SUPPOSE SO.
YES. WELL.
YOU... SHOULD REST.
BUT YOU WANT TO FLY, DON'T YOU?
GO, ORORO.
YOU DESERVE IT.
WE'LL HOLD DOWN THE FORT.
SMEK

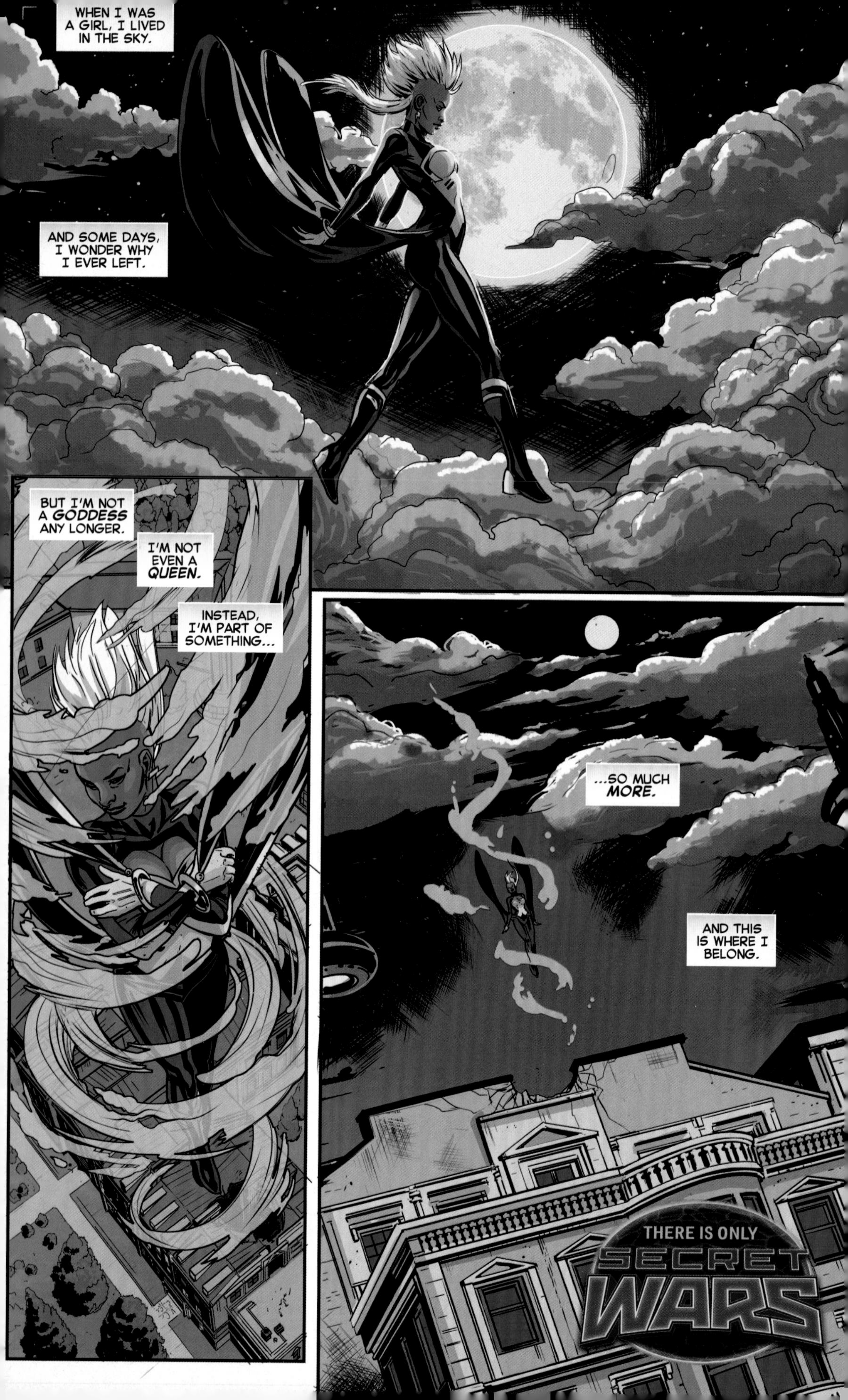
WHEN I WAS A GIRL, I LIVED IN THE SKY.
AND SOME DAYS, I WONDER WHY I EVER LEFT.
BUT I'M NOT A GODDESS ANY LONGER.
I'M NOT EVEN A QUEEN.
INSTEAD, I'M PART OF SOMETHING...
...SO MUCH MORE.
AND THIS IS WHERE I BELONG.
THERE IS ONLY SECRET WARS

▼ #6, PAGE 16 PENCILS BY **AL BARRIONUEVO**

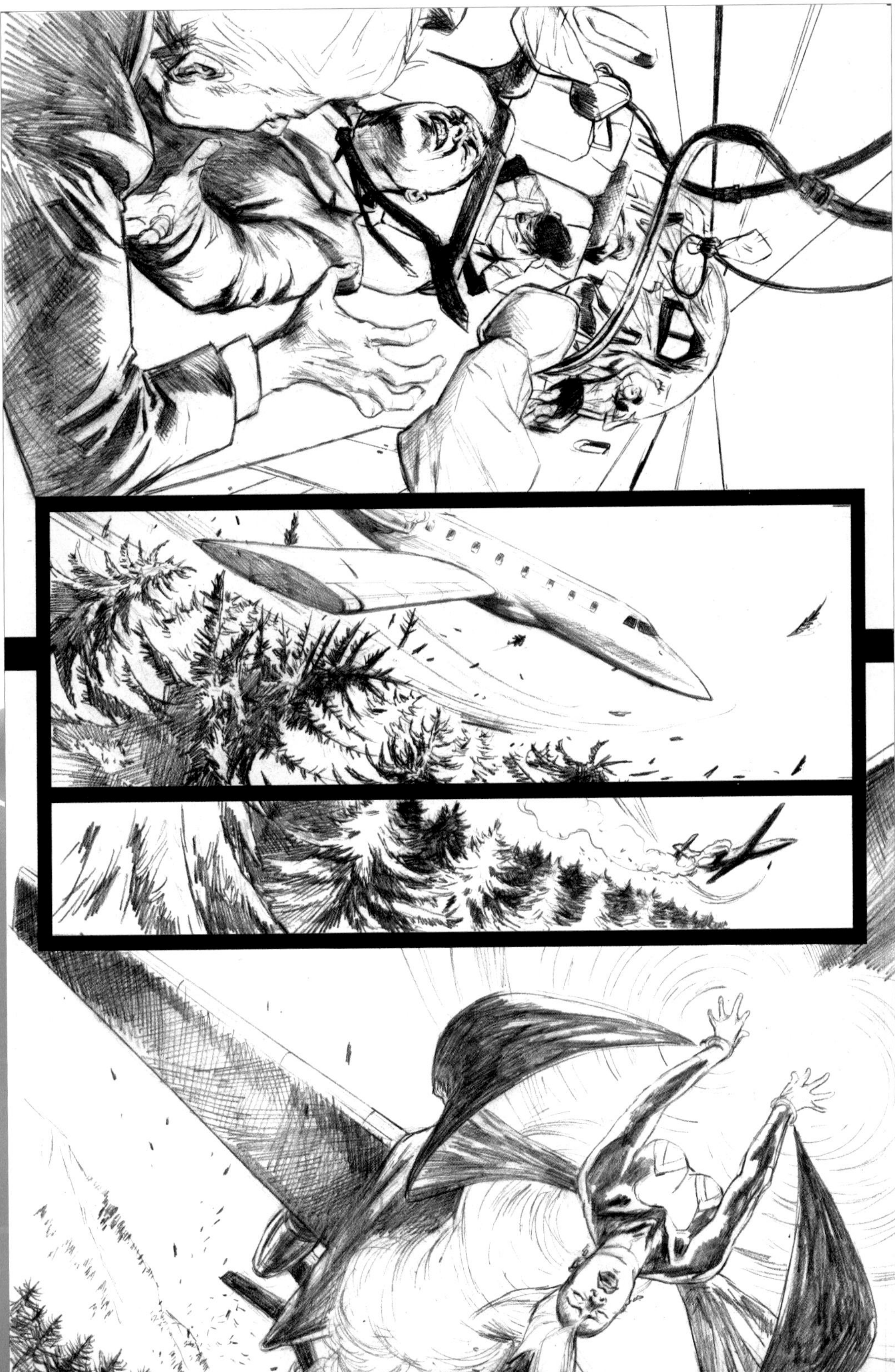

#6, PAGE 18 PENCILS BY **AL BARRIONUEVO** ▼

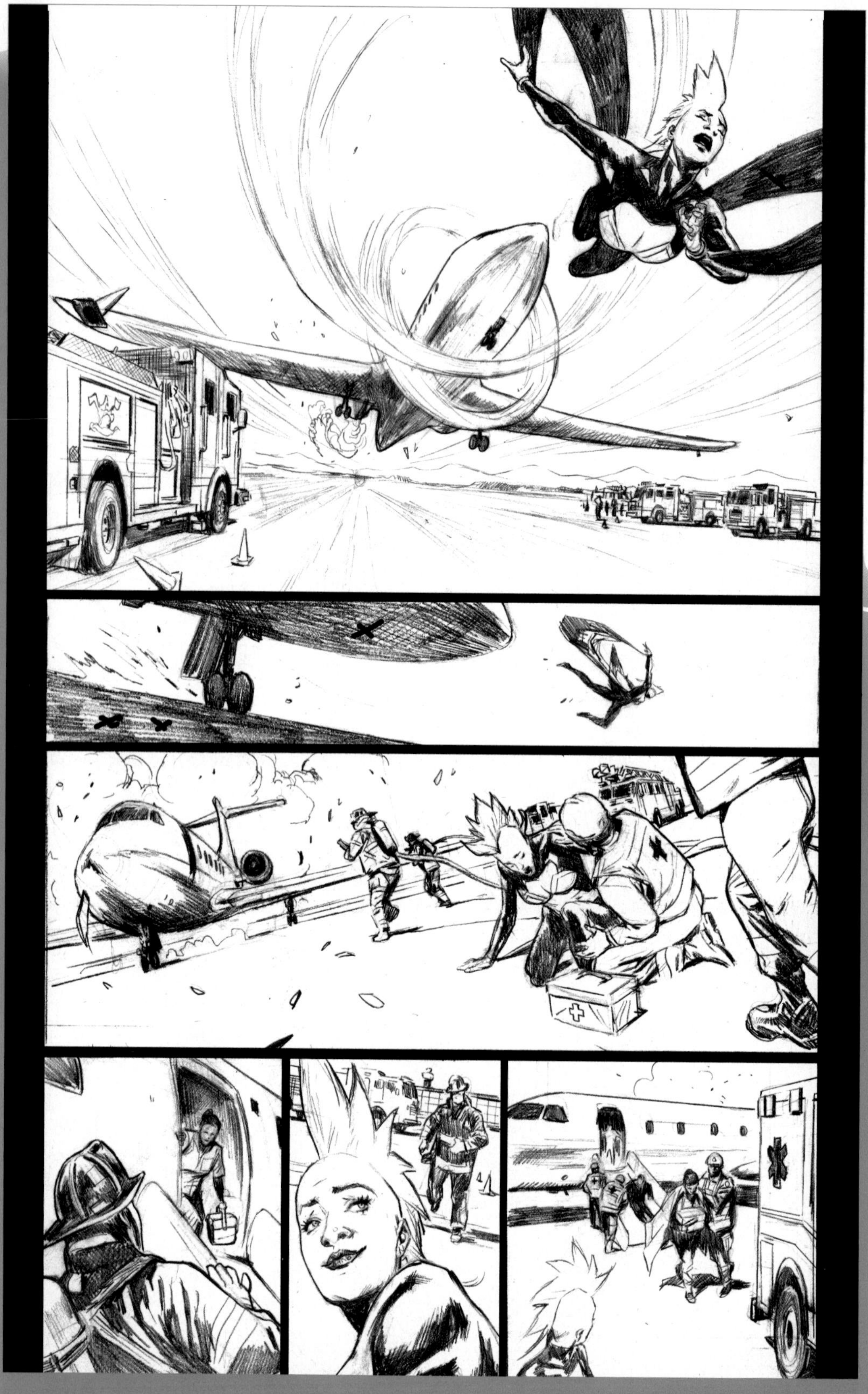

▼ #6, PAGE 20 PENCILS BY **AL BARRIONUEVO**

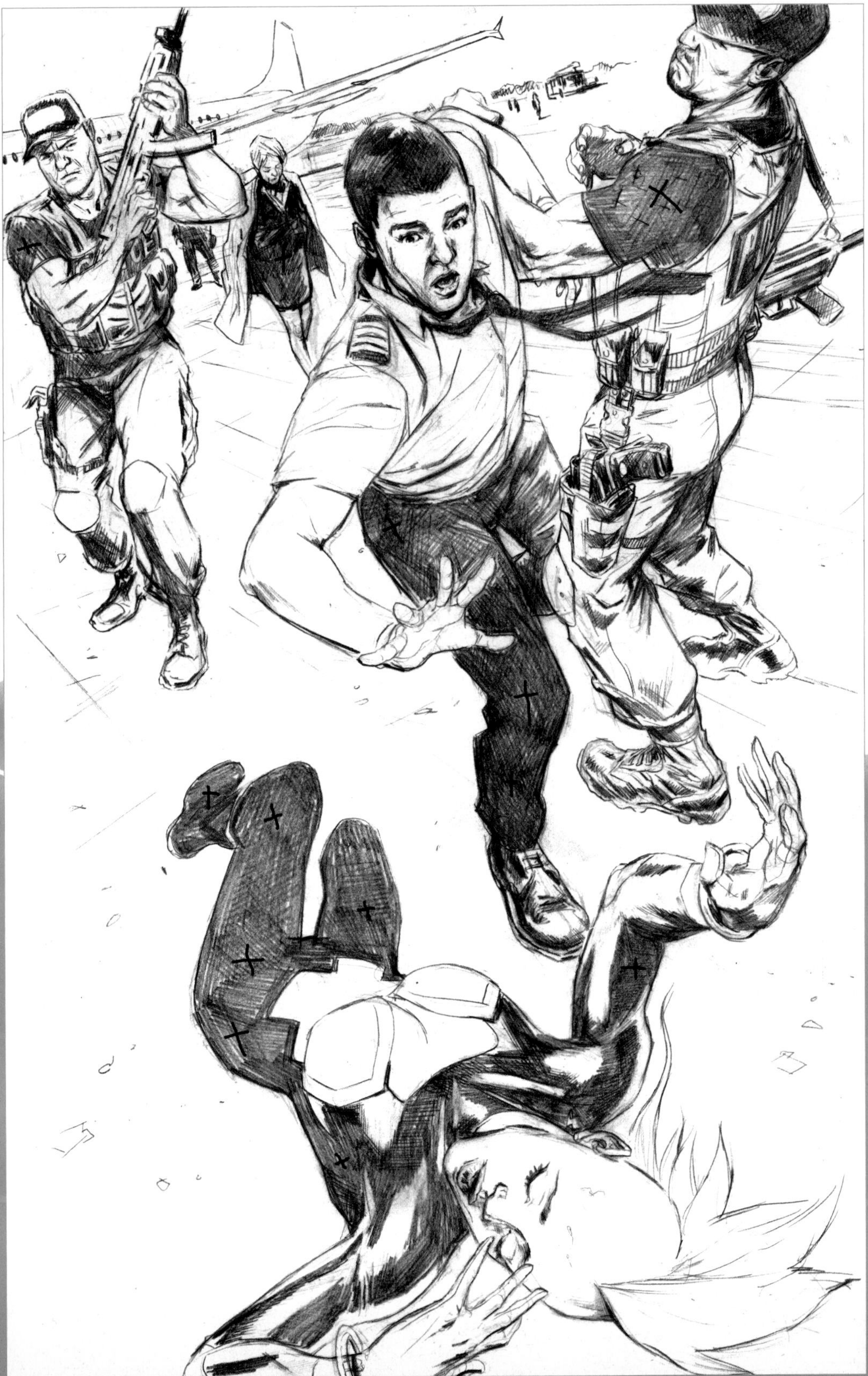

#7, PAGE 17 PENCILS BY **AL BARRIONUEVO** ▼

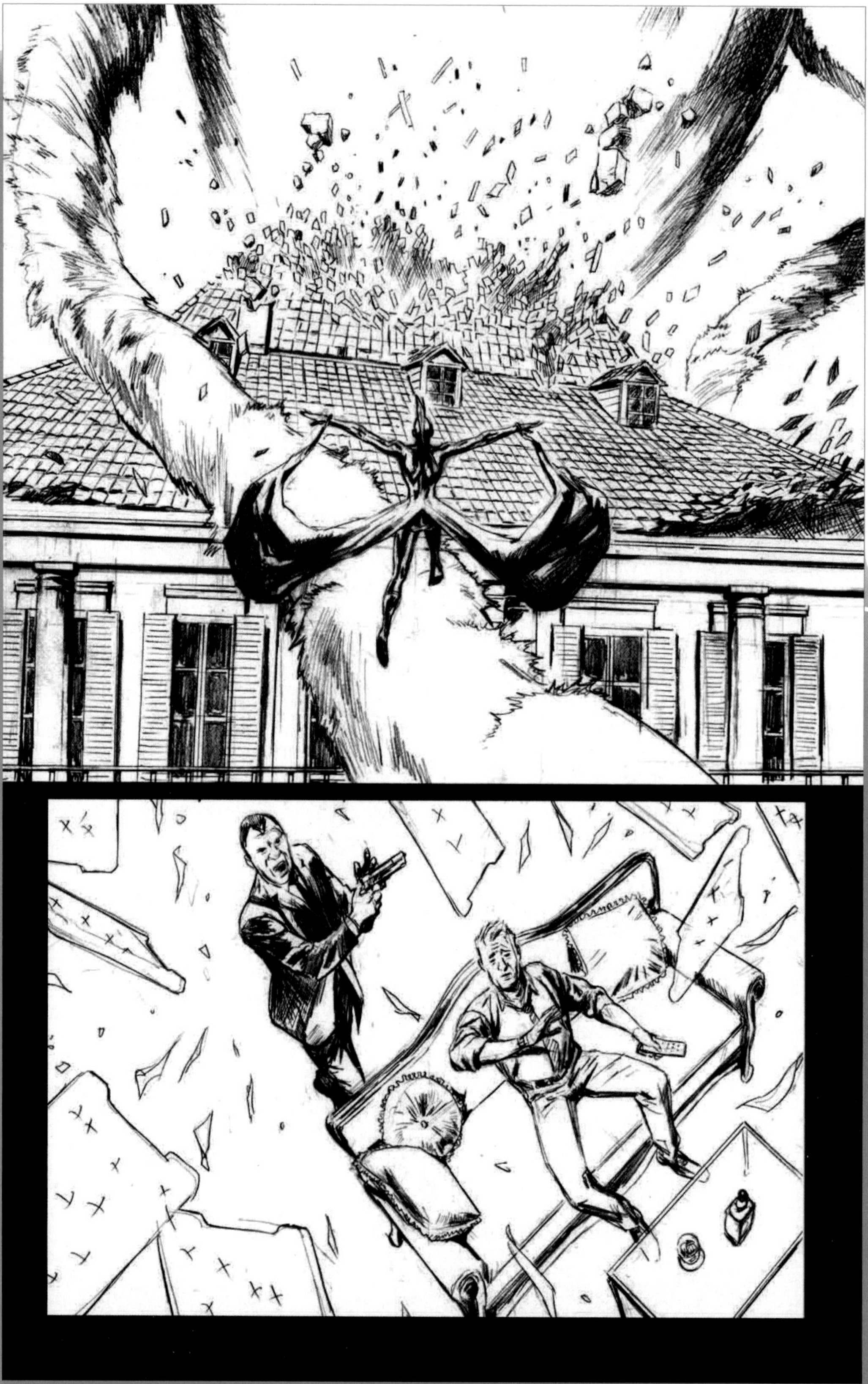

▼ #7, PAGE 19 PENCILS BY **AL BARRIONUEVO**

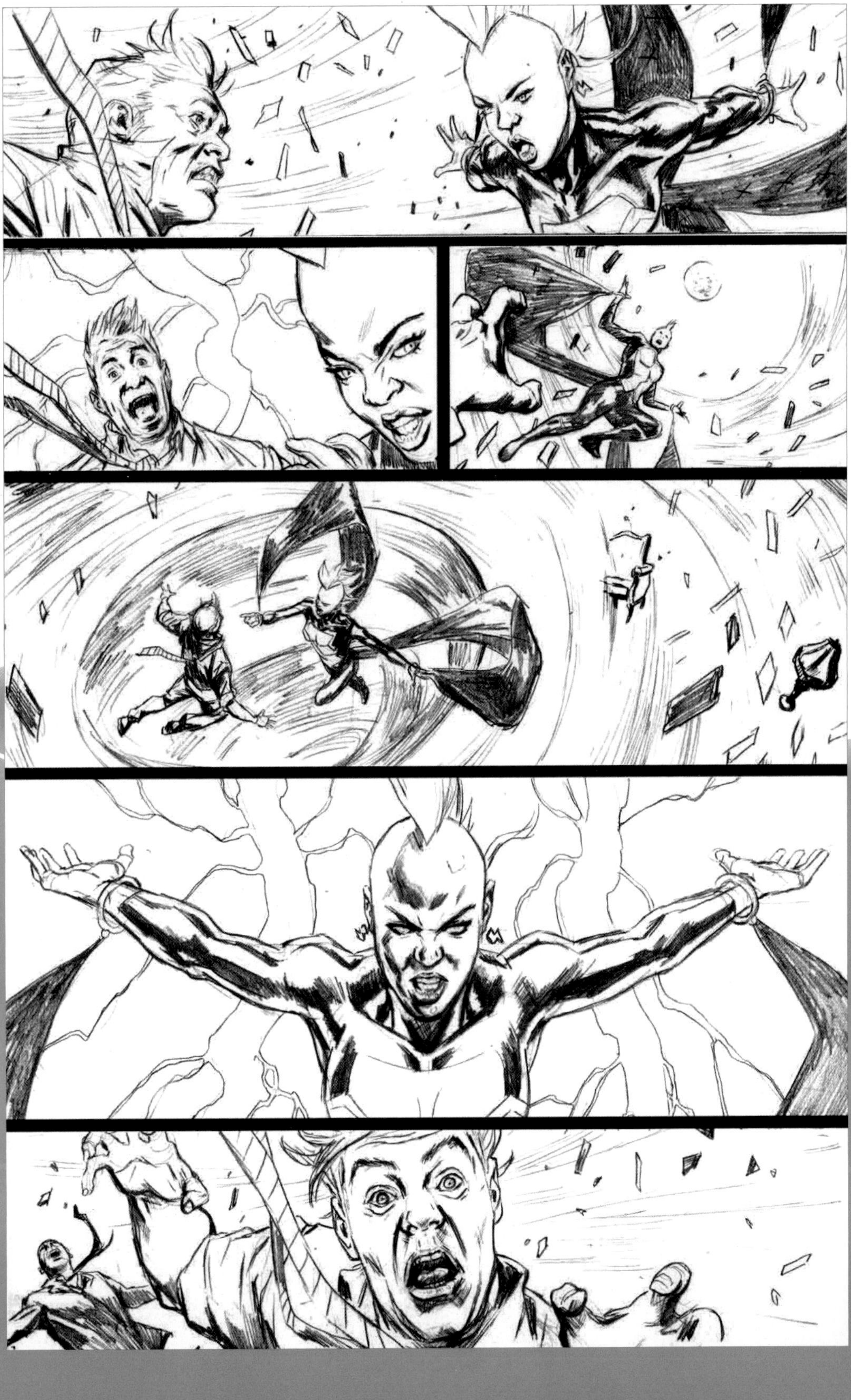

#8, PAGE 16 PENCILS BY **AL BARRIONUEVO** ▼

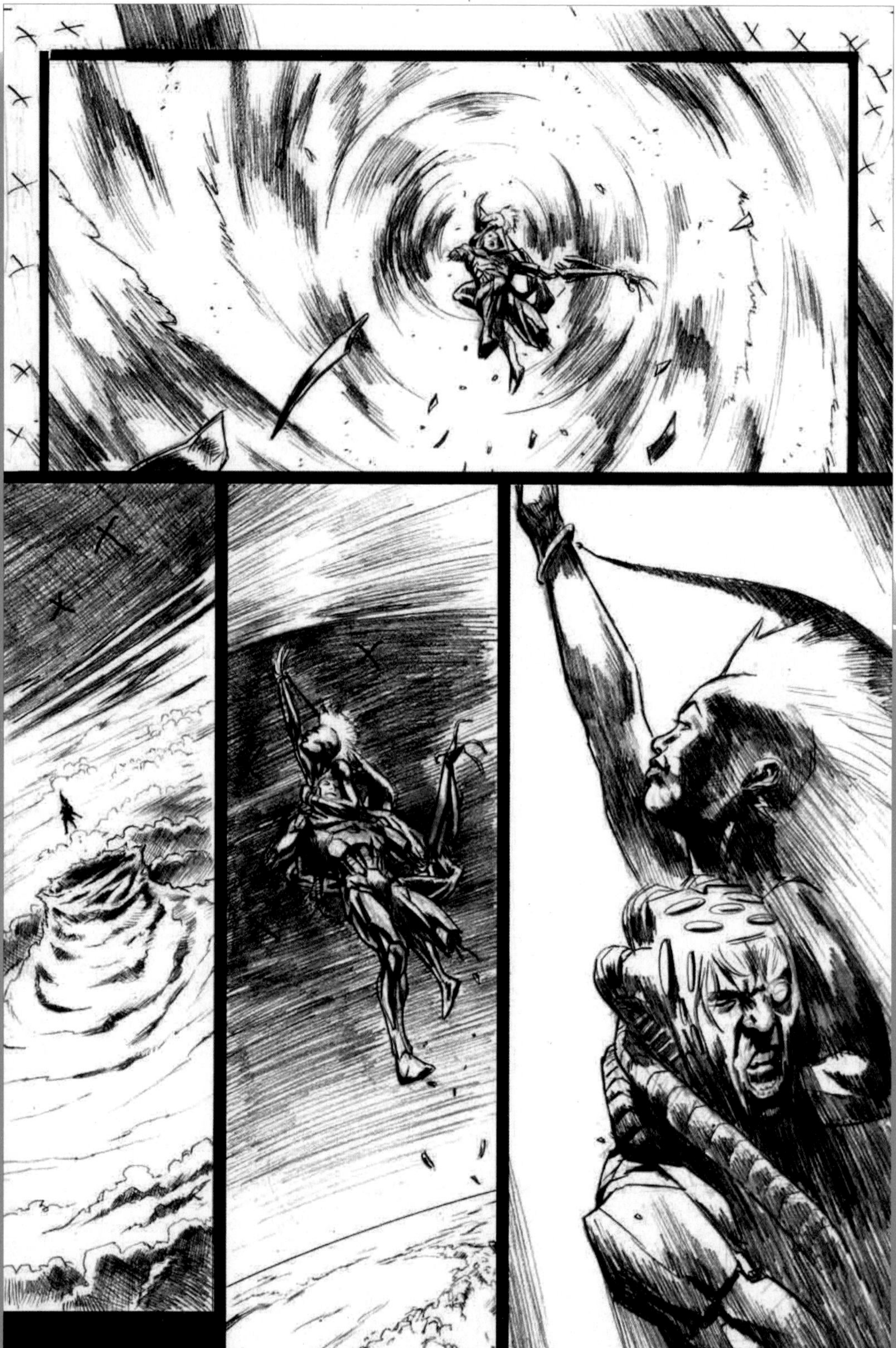